WARNING!

DO NOT READ OR USE THIS BOOK UNLESS YOU HAVE READ AND AGREE TO THE FOLLOW-ING STATEMENT:

Rock Climbing and Bouldering are inherently dangerous activities which may result in death, paralysis, or injury. Using this guidebook may increase that danger.

This book is not intended to be used as an instructional manual, and should not be used as one. Do not use the information in this book as, or in place of, instruction in rock climbing or bouldering.

Assumption of Risk:
This guidebook is a compilation of opinions. These opinions derive from the author and the people he consulted with. The information within is not verified, and should not be treated as factual. Information in this book pertaining to ratings of boulder problems or climbs, descriptions of problems, or recommendations pertaining to seriousness of a problem or climb, such as how "scary," "nuts," or "sketchy," a problem is, are based upon the personal opinions of the author and are entirely subjective. Difficulty and risk must be assessed as an individual, and one person's opinions about difficulty and risk do not always match another's. Use your best judgement, and do not rely upon this book, or the opinions expressed within, to make risk based judgements. Just because a problem is not described as being dangerous does not mean that it is not. A person can fall from any height, however short, and still hurt themsleves. Additionally, the use of protective crash mats, helmets, and/or attentive spotting technique, may not save a falling boulderer from injury. Do not assume that using safety equipment or technique will save you from injury or death in the case of a fall.

Be aware that any or all of the information in this book may have changed due to factors beyond the publisher's or author's control. Man-made changes, changes due to weather, changes in vegetation, from wildlife, or by erosion, may have occured to any boulder, area, or problem described within. Additionally, this book has been through a long process of writing, editing, proofing, and through this process, many different people have left their mark. Inadvertent changes or mistakes may have taken place during this process. Also, there are many other risks and hazards associated with rock climbing, bouldering, and being outdoors in general, which are not recognized within this book. Do not assume that the information presented in this book is accurate, or that it accurately represents all the dangers associated with rock climbing, bouldering, or being in an environment where these activities are taking place.

The author and publisher make no promises, warranties, or representations about the accuracy of the information printed in this book, and are not liable for mistakes within. If you use the information printed in this book, for any purpose, you do so at your own risk.

Disclaimer of Warranties:
THE PUBLISHER AND AUTHOR MAKE NO REPRESENTATIONS OR WARRANTIES, EXPRESSED OR IM-PLIED, ABOUT THE ACCURACY OF THE INFORMATION CONTAINED WITHIN THIS BOOK. THE PUB-LISHER AND AUTHOR MAKE NO WARRANTIES REGARDING FITNESS FOR A PARTICULAR PURPOSE AND/OR MERCHANTABILITY OF THIS BOOK. THE PUBLISHER AND AUTHOR EXPRESSLY DISCLAIM THEMSELVES OF ALL LIABILITY ASSOCIATED WITH, AND NOT LIMITED TO, THE USE OF THIS BOOK.

THE READER AND USER OF THIS BOOK ASSUMES ALL RISKS ASSOCIATED WITH ANY USE OF THIS BOOK, INCLUDING, BUT NOT LIMITED TO, ROCK CLIMBING AND BOULDERING.

r. jenkins, chattanooga, t. donoso. photo.

ORGANIC

www.organicclimbing.com

Stone Fort Bouldering

by Andy Wellman

Published and distributed by Rockery Press
ISBN 13: 978-0-692-50024-8

Cover Photo: jill Sompel on Deception, V7 (photo by Lucas Sinclair)

Boulder photos: Andy Wellman.
Maps: Andy Wellman.
Words: Andy Wellman, unless otherwise noted.
Editing and Design:

Printed in Korea.

ACKNOWLEDGEMENTS

There are a lot of people who deserve credit for helping with this book. First of all thanks to Jillian for everything you have ever done. And thanks to my Mom and Dad for supporting my fledgling company.

Thanks to everyone who played a hand in making this book happen in the first place. Thanks to Luke and Mel Laeser for being good friends and supporting the process, Chad Wykle and John Dorough for all the help and support, and Adam Henry for the advice. Thanks also to Lynda Childress and Tammy Babb for agreeing to let me have this opportunity.

Many thanks to everyone who contributed something to the making of this book: Luis Rodriguez, Jeff Drumm, Gary, Marvin Webb, Travis Eiseman, Sam Adams, Ben Ditto, Jonathan Clardy, Anthony Meeks, Michael Field, Bob Cormany, Jody Evans, Ana Burgos, Ronnie Jenkins, Tony Lamiche, Jimmy Webb, Brion Voges, Matt Stark, Dan Brayack, Adam Johnson, Stephan Denys, Raphael Legrange, Jerry Roberts, John Sherman, Andrew Kornylak, Chris Brown, Sam Silvey, Dan Lubbers, Aubrey Wingo, Wills Young, Kasia Pietras, Bonnie Sarkar.

Thanks also to the advertisers that helped support the project and the people who arranged that support: Marvin Webb, Dawson Wheeler, Mark McKnight, Tim O'Brien, Gustavo Moser, Jamey Sproull, Pi Vongsavanthong, Rebecca Robran and Chris Gibson, Josh Helke, Jason Karn, Tim Hovey, John Evans, Andy Stratton and Chris Sierzant, Lindsay Brown, Holly Stewart, Paul Morley, Joe Ortega, and Jim Horton.

Last but not least, special thanks to Henry Luken for letting us climb on his land, and anyone and everyone who has contributed time, effort, money, or all three towards making the Stone Fort what it is today.

BROADVIEW BUTTRESS

CB

2 DAYS

BROADVIEW BUTTRESS

Carl Buch on Real Estate Man 5.12e   Photo Credit: James Arnold

❶ Handy Man 5.10+ ★★★★★ ❏

This beaut' looks even better after a little elbow grease. Start 118 miles north of Atlanta. Work out the huge cantilever before leveling out to face the prominent tapering crack that starts as thin fingers and erupts into an all-out off-width war zone--you may as well just call a real Handy Man to do it. **Chuck Berry 1958**

❷ Property Man 5.12e ★★★★★★★ ❏

Searching for your next dream line? Property Man begins just right of Handy Man. Start low and sell high on this investment opportunity. And with the proper guide, you won't need to bring your big nuts to the sale. Find your sequence through the opening moves to the quaint two finger pocket for the frantic lunge to the garage sized hueco where you can park that new caddy before the run out finish—are you a Property Man? I am…
Mark Livasy 1981

❸ Rock Climber Man (project) ❏

You warmed up on Handy Man, sent Property Man and still have time for more? May as well hop on the 'ole proj, right? Rock Climber Man is the 2,000 ft. extension of Real Estate Man. Personally, I'd ask Carl Buch and Broadview Property Solutions what they would do before buying a 1200 meter rope.
The advertisement is just below!

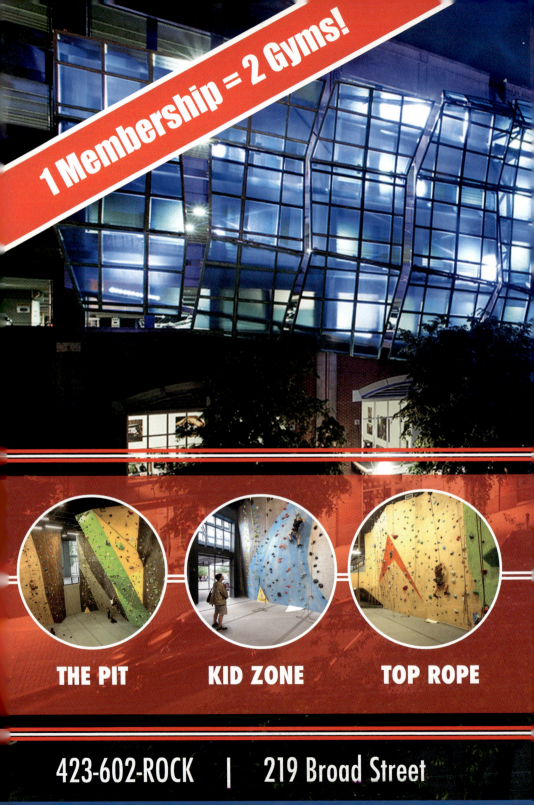

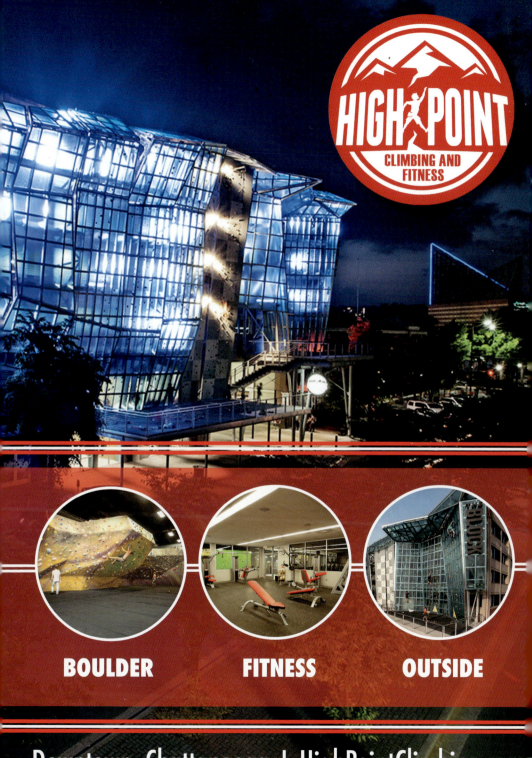

TABLE OF CONTENTS

INTERVIEWS AND ESSAYS

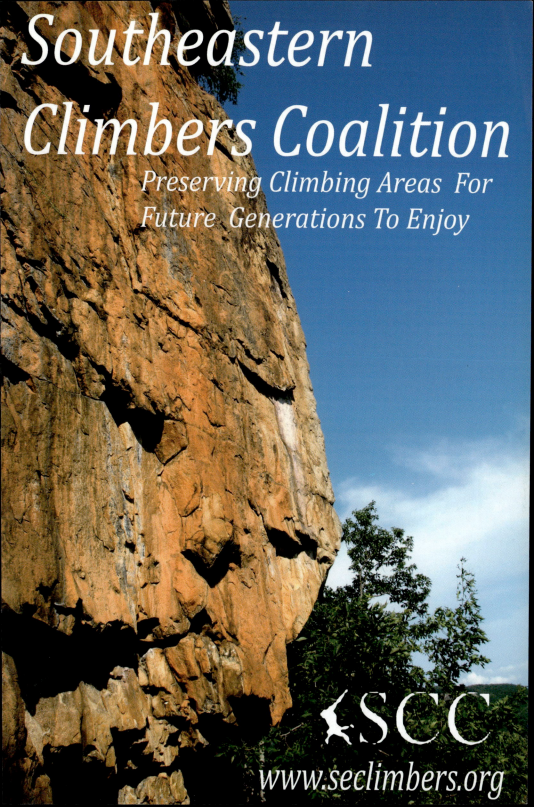

Southeastern
Climbers Coalition

Preserving Climbing Areas For Future Generations To Enjoy

SCC

www.seclimbers.org

Handmade Climbing Goods

dirtbagclimbers.com

Atlanta, GA

Follow us on Facebook and Instagram @Dirtbagclimbers

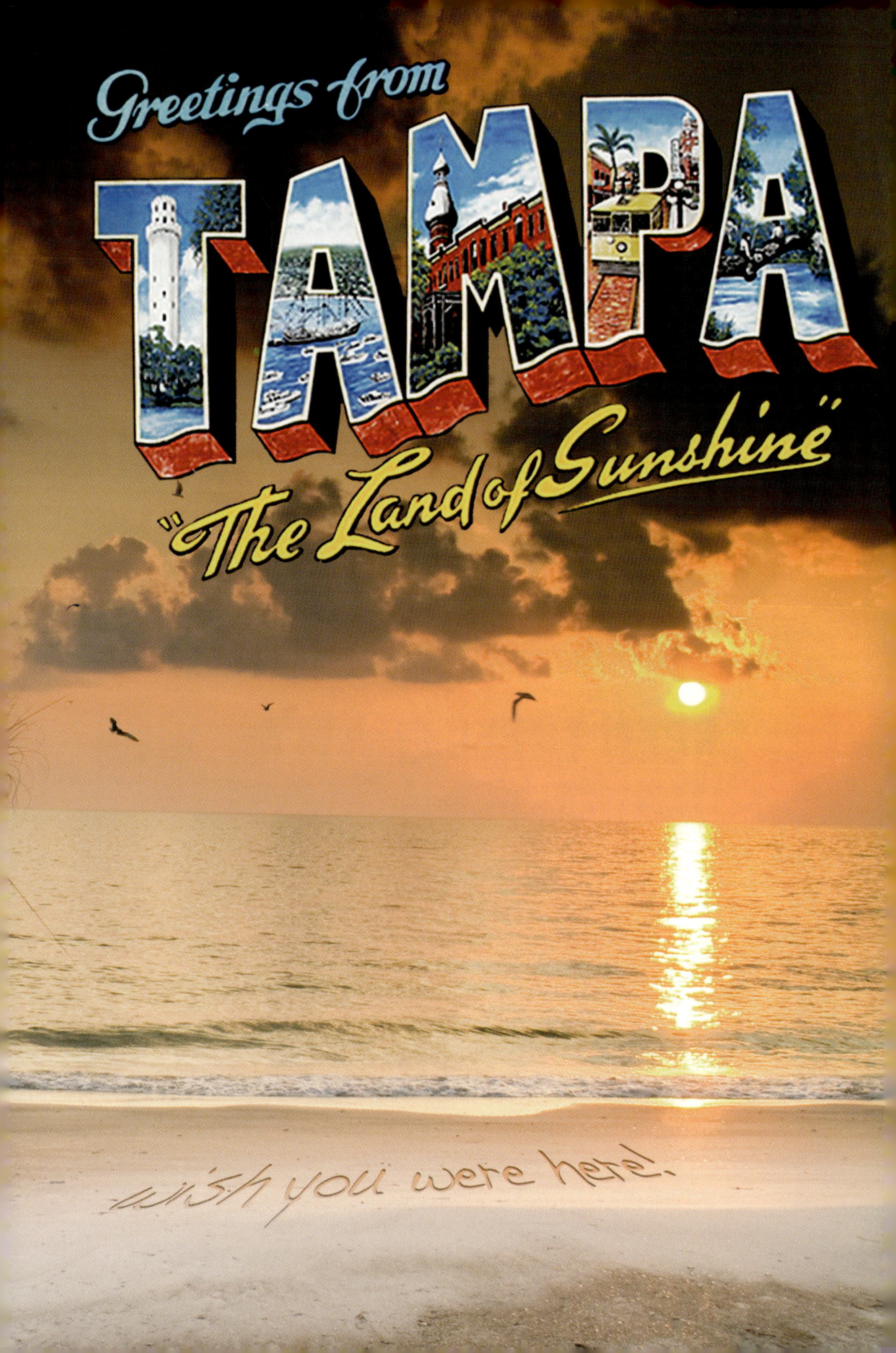
Greetings from
TAMPA
"The Land of Sunshine"
wish you were here!

GREEN TREES CHATTANOOGA

 (423) 508-4042

GreenTreesChattanooga.com

Hemlocks are the Redwoods of the East Coast, but our Majestic trees are under threat of total annihilation from the Hemlock Wooly Adelgid. Hemlocks live 600+ years, guarding over the stream cooling waters for our rich ecosystem. All the Hemlocks with die without our help!

Spread the Word. Donate. Volunteer.

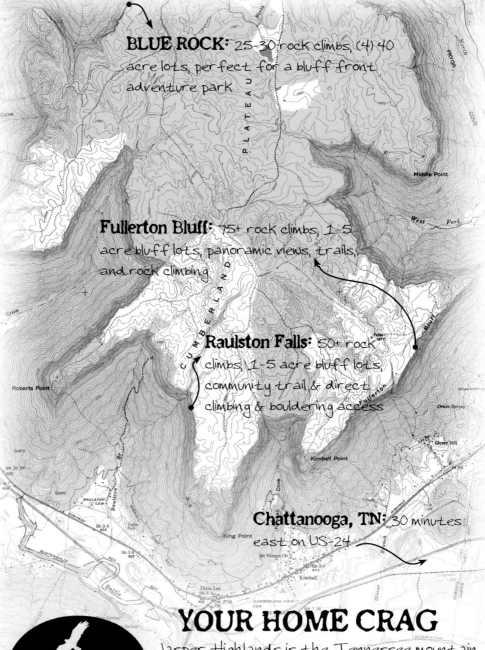

BLUE ROCK: 25-30 rock climbs, (4) 40 acre lots, perfect for a bluff front adventure park

Fullerton Bluff: 75+ rock climbs, 1-5 acre bluff lots, panoramic views, trails, and rock climbing

Raulston Falls: 50+ rock climbs, 1-5 acre bluff lots, community trail & direct climbing & bouldering access

Chattanooga, TN: 30 minutes east on US-24

Two Gyms, One Membership

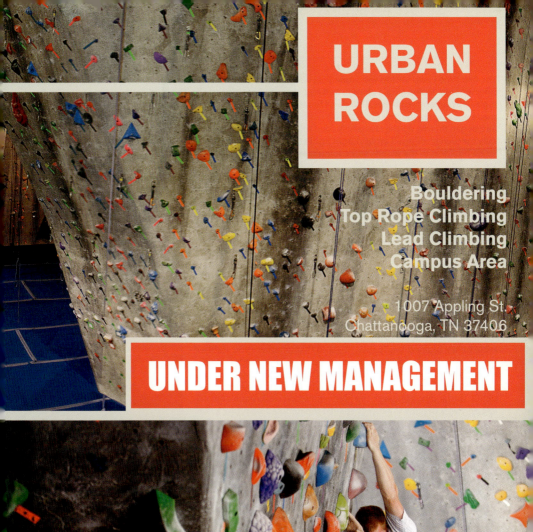

URBAN ROCKS

Bouldering
Top Rope Climbing
Lead Climbing
Campus Area

1007 Appling St.
Chattanooga, TN 37406

UNDER NEW MANAGEMENT

INTRODUCTION

The first time I ever visited the Stone Fort was on a brief spring break visit to Chattanooga. My girlfriend Jill and I were looking for a change and had come to Chattanooga for the week to investigate the climbing and living opportunities. One day, I found myself in the front seat of my friend Luke Laeser's car as we made our way north from Chattanooga into the hills and forests of the North Chickamauga River Gorge and began driving up the steep hilly road to gain the flat top of Mowbray Mountain. As Luke, an amateur rally car driver, whipped around tight uphill curves, I caught desperately short glimpses of massive sandstone boulders in the woods and couldn't help but ask, "Did you see that boulder?" Luke just laughed.

Moments later Luke was negotiating our car into a spot at the back of a large parking area in front of a golf course clubhouse. After signing our names and paying five bucks inside the clubhouse, we were off to the boulders, hidden in the deep green forest beyond the breathtaking 18th green. Within about 30 seconds we were parting the leaves which had grown over the trail and what from the outside appeared to be a solid wall of vegetation was transformed into a cathedral of massive grey boulders. The huge square cut blocks leaned against one another in impossible numbers, and my eye followed them as they disappeared over a slight hill. "Holy cow," I thought, "this place is incredible." I hadn't even touched the rock yet.

As Luke led me down pathways and corridors, around huge blocks and through tunnels to more boulders, I realized that this boulderfield was much different than the bouldering I was used to in my home state of Colorado - it was much better! The smooth grey rock was comfortable to the touch and molded into the perfect shapes for handholds. It was also grippy beyond belief – the texture, comparable to fine grained sandpaper, ensured that wherever you stabbed your foot it would stick! And this was all a mere 30 seconds from the car and a clubhouse that sold beer! In Colorado, the most popular and best bouldering areas require close to an hour to approach, all uphill. The landings beneath the high alpine boulders require incredible amounts of pads to protect against the jumbled talus blocks beneath the problems. Not to mention that one considers themselves lucky if they are not caught in a July snowstorm, or even worse, a horrendous alpine electrical storm. I knew within seconds that I was going to love climbing at the Stone Fort.

Luke is a fantastic host – he can't help but try to show you everything there is to see. After what seemed like hours of wandering around, with Luke happily shouting out names and grades, I was completely lost. It was all starting to look the same, not to mention that the boulderfield was massive. We made stops at the ultra classic problems *Tristar* and *Super Mario* along the way. I remember stopping to stare at the incred-

The author on Mousetrap V2, pg. 116. Jim Thornburg photo.

ible rock on the *Shield* and *Deception*. But soon we were leaving, it began to rain, and a mere three days later I was back home in Colorado, dreaming of the Little Rock City.

So what's with the name anyway? Is it the Stone Fort, is it Little Rock City, or LRC for short? Why does this bouldering area have two names? Well, the first name that it came to be known as by climbers was Little Rock City. This name was probably coined by a climber and outdoor program leader named Chris Moore, and is a reference to the famous tourist attraction on the top of Lookout Mountain, which towers over Chattanooga, called Rock City. I'm sure you've seen the billboards. Check out the interview I did with Marvin Webb, the first true rock climber to explore Little Rock City, on page 18, for more information about how the name came to be. It had always been referred to amongst climbers as Little Rock City until the time when the SCC and the Triple Crown Bouldering Series organizers negotiated with the current land owner, Henry Luken, to allow public climbing access. A commercial real estate tycoon, Luken preferred that the name be changed to not infringe upon the name of one of the most recognizable tourist spots in Chattanooga – Rock City. So, the new name was decided to be the Stone Fort, which is the only name I have used within this guidebook (some of the contributors have continued to refer to it as Little Rock City, which I have not altered). Throughout the climbing world it is commonly referred to using both names (on the SCC website it is called LRC, the Triple Crown calls it the Stone Fort, and on 8a.nu and mountainproject.com it is called Little Rock City).

Two months after our first visit, Jill and I moved to Chattanooga. Despite the oppressive heat and astronomical humidity, we spent the majority of the summer bouldering at the Stone Fort. As fall arrived and the temperatures and humidity began to drop, we happily took advantage, climbing at the Stone Fort as often as four or five days a week. With each visit I would discover a new problem, or talk to somebody I'd never met and learn something interesting about the history of the area. I would also see countless visitors wandering around aimlessly on their first visit, lost like I was, but without the help of a local guide. I began to think that a proper guidebook was exactly what the Stone Fort needed.

I brought the idea up with many people over a period of many months. Most people I talked with thought it was a great idea, but I also heard countless reasons why there should not be a guidebook to the Stone Fort: The golf course owners didn't want one, the Triple Crown organizers didn't want one, the locals didn't want one, the access was too touchy, the problem names that everybody knew were all wrong, the history was forever lost and would be impossible to track down, and on and on. To me, none of these reasons seemed like they could not be overcome, but it also seemed like nobody else was willing to take on the project. So I began collecting information about the place myself. I spent many days out in the boulders drawing the map that is used here in this guide. I also set out to climb or attempt to climb every peice of conceivable stone in the boulderfield and document it all. I started this effort by setting myself the goal of 40 new problems per day, which initially I was hopelessly unable to reach. Months later I was frequently documenting up to 70 problems per visit.

As I was collecting information about the Stone Fort and pondering how to transform this info into a guidebook, I heard the rumor that the owners of the Montlake Golf Course actually *did* want there to be a proper guidebook to the area. So I went into the clubhouse and brought up the idea with the guys working there and they loved it. They passed on my information to the higher ups, and before I knew it I was being contacted by Chad Wykle, the organizer of the Triple Crown, who had been consulted about the guidebook idea by the golf course people. I wasn't sure whether he would be for or against the idea, but as it turned out he was one of the biggest supporters, and along with his friend John Dorough, proved to be invaluable in helping to fill in the gaps in my research. With Chad and John on my side we did not have a hard time convincing the owners of the golf course that a guidebook would be a good idea. Another crucial supporter was on board, and bolstered by this confidence, I began to approach other local boulderers, hoping for their help as well. The Chattanooga climbing community is known for its secrecy, and I thought there was a good chance that I would receive nothing but a cold shoulder. Instead, the locals seemed more than happy to help out, many of them meeting me at the boulders for walk-throughs, or having long conversations over the phone or in person about the problems they had done, or regaling me with stories of the old days. In a matter of a few short weeks, all the obstacles that I thought would be major hurdles to the publication of a guidebook had been ironed out, and the project had a momentum of its own.

The lone obstacle left in my mind was unearthing the climbing history of the Stone Fort. In Colorado, California, New York, and other old and famous climbing areas, the history of rock climbing has been well documented, and one of my favorite parts of guidebooks is the history section. Reading the stories about an area, a climber, or a particular climb as a young adult obsessed with rock climbing gave me an intense respect for those who came before me and added meaning to visiting that area, or attempting a famous or historic climb. As a newcomer to the south, there was no way that I could write such a history about the Stone Fort myself, and due to reasons both cultural and practical, virtually none of the 30 year climbing history of the Stone Fort had been documented or preserved.

To overcome this challenge I decided to track down and speak with Stone Fort climbers of as many different "generations" as I could, and convince them to write something about their time spent bouldering at the place. The goal was to be able to paint a picture with the words of many about the history of the area. This proved to be a seemingly never-ending process, one which I admittedly had to bring to a halt so that this book could be finished. Although there are still many gaps and holes unfilled, I hope you will find that after reading the essays from the 12 separate contributors found within this book, you will understand and have more respect for this place and its climbers than you did before. The essays are arranged in chronological order throughout the book, beginning with the Marvin Webb interview on the next page.

Thank you for purchasing this book, I hope it guides you through many fine adventures, and welcome to the Stone Fort!

MARVIN WEBB INTERVIEW

In May, 2010, I met with Marvin Webb for about half an hour to conduct an interview about the beginning of climbing at the Stone Fort. Marvin is a co-owner of Rock/Creek Outfitters, the local gear shop in Chattanooga, and we met in his office at the Rock/Creek Warehouse. Here is a somewhat edited version of the discussion that took place.

Andy: Thanks for meeting with me.

Marvin: No problem.

Andy: So, one of my main goals with the guidebook, or with the history section of the guidebook, when I'm talking to you or other people, is that... I grew up in Colorado and as I grew up as a climber I would read. The history of climbing was really well documented in Colorado and California and all over the west and reading as a kid all this stuff about Layton Kor and the development of Eldorado Canyon and all that, not only does it add meaning to climbs – I mean when you get to go climb the Bastille Crack knowing the history of it, it's a more special experience than a little 3-pitch 5.7 – but also I think it just taught me, and the community in general, a lot of respect, knowing the history. And I feel like that's not something that is neces-sarily lacking – but in a way I do – with the younger generation. Climbing is snowballing in terms of growth, and I think it's going to continue to do that, and especially bouldering, and people coming out of the gym. I feel like in the south in general, the history just wasn't documented in a way that anyone can get their hands on and understand and I feel like it's a duty – I would like to read all this info! And I have an opportunity to collect it in a way that can be passed down and hopefully that is something that will be good for the community. And it's interesting to know that I'm sure when you guys found [the Stone Fort], it [was] just a little practice bouldering area, but I think the meaning and the significance of that area... If you were to ask people these days what they think the best climbing area in Chattanooga is, a lot of them would say [the Stone Fort]. So, I think it will be a good thing to collect the 30 years of history as well as we can. So [to start things off] that is my mission in talking to you.

Marvin: My experience, I climbed in the early '80s. I climbed more out west in blocks of time and a lot in Eldorado, and the book "Climb" was our Bible. Looking at pictures from a 5.7 climb in the '70s, looking at "I'm gonna do every one." In Boulder, it was like turn a page, and "OK, today I'm gonna do this." And [I] spent two or three summers in Boulder. Jim Erickson – huge, huge impact on us – we lived by anything that was written about him. One ascent, if you fall, that was it, climb as if there was no rope. Back then, even if you were bouldering, falling was almost a taboo thing within us. It wasn't taboo, but everything was about being able to do whatever you set out to do without falling, and to potentially downclimb out of anything you got into without falling, stepping back onto the ground. But our generation, you know, even cragging, bouldering was to improve your cragging, cragging was to improve your big walls, big walls was to prep you for mountains, and the majority of climbers in the '70s and '80s, there were so many, proportionately more seemed to have targets and aspirations to bigger things. Whereas now, it's so compartmentalized, it's still sport climber, this is what I do, I don't have an aspiration to do anything else but sport climb. Or, boulderers, that can go to some of the best climbing areas in the country, and expense of travel and all this, and not even bring a rope.

Andy: People go to Yosemite to boulder.

Marvin: I know, and it blows my mind. We loved bouldering. In Boulder, you know, we'd work all day casual labor at a job and work for a while and then come home and eat whatever was the cheapest thing we could afford to eat, then go back out to CU and boulder till 10 o'clock, on the buildings, or run up Flagstaff [Mountain] or something like that. It's different now.

Andy: So how did you first hear about [the Stone Fort]?

Marvin: Well hear, I don't know who, I think. I think this is vaguely correct. That property was owned by several men, maybe doctors, that were old Baylor School graduates. But they were older, they would have been graduates in the '50s or whatever. And, Chris Moore, he's a MD, worked with Baylor – the Moore's were very involved with Baylor. He was a climber, quasi-climber, years ago, really good boater, just an outdoors person. But anyway, he was connected to the school working with them on the development of this outdoor program and it was an adventure camp kind of model [like] Outward Bound. And I think it was he or Larry Roberts told me about this, because, or I heard through them, because they took some Baylor students. Probably being at a party and talking to one of these doctors who mentioned this land that they owned that had all these rocks on it. So they took a field trip or two with some kids and ran around and probably hung some ropes and did stuff.

And then we heard about it, and that was when I was back teaching at Baylor running their outdoor program. I believe, maybe, I don't think anybody had heard about it, but I remember the day. Rob [Robinson] and Forrest [Gardner] and I went out, and it was basically a jeep road, just a grown up logging road. And it went in about where the clubhouse is, cause we walked down and then weaved our way through the woods, and it was kind of oriented the way the trail is now, the way we first went in. And I remember it well that day cause the three of us, we were the only ones there. I mean nobody knew of this place, and it was like kids in a candy store! We walked in, and I had a lot of experience traveling around and being on Flagstaff [Mountain, Boulder] and being in other areas with developed bouldering, but nothing – there wasn't anything like that in the south. There

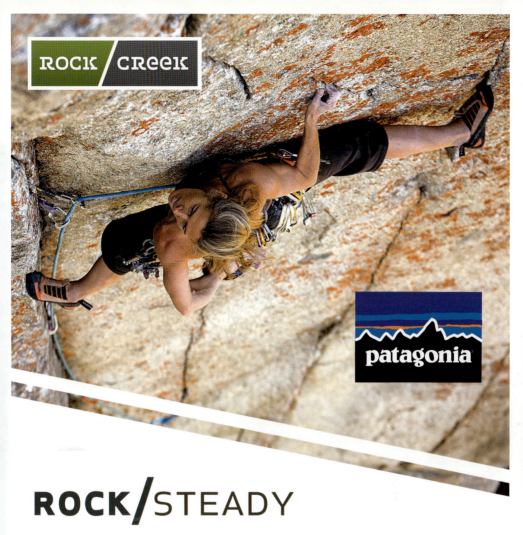

ROCK/STEADY

With lightweight, bomber, tear- and abrasion-resistant nylon ripstop, Patagonia's new climbing packs are super clean and stripped down to the features that matter most. Shop online at rockcreek.com/patagonia or stop by one of our Chattanooga-area stores to check them out.

Photo by Andrew Burr for Patagonia: Lynn Hill climbing in Little Cottonwood Canyon.

was a boulder problem or two that they said that Frost had done at Sunset, there were things that we worked out on, but, nothing like Little Rock City – not even the concept really. So we went out there and just went apeshit. Rob screaming, and we were looking for the perfect crack, and there were some. Back then you looked for something really hard that was a crack, it wasn't esoteric blank faces with sparse holds. It was classic, "here's a problem," and you'd see features – but the real limelight was looking for really cool crack problems. So we jumped on all kinds of stuff. Bouldered all that day, and from then on it just started evolving. There's a classic problem… star… there, um… it's kinda in an alcove…

Andy: Oh. Tristar.

Marvin: Tristar, yeah. I mean we went right to that. That was something we put our hands on the first day, but I don't think any of us got it that day. But like two weeks later I think Forrest went back out there and got it, and then all the little crack things that are around there, those were the first that we got and messed with, and then started getting more on the facey stuff. Back then there were a lot of days like that. You would find, and it wouldn't be just a little thing somewhere, it was like, you walk into the T-Wall, or just walk into someplace for the first time and just be exploding, another thing in our backyard, running around.

Andy: What did it look like, was it all overgrown? Did you guys have to clean very much?

Marvin Webb in the Rock/Creek Warehouse in Chattanooga, 2010. Andy Wellman photo.

Marvin: Like, Tristar? No. There were a lot that you could just look at the rock, even now, after all the traffic, and see what might have been grown up. There were definitely a lot of things that we had to clean, but a lot of it was pretty clean anyway. The woods weren't thick. [It was] nothing like it is now. I go there now and it's hard trails and established this and that, but nobody had been in there.

Andy: Nice, sounds like fun!

Marvin: But we were used to that, and relative to going to school, I would always be gone in the summer. Rob and them maybe taking a trip or so but, like again, Little Rock City was just kind of a special fun day, cause the real effort and focus was, all these lines everywhere – Steele, Yellow Creek, Sunset – a ton of stuff. There was two or three years where there wasn't a need to go [anywhere] else cause it was all about new routes and you'd kind of have your plan. Sunset ate up a summer or two cause nothing had really been done there either. There was some old established aid lines and a few things, but,there was a lot of cleaning involved there.

Andy: So how long did you guys – you and your crew – keep climbing at [the Stone Fort]?

Marvin: From then on. I think.

Andy: And what year was this, do you know, when you found it?

Marvin: Probably would have been '80, right around '80 - '81. And that's why, Chris Moore, he's 10 years older than I am, so he would have information on literally, walking around with a group of kids to explore around. And around that same time period, I gotta think of his name… Bob Mitchell. [He's] a guy who used to live in North Carolina and moved to Chattanooga and taught at McCallie, the other prep school. He has his name on the old guidebooks in North Carolina. He did a lot of significant routes at Looking Glass and Whitesides [Mountain]. He moved to Chattanooga and started taking McCallie kids out there, and then that kind of evolved along until the next generation came along. But still, bouldering hadn't become even remotely what it is now…

And it was real volatile. We worked with the owner, the name was Earl Spears – which struck me cause as soon as I heard his name I kinda knew it had a negative connotation to it, in the literary sense – and it turned out he was kinda tough. One day he'd be fine with us coming in and other times not. And then you could just see the writing on the wall, the conflict between … once he learned of liability and people started coming in, you saw the writing on the wall that it was something that would have to be addressed at some point.

Andy: Did you guys name anything that you climbed out there?

Marvin: I think Forrest, um, I wouldn't. Forrest might have named, seemed like Tristar got…maybe it didn't. Typically no, we wouldn't name a boulder problem, unless it was just so spectacular, or we were just goofing around and named it as a reference. But, everything we did that day, going back out, cool face here, crack next to that. I think the first time that someone was trying to describe something I had done and they kept saying – it was [what is now] Tristar – and they were like, "you did that right," or don't know what your talking about, and trying to describe it, but I think there was a point were I was struck with [how it is] kinda funny that they're calling everything by name. I mean, they're boulder problems.

Andy: That's funny. So, who did you pass the torch to, figuratively speaking, who was the next crew, so to speak, to come in and go nuts? Do you know?

Marvin: Well it would have been Chad [Wykle's] generation, Jonathan Clardy. [Note: This wouldn't have been quite accurate. Chad was only climbing there very intermittently on short trips from North Carolina from about 1995 till he moved to Chattanooga in 2001.] There were a lot of Rock/Creek staff, and I might of been in my 30's, and there started to be this energy – going out there every day, going out. And then a lot of other climbers in town [were] going out. Less of our generation and more of the youger generation, cause eventually we were just running businesses and having babies. I think it, well, Ben Ditto. I think he's in Chad's age range. But, uh, Ben and his dad would be out there. Chris [Gibson], who owns the [Urban Rocks] gym here, he would have been a youngster, going out with his dad and his brother, piddling around out there. More of the people who were in the whole climbing scene, but then there was a point where, I think when Chad and that group started going out there and climbing, I think that's when the word started getting out where you had Atlanta, Nashville, Knoxville, starting to come in. That was also an era when sometimes it was OK to go out there and climb and sometimes it was like, don't go out there, you'll get arrested. And people were sneaking in the back, trying to get in any way they could. And then it just mushroomed into a lot of kids I wouldn't even have known, hanging out.

Andy: That's cool. Do you remember when John Sherman came through for the first time?

Marvin: Yeah, um, I do. I think he came and he loved it so much, and he… Jennifer Cole, might of been working with us at the time. But he ended up staying with somebody for like a month or so, to where they were kinda like, "aah, is he ever gonna leave." But, I had friends from out west… You know there were a lot of good climbers that weren't recognized names, coming in to visit, whatever, and anyone who went out there was blown away. Cause in the south you didn't know any better, [you thought,] "this is just a cool place." But if you traveled around and had been climbing all over, and saw Little Rock City, then you knew the potential.

Andy: You were still blown away.

Marvin: You were still blown away. Cause then, that was kinda my thing, but to go back to your very first deal, you know, the west was very well documented. The south, it's almost a cultural thing – for the most part we didn't want documentation. You know, I'm not judging Rob and his guidebook, but nobody was into documenting, publicizing anything. It was like, this is our backyard, there wasn't even a thought to get the word out, or let people know. In fact Rob used to get mad at me cause I wouldn't even name a climb I did. I'd just go do a new route and I'd get a call like, "what's the name, describe it," and I'd be like, "I didn't name it. You name it. I don't care what the name is, it's just a cool route." So…

Andy: Cool… Oh yeah, do you know who coined the name Little Rock City? How that came about?

Marvin: If it were my guess, it would have been Rob, Forrest and I. Well, it might not have been, it could have been Chris. I bet you, I think it might have come from Chris, with Baylor kids going out there, cause I keyed into, yeah, I think they were using that.

Andy: And was Rock City already known as Rock City at that time?

Marvin: Oh yeah. And Chris is from Lookout Mountain, so that would make sense. Forrest lives right next to Rock City, but I almost think that the first time it was mentioned to me… Chris, he's not, wasn't even really a serious climber or anything like that, was like, "here's this place, we call it, its like a little Rock City. And that's what stuck, and it just became Little Rock City…

Downtown Chattanooga with the Tennessee River and Lookout Mountain. Andy Wellman photo.

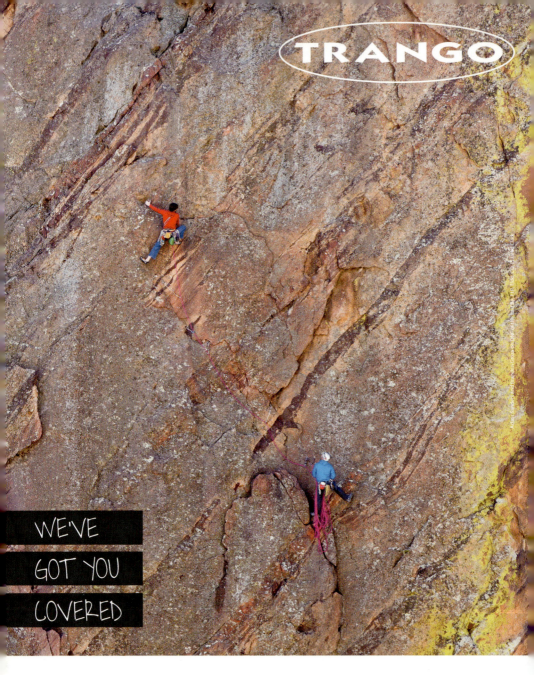

TRANGO

WE'VE
GOT YOU
COVERED

Meet the complete line-up of new products at **www.trango.com**

BOULDERING ETHICS

Bouldering is not a sport or a game or a competition. It is an activity, something cool to do, it's fun. I think of it like weight lifting or karate: you can't win it and there are no rules. That's right, there are no rules. Or looked at another way: there are rules, but like reality, you create them for yourself. At the end of the day, if you can live with yourself and what you did with your day, then that's all that matters. However, nobody can deny that there are a lot of boulderers, it is becoming more popular all the time, and that bouldering DOES have an environmental and social impact. For this reason there are Ethical Rules to bouldering which need to be followed for continued access to the boulders, and for the sanity of us all. Here are some suggestions:

MINIMIZE YOUR IMPACT

Minimizing your impact is important for a variety of reasons, but the most important is that bouldering pretty much only exists on either private land, or public land that is managed by an appointed agency. Private land owners don't like to see a bunch of people they don't know trash their land, and public land managers usually have mandates to follow which include human impact concerns. In order to retain and expand access into the future, it is essential that boulderers do their best to leave as little impact as possible.

• **Litter:** Litter is unacceptable. DO NOT LITTER. This includes cigarette butts. Pick up trash when you see it.

• **Trails:** Following the trails which are already in place helps prevent new ones from forming. When new trails form all over, they become a visual impact, and people like land owners and managers start to consider the changes that are taking place on their land due to boulderers.

• **Smoking:** A lot of people like bouldering cause its outside, in nature, where it's supposed to be clean and fresh and beautiful. Respect others and don't ruin their experience by forcing them to inhale your smoke. Ask first, or better yet, just move a reasonable distance away before lighting up. Always pick up your cigarette butts.

• **Pads:** Throwing a giant mat down on the ground and then repeatedly landing on it squishes anything which might be underneath. Pay attention where you put your pad and do your best to place it on a durable surface such as dirt or rock, and not directly on top of vegetation.

• **Brushes:** It is pretty much standard practice to brush holds clean of excessive chalk and grease. But remember, this rock is sandstone, and it does wear away. **Do not use steel brushes on any rock!** At the Stone Fort, the use of nylon and horse or hogs hair brushes is acceptable.

• **Dogs:** Dogs should be left at home.

• **Stereos:** Not everyone will agree that 90's gangsta rap is the best music to send to. Blaring your tunes in the boulders is a lot like smoking: chances are that your fix is ruining someone else's experience. Keep it to yourself, keep it discreet, and turn it off when others are around.

SPRAY

Like my friend Adam Henry has said, "Spray should only come from a metal can." Spraying is the practice of opening one's mouth for the purpose of receiving a self-induced bump to the ego. Bouldering is not about making money, or receiving props or recognition, or becoming famous. Bouldering is an escape from all of these unfortunate realities. Telling people about how rad you are for one of these purposes will only make you look foolish. Stay humble, and realize that in the end it doesn't matter, there is no point, and there will always be someone better than you are.

BE SOCIALLY RESPONSIBLE

• **Entitlement:** By the time any of us retire, the government will be bankrupt and entitlement programs like Medicaid and Social Security will cease to exist. Lets start acting like it's already happened and realize that we are not entitled to anything! Unless you personally own the land under the boulder you are climbing, you are a guest, and can be kicked out at any time. At all times act like a guest and do whatever it takes to maintain a good relationship with the powers that be.

The Stone Fort has been closed to bouldering for the majority of its history. The only reason that we all have access to this boulderfield now is because climbers were willing to forge a relationship with the owner and have acted responsibly enough to maintain that access. It has been a bumpy road at times. Pay the fee if you want to climb here, and realize that this place doesn't have to be open at all.

• **Giving Back:** Realize that if you boulder regularly, you WILL have an impact, regardless of whether you follow these practices or not. Mitigate this impact by giving back. Volunteer for trail days or donate money for improvements to the climbing areas. When landowners see a huge posse of volunteer climbers that care so much they are willing to donate their time, labor, and money to improving the climbing area, there is no better impression that can be made. It also feels good, gains you good karma, and chances are you will meet some cool people.

gearX.com

GearX Web Manager Ivan Tighe keeping his composure on Fear and Loathing in Keene Valley (11b) in the Adirondacks, NY

FIVE TEN

The Best Selection of New & Discounted Gear Everyday Online.

Find our brick and mortar store in Burlington, VT

gearX.com
Outdoor Gear Exchange

LOCATION

The Stone Fort is located on the property of the Montlake Golf Course, located on Mowbray Mountain, in Soddy-Daisy, Tennessee. It is about a 20 minute drive from downtown Chattanooga, TN.

For visiting climbers, the first step is to point yourself towards Chattanooga. Chattanooga is conveniently located at a crossroads of four Interstate Freeways which arrive at it from Atlanta, Birmingham, Nashville, and Knoxville. It is located within 500 miles of almost every major city in the eastern US, making it no more than a day's drive from about 100 million people.

For climber's wishing to use an airplane to reach the Stone Fort, the nearest commercial airport is in Chattanooga. This is a small regional airport, however, and so flights tend to cost a bit more. The closest major airports which may have cheaper flights are in Atlanta and Nashville. Each are about a two hour drive from Chattanooga. Regardless of where you choose to fly in to, you will need to rent a car, as there is no public transportation that will deposit you at the Stone Fort.

DRIVING DIRECTIONS

I am going to assume that you have made your way to Chattanooga, and these directions are going to start from where US Hwy 27 splits off from I-24 near downtown. If you are arriving on I-75 from either north or south, follow signs towards Chattanooga as you merge onto I-24. If you are coming from Nashville or Birmingham, you will already be on I-24.

Take US 27 North where it splits off from I-24 (signs will say Downtown Chattanooga). Drive North on 27 for 15.7 miles to the Thrasher Pike exit. Take a left on Thrasher Pike and follow it to the stop light. Take a right on Dayton Pike at the stop light and go 0.7 miles to a stop light at Montlake Road. Turn left and follow Montlake Road up the mountain, and once on top, take a right onto Brow Lake Road. Brow Lake Road forms a loop and encounters Montlake Road twice. Turning right at either junction will bring you to the Montlake Golf Club parking area and Clubhouse, which should be obvious. Park here in the area marked "Climber Parking."

CAMPING

Depending on what kind of set-up you are looking for, finding adequate camping close to the Stone Fort could be your biggest crux. Here are the options:

Wal-Mart

Everyone knows that Wal-mart allows people to "camp" in their vehicles free of charge and with no hassles in their parking lots. If you are in a van, or can sleep in your car, this will be the closest and cheapest sleeping option to the boulders. Not much ambiance though. The closest Wal-mart to the Stone Fort is at 9334 Dayton Pike in Soddy-Daisy.

Cost: Free. **Alcohol:** Sure. **Campfires:** No. **Open Year Round:** Yes. **Water:** Yes, inside. **Toilets:** Yes, inside. **Distance from Stone Fort:** 15 mins.

Directions: From the Montlake Parking lot, take a right, and then a left on Montlake Rd. Follow this to the bottom of the hill. At the stoplight at Dayton Pike, turn left, and drive about one mile till you see it on your right.

Chester Frost State Park

Chester Frost is a state park located on the banks of the Tennessee River. It has tent camping sites which are flat, maintained, and located next to the river and your car. It is about 25 minutes drive from the boulders, and is the closest family camping option. The park is patrolled by rangers, so it is safe, but at times in the winter the tent camping sites are closed. Call ahead to make sure at 423-842-3306.

Cost: $16 per site per night. Two tents and two cars allowed per site. **Alcohol:** No. **Campfires:** Yes. **Open Year Round:** No. **Water:** No. **Toilets:** Yes. **Distance from Stone Fort:** 25 mins.

Directions: From the Montlake Parking lot, take a right, and then a left onto Montlake Rd. Follow it to the bottom of the hill. At the stoplight, go right on Dayton Pike. Take a left at the next stoplight onto Thrasher Pike. Follow it till it dead-ends at Hixon Pike and go left. Take your first right onto Gold Point Circle, where there is a small sign for Chester Frost Park. Follow this road to its end, where you will be at the park.

Tennessee Wall Parking Lot

The parking lot at the T-Wall has long been the climber camping spot of the Chattanooga Area. It is free, although being right next to the road it is usually trashed, and has limited quality tent sites. There have also been major problems with break-ins here, but no reported problems of people being hassled while present. There is a nasty pit toilet you won't want to use, and your cell phone probably won't work.

Cost: Free. **Alcohol:** For sure. **Campfires:** Yes. **Open year Round:** Yes, except on managed hunt dates. Check this website for dates: http://tennessee.gov/ agriculture/forestry/stateforest07.html. **Water:** No. **Toilet:** Lets just say no. **Distance from Stone Fort:** 45 mins.

Directions: From the Montlake Parking lot take a right, then a left on Montlake Rd. Drive to the bottom of the hill and take a right at the stoplight onto Dayton Pike. Follow it until you encounter US-27 and get on it going south (entrance ramp will be on your right). Exit onto Signal Mountain Rd. and go right(west) at the base of the ramp. Follow it until you make a left turn for TN-27 Suck Creek Rd. Follow this about three miles till you come to a short concrete bridge crossing Suck Creek. Make a hard left just after the bridge onto River Canyon Rd. (unmarked). Follow this winding and narrow road about 6.6 miles till you encounter the parking lot on your left. The camping is a short ways downhill.

Hunter Check Station Camping Area

This camp area is quite a ways from the Stone Fort, but offers the largest, cleanest, and safest camping option for a visiting climber, not to mention it is free. It is open even during the hunt dates, and has a maintained pit toilet.

Cost: Free. **Alcohol:** Yes. **Campfires:** Yes. **Open Year Round:** Yes. **Water:** No. **Toilet:** Yes. **Distance from Stone Fort:** 40 mins.

Directions: From the Montlake Parking lot take a right, then a left on Montlake Rd. Drive to the bottom of the hill and take a right at the stoplight onto Dayton Pike. Follow it until you encounter US-27 and get on it going south (entrance ramp will be on your right). Exit onto Signal Mountain Rd. and go right(west) at the base of the ramp. Follow it until you make a left turn for TN-27 Suck Creek Rd. Follow this as it climbs up the long hill of Suck Creek Canyon. As you approach the top of the mountain, you will see a Prentice Cooper Sign on your left, turn here onto Choctaw Rd. Follow the road as it winds and splits in the neighborhood, following little brown Prentice Cooper Signs. The road will turn to dirt, and shortly you will encounter a gate and a Hunter Check Station on the left. The camping area is before, outside, the gate, on the right hand(west) side of the road. There are no signs signifying it as a camping area, but there are many dirt roads and campsites.

WRESTLE WITH THE THONG.
COME BACK TO CRASH.

PHOTO: EMILY VARISCO

JOHN YING ON TENNESSEE THONG

HOTELS AND MOTELS

Cheap hotels and motels are abundant in Chattanooga and should not be dismissed for those spending a few days in the area. Rain is unpredictable and an ever present threat, and having a roof over your head when it decides to soak can make things a lot less miserable. There are too many options to list here, I would consider doing an internet search before you come.

GROCERY STORES AND GEAR

There is a Bi-Lo and a Wal-mart in Soddy-Daisy at the bottom of Mowbray Mountain. Follow Montlake Rd. down the mountain and take a left at Dayton Pike, at the stop light. Follow this for about two miles to the shopping center. Greenlife (Whole Foods) is a huge organic grocery in North Chattanooga. To get there get on US-27 going south and get off at the Manufacturers Road exit. Take a left and you will see it on your left very soon. Rock/Creek Outfitters is located in the same shopping center and is your best option for climbing or camping equipment or beta.

SEASON AND WEATHER

There are climbers wrestling the boulders of the Stone Fort almost every single day of the year. That's no lie. But, the best temperatures for bouldering are typically found in the winter, between November and March. The shoulder seasons also offer a decent chance of cool temps and low humidity, making a visit in October, or April and May, probably worth your while. Hard core boulderers should avoid visiting during the summer, as the heat and humidity are oppressive. For those select few who believe that summer is climbing season, there will undoubtably be plenty of like-minded people out there suffering with you.

A bigger issue than choosing when to find the best temperatures and lowest humidity is the ever-present threat of rain. It rains pretty much every single week of the year in Tennessee. You really never know what you are going to get with the rain, but if you have the luxury of planning your trip for a certain window of time, and then checking the weather reports religiously before you commit to a drive, you will have a better chance of finding dry rock.

The rock can dry surpisingly quick after a rainstorm, although I'm not making any promises. A couple hours after a rainstorm can be the perfect time to climb some of the harder friction problems, as they will have been washed clean of chalk and hand grease.

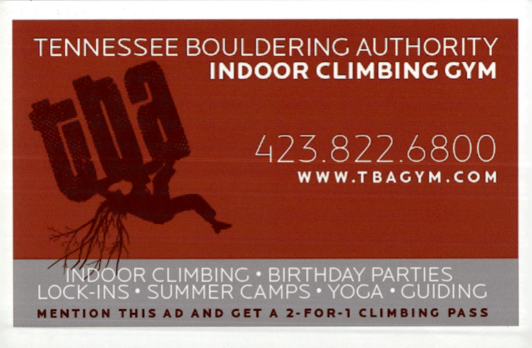

STONE FORT VISITATION RULES

The Stone Fort is on private property. Use your best judgement and avoid any behavior that could compromise our opportunity to climb there. Please abide by these rules which were set forth by the landowner and encourage others to do the same. Your cooperation is key to keeping the Stone Fort open. Please contact the clubhouse at 423-332-3111 if you have any questions.

GOLF COURSE AND BOULDERING RULES

- All visitors must sign in the clubhouse and pay the daily ACCESS FEE, climbing or not you need to pay and wear the wristbands on your person (wrist, ankle, or belt loop) while you are on the property. Anyone caught in the field without the wristband will be asked to leave immediately.
- The ACCESS FEE is good for both Stone Fort and Leda climbing areas, although Leda does require a parking pass. Without the parking pass to Leda you will be ticketed.
- Everyone must be out of the area by dark. The neighborhood patrol will report any vehicles in the area.
- No dogs are permitted in the field. Do not leave your dog in the car.
- No metal brushes are allowed to be used in the cleaning of the boulders. Boar's hair brushes are the recommended brushes to prevent damage to the boulders.
- No outside alcohol is permitted, anyone caught with outside alcohol will be asked to leave. Beer is available in the clubhouse.
- Maintain a low profile (no yelling or swearing). No loud music.
- Stay off the golf course and fairways.
- No climbing on closed areas or boulders. Closed areas are marked with signs and are not described within this guide. There is no climbing on boulders which reside on the golf course.

- Always yield to golfers.
- Shirts must be worn at the Clubhouse and in the parking lot.
- Make every effort to stay on the trails and to avoid short-cutting.
- Place crash pads on durable surfaces to lessen impact.
- Pack out all trash that you bring in. Pack out all trash that you see, even if it is not yours.
- Do not cut down trees or partake in excessive cleaning of boulders or moss and vegetation on the boulders.
- There are no seasonal or annual passes available

THE MONTLAKE GOLF COURSE CLUBHOUSE

The Montlake Golf Course Clubhouse is located next to the parking lot for the golf course, and is conveniently located in between the climber parking area and the entrance trail to the boulders. The Clubhouse is run by a friendly group of fellows who are always ready to chat about the weather or whatever is on your mind, and will graciously answer all of your questions. Leave bouldering pads outside and sign in and pay the climber day use fee at the front desk, just inside the front door.

The Clubhouse has lots of amenities for sale to help you enjoy your bouldering day. They sell bouldering gear such as chalk, chalk bags, brushes, guidebooks, and tee shirts. Climbers can rent bouldering pads. The clubhouse is a great spot for the end of your day as well. There is free WIFI and they also sell tasty and refresing beverages such as canned beer, soft drinks, sports drinks, and water, as well as a selection of snacks. There is also a small grill which operates year round although the menu may be limited during winter months. Hours of the clubhouse vary depending on the time of year, but check out their page on Facebook under Montlake Golf Club or Stone Fort Bouldering.

CLIMB HARD.
EAT HARDER.

German-American Gastro-Pub

Featuring 12 continually rotating draft beers

Extensive craft & import bottle selection

Chef driven food with a view

Located on Chattanooga's Northshore
Monday-Saturday 11am-12am
Sunday 10am-10pm {Sunday Brunch 10am-2pm}

224 Frazier Ave.   www.BrewhausBar.com   423. 531. 8490

THE SOUTHEASTERN CLIMBERS COALITION

The Southeastern Climbers Coalition (SCC) is a non-profit group dedicated to pre-serving southern climbing areas for future generations to enjoy. In 2003, the SCC negotiated with the owners of the Montlake Golf Course to institute a day use permit system which, for the first time, allowed public access to the boulders of the Stone Fort. Through ongoing communication and continued support, this arrangement is still in place today, and has evolved to allow greater climber access to the boulders, while at the same time meeting the goals of the property owner. The SCC sponsors an annual trail and clean-up day at the Stone Fort, which usually takes place the same weekend as the Triple Crown Bouldering Series. To join the SCC, learn more about their climber advocacy work, donate money to the cause, or check out the calendar of upcoming events, go to their website at www.seclimbers.org.

In an effort to support the causes championed by the Southeastern Climbers Coalition, Greener Grass Publishing is donating 5% of all sales of this guidebook to the SCC.

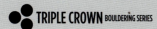

THE TRIPLE CROWN BOULDERING SERIES

The Triple Crown Bouldering Series is a competition made up of three venues on three different days - Hound Ears in North Carolina, Horse Pens 40 in Alabama, and the Stone Fort in Tennessee. At press time, the competition was getting ready to be held for the eighth consecutive year. Typically, the competitions take place on the first Saturday of the months October, November, and December. It is the largest outdoor bouldering competition in the country, and the model for how community activism can make a positive difference for climbing access.

The goal of the Triple Crown Bouldering Series is to raise money to give to the SCC and the Carolina Climbers Coalition, as well as local rescue groups and non-profit causes. The organizers of the Triple Crown, Jim Horton and Chad Wykle, have played a tremendous role in securing climber access to the boulderfields of Hound Ears and the Stone Fort. Without these two guys, it would probably be safe to say that these climbing areas would not be open to the public. Registration for the Triple Crown is always open, if you are interested in competing, sign up at www.triplecrownbouldering.org.

USING THIS GUIDEBOOK

GRADES

The grading system used within this book is the V-scale, also known as the Vermin scale, originally invented by guidebook author John Sherman in his bouldering guidebook to Hueco Tanks, Texas.

Grades for bouldering are a controversial thing, and grade debates seem to have taken the place of ethics debates as the most heated, overblown, and sometimes downright silly arguments in climbing. Many people focus far too much energy on what grade they are climbing, have climbed, or want to climb – usually ignoring the uniqueness of the individual problem in the process. Like my high school math teacher told me – grades are not important. I believe that grades are meant to be a guideline as to whether this is a problem you would be interested in trying or not, and nothing more.

Accordingly, I have attempted to grade climbs in the least controversial manner possible. In most cases, I gave each problem the grade that it is most often reported to be, consulting many sources such as word of mouth, the most recent Triple Crown pamphlets, and multiple internet sources, as well as my own experience on the problem. In other cases where the problem is very obscure or never before published, I gave it the grade I felt fit the most after either sending it or attempting it many times. In some cases, problems were reported to me which I could not climb, in which case I gave them the grade that they were reported to me as being. As Adam Henry would say, "If only we could afford to package these books with white out, the grades could be whatever you want them to be."

STARS

This book uses a 3 star system. It is meant to be a simple system for determining quality, and strives to not have to split hairs between good problems. The main considerations in determining the stars that a problem receives are: aesthetic quality, quality of movement, and rock quality.

⭐⭐⭐ – A unique and world class boulder problem. If this is your first visit, seek these out.

⭐⭐ – A very good problem. You won't be disappointed.

⭐ – Fair. Worth doing.

No stars – A bit lacking. Usually due to the fact that the problem is dirty, chossy, ugly, contrived, or just not very fun to climb.

LAYOUT AND MAPS

For the purposes of this guidebook I have divided the Stone Fort into 12 sections and given each of these sections its own chapter. The sections are described from front to back in the order that you would come to them if approaching from the parking lot and Clubhouse. The sections roughly mirror the sections used to divide up the boulderfield in the Triple Crown pamphlets, although there are some variations of names and areas that are designed to hopefully make things more intuitive. Each section of the Stone Fort is given a roman numeral to denote its order in the book. Take a peek at the Overview Map on the opposite page to understand how the sections are divided up.

At the beginning of each chapter there is another overview map, which describes and names the boulders located within that chapter. There is also a small inset map which highlights the area of the boulderfield that particular chapter describes. Each separate boulder also has its own map, which shows where on the boulder the respective problems are located.

The only special symbol found on the maps that is not found on the photos of the problems is:

 – A red arrow designates where the easiest or most commonly used down climb off the boulder is to be found.

The maps in this book were originally drawn by hand, before being pieced together and digitized. They are as accurate and to scale as an obsessive, yet sane (I think), person could make them, but they are not perfect. They are oriented the same way throughout the entire book to hopefully avoid confusion.

OVERVIEW MAP

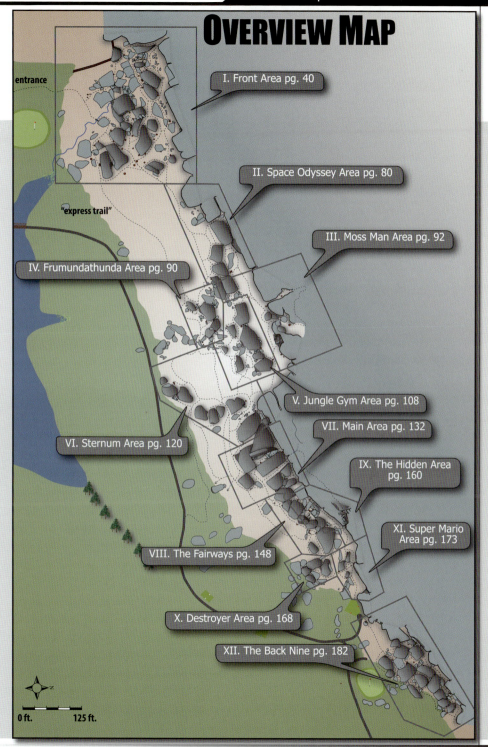

entrance

I. Front Area pg. 40

II. Space Odyssey Area pg. 80

III. Moss Man Area pg. 92

IV. Frumundathunda Area pg. 90

"express trail"

V. Jungle Gym Area pg. 108

VII. Main Area pg. 132

VI. Sternum Area pg. 120

IX. The Hidden Area pg. 160

XI. Super Mario Area pg. 173

VIII. The Fairways pg. 148

X. Destroyer Area pg. 168

XII. The Back Nine pg. 182

0 ft.   125 ft.

NUMBERING AND COLOR CODING

I. – Roman numerals represent the section of the boulderfield, and chapter, that the boulder is within.

2. – Numbers represent the individual boulders or groups of boulders described together. There are 82 boulders or areas described in this guide, and the numbers do not repeat themselves.

a. – Lower case letters represent the individual problems on that boulder. All problems are represented with both the number and letter together.

☐ **1a** – Each problem is assigned a number and a letter. Numbers are used to describe the boulder that the problem is on. Letters denote the separate problems.

☐ **1b** – **Indented problem** descriptions, like this one, are variations of the problems above them.

Every problem in this guide is given a color coding depending on how hard that problem is. This is designed to make it easier to quickly find problems which might suit you. The idea is that you can glance at a page, map, or photo, and instantly see roughly how hard the problems are, without having to look all that information up. If you are looking to climb easy (green) problems, you can glance at a page and know whether it is an area or boulder which might suit you by how many green problems that you see.

The color codes go like this:

V0 - **V3** – **Green** represents problems of the grades V0, V1, V2, and V3.

V4 - **V7** – **Yellow** represents problems of the grades V4, V5, V6, and V7.

V8 - **V12** – **Red** represents problems of the grades V8, V9, V10, V11, and V12. Currently there are no problems graded harder than V12 at the Stone Fort, but hard men take note that there a number of extremely worthy projects that will be far harder than what has been climbed thus far.

■ – **Black** represents projects. These problems have not yet been climbed. Have at them.

■ – **Blue** represents problems which have been given a route climbing grade instead of a bouldering grade, usually due to height or length. Blue also represents problems which have been climbed but which do not lend themselves to a V grade, or the grade is unknown.

SKETCHY AND SCARY

Many problems are described within as "Sketchy," or "Scary." This classification is designed to let the climber know how serious a problem might be. These descriptions are purely subjective, and should not be used in place of common sense and good judgement. Just because a problem is not described as "Sketchy," or "Scary," does not mean that you could not get seriously injured or die in a fall. Please re-read the WARNING in the front of the book for more information.

"Sketchy." – Means that the problem does not have an ideal landing beneath it, or that the problem is somewhat to very tall. Sketchy problems should be considered carefully before they are attempted, and every effort should be taken to mitigate the risk of a fall.

"Scary." – Means that regardless of crash pads and spotters, a fall from this problem is a very serious endeavor. In most cases these problems are VERY tall. This is not child's play, don't say I didn't warn you.

A NOTE ABOUT NAMES

Many amongst the older generations have assured me that the majority of the names in this guidebook are wrong. The reality is that for 20 odd years of climbing, problems were established and never named. When the first Triple Crown competition was held at Stone Fort, some unnamed problems were given names to avoid confusion during scoring. These new names were printed in successive generations of competition pamplets, and are now generally the names which the problems are known by. I have preserved the names from these pamphlets. When I encountered an unnamed problem and was told who did the first ascent (supposedly) I named the problem after that person. When I encountered a truly unknown problem, I have just called it by its grade, choosing to not invent names if I didn't know them.

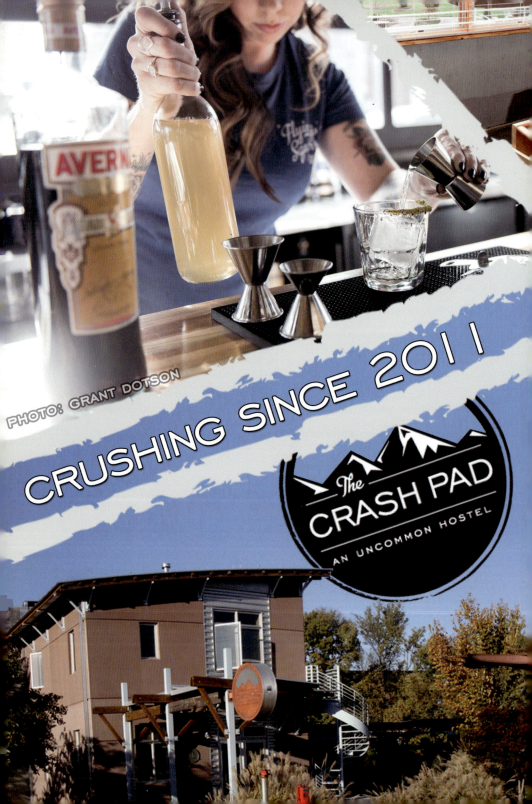

PHOTO: GRANT DOTSON

AVERM

CRUSHING SINCE 2011

The
CRASH PAD
AN UNCOMMON HOSTEL

PHOTO: MANDY RHODEN

CHATTANOOGA, TN

PHOTO: OSBORN SONG

Flying Squirrel

I. FRONT AREA

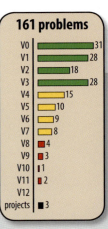

161 problems

V0	31
V1	28
V2	18
V3	28
V4	15
V5	10
V6	9
V7	8
V8	4
V9	3
V10	1
V11	2
V12	
projects	3

The Front Area in winter. Luke Laeser photo.

The Front Area, also known as the Forbidden City, is the first collection of boulders that you encounter when you walk into the woods from the Clubhouse. And what a first impression it makes! This tightly packed zone of bleached grey boulders has it all. In this zone are classics and obscurities, tall slabby faces and short powerful roofs, easy problems by the bucket load as well as some of the hardest problems in the South. This collection of blocks could easily stand alone as one of the best local boulderfields around – never mind that there's about half a mile of blocks stretched out beyond. Conveniently enough, it is also the best area to warm up, offering the largest variety of easy and moderate problems to get the blood flowing and the fingers loosened up.

As you walk along the trail by the 18th green of the golf course and then enter the woods, the boulders spread out below you and to the left. A short stone staircase takes you to a shallow stream, and then after strolling over a small slab, you walk through a narrow corridor on your left into the heart of the Forbidden City. As you stare at the crenulated jugs on the *Incredarete* or the tall white "eyebrowed" faces on all sides, it's easy to imagine that you are standing in the middle of some ancient Terra Cotta Pagoda Village – made for boulderers! (Never mind that the Forbidden City was the ancient secluded home of the Japanese royal family in Kyoto, while the Terra Cotta warriors were discovered in underground vaulted tombs in Mongolia thousands of miles and an ocean away – you get my point!)

If you are following the directions (and probably even if you aren't) you will end up in a small open area where most people choose to throw down their junk and start getting their climb on for the day. Set a little bit apart is the Fire Crack Boulder, with its obvious detached flake, and making up the corridor you just walked through is the Slice and Dice Boulder, the Mystery Machine Boulder, and the Brain Boulder. The descriptions start in this area and then branch out and back towards the cliffline from here, see the map on the opposite page.

NOT TO BE MISSED:

V0 Spare ★★★ – Awesome sloper climbing up the prow of the Bowling Ball. One of the best V0's at the Fort.

V1 Incredarete ★★★ – You won't find holds like these anywhere else, not even the gym.

V1 The Crescent ★★★ – An awesome arcing seam that will school you on footwork and balance.

V1 Storming the Castle ★★★ – Tall, smooth, and with ramparts guarding the top. Just be happy that all you have to worry about is the climbing.

V3 Mystery Machine ★★★ – One of the most interesting slabs in a boulderfield packed with interesting slabs. Good holds, but how to reach them?

V3 Swingers ★★★ – You're so money and you don't even know it! Now show this roof what's up.

V4 Mystery Groove ★★★ – The mysterious climbing groove required to climb this pinch problem may elude you...

V5 Genghis Khan ★★★ – Probably the most popular V5 at the Stone Fort, this quality problem certainly attracts the hordes.

V6 Manute Bol ★★★ – A classic reach problem named after one of the tallest humans to ever play basketball.

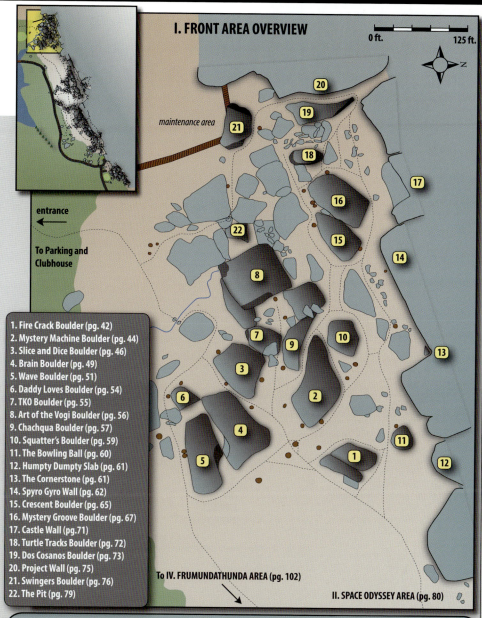

I. FRONT AREA OVERVIEW

0 ft.   125 ft.

maintenance area

entrance

To Parking and
Clubhouse

1. Fire Crack Boulder (pg. 42)
2. Mystery Machine Boulder (pg. 44)
3. Slice and Dice Boulder (pg. 46)
4. Brain Boulder (pg. 49)
5. Wave Boulder (pg. 51)
6. Daddy Loves Boulder (pg. 54)
7. TKO Boulder (pg. 55)
8. Art of the Vogi Boulder (pg. 56)
9. Chachqua Boulder (pg. 57)
10. Squatter's Boulder (pg. 59)
11. The Bowling Ball (pg. 60)
12. Humpty Dumpty Slab (pg. 61)
13. The Cornerstone (pg. 61)
14. Spyro Gyro Wall (pg. 62)
15. Crescent Boulder (pg. 65)
16. Mystery Groove Boulder (pg. 67)
17. Castle Wall (pg.71)
18. Turtle Tracks Boulder (pg. 72)
19. Dos Cosanos Boulder (pg. 73)
20. Project Wall (pg. 75)
21. Swingers Boulder (pg. 76)
22. The Pit (pg. 79)

To IV. FRUMUNDATHUNDA AREA (pg. 102)

II. SPACE ODYSSEY AREA (pg. 80)

V6 The Wave ★★★ — One of the most attempted climbs at the Fort, this wave won't break. Ride the lip.

V6 Kingpin ★★★ — A power slab classic on the back of the Bowling Ball. Just add about six more moves and you have *Space*.

V7 Tennessee Thong ★★★ — Maybe I'm just ignorant, or perhaps sheltered, but this one I had to look up. The most interesting thing I found, besides YouTube movies that didn't involve rock climbing, was a comic book hero named Thong Girl, who finds a magic thong which allows her to fly and shoot laser beams from her rear, all in the name of fighting crime in Nashville.

V7 Spyro Gyro ★★★ — Like those circular pen drawings you did as a kid, your efforts on this problem could get repetitive...

V7 Kaya ★★★ — Like Bob Marley as he sang his songs, the goal on this problem is to get higha' mon.

V11 Flying High ★★★ — This huge dyno first climbed by Tony Lamiche is a classic. If you like big lunges, you should also check out *Watch Your Back*, to the left.

1. FIRE CRACK BOULDER

1. FIRE CRACK BOULDER

1. FIRE CRACK BOULDER

This boulder, or rather two boulders leaning against each other, is easily recognizable by the large detached flake on its downhill corner. The Fire Crack Boulder has a few really mellow warm-ups on it, making it a very popular first stop when arriving at the boulders. **Problems are described from left to right if looking at the boulder.** The easiest downclimb is to just walk off the back side.

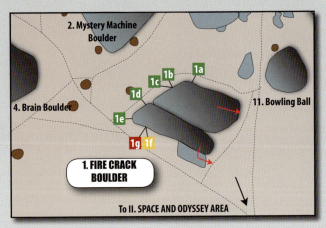

2. Mystery Machine Boulder

4. Brain Boulder

11. Bowling Ball

1. FIRE CRACK BOULDER

To II. SPACE AND ODYSSEY AREA

☐ **1a Slab** V0-
Around the corner to the left. Use it as a downclimb, or as a first climb for your tennis shoe clad non-climbing friends - or your kids!

☐ **1b Needless Things** V0- ⭐
The brown face covered in large flakey holds is a very popular first problem of the day. Stand start and climb straight up from the bottom and finish left.

☐ **1c Costume Rings** V0- ⭐
Just to the right of *Needless Things*. Stand start at the bottom and angle up and right.

☐ **1d Seam Eliminate** V3
Climb the rightward angling seam to the left of the big detached flake. Stand start on crimpers by the seam and climb crimps and sidepulls up the seam and using the left arete to the top. You have to ignore the good holds further left.

☐ **1e Fire Crack Flake** V1 ⭐
At the corner of the boulder is a huge dinner-plate thick spike sticking out of the ground. Climb it to its top, then make moves to finish off the boulder. Feel it flex?

☐ **1f Aneardon** V6 ⭐⭐
Stand start to the right of the detached flake with right hand really high on sidepull crimper and left on blocky sidepull. Follow crimpers and the obvious flake to the top of the boulder.

☐ **1g Aneardon Low** V8 ⭐⭐
Stand start with right hand on low sidepull crimper and left on the same blocky sidepull. Do one move to high right crimp (normal start) and then follow more crimpers and the flake to the top of the boulder.

Elden Earhart on the V2. Micah Gentry photo.

2. MYSTERY MACHINE BOULDER

The Mystery Machine Boulder is one of the most popular boulders in the field - and for good reason! There are classics on all sides of this boulder of all grades. From the awesome sculpted holds on the *Incredarete* and the climbs to its right, to the heinous crimper problems on the boulder's steep side, to the lower angle introductory climbs on the uphill side, this boulder holds something for everyone. **The problems are described starting with *Incredarete* and then continue right all the way around the boulder.** The easiest way off is to downclimb the problem *Easy Does It*.

☐ **2a** **Incredarete** V1 ★★★
"Sketchy." Maybe the funnest V1 you will ever climb! Stand start on underclings and climb straight up the tall arete on awesome sculpted holds.

☐ **2b** **Incredarete Sit** V3 ★★
"Sketchy." Sit start on low scooped holds directly under the underclings and climb upwards.

☐ **2c** **Incredarete Left Sit** V4 ★★
"Sketchy." This low variation adds a couple interesting moves to this super classic arete. Sit start to the left of the arete on crimpy edge. Use the arete to the right for a right heelhook and make a hard move to the left-facing arcing sidepull above before rocking over right to *Incredarete* and finishing up it.

☐ **2d** **Sister Sarah** V3 ★★
"Sketchy." Stand start about three feet right of the arete on underclings and climb the cool face above using slopers and more underclings. Top out in a crack/groove.

☐ **2e** **Ruby Roo** V2 ★★
"Sketchy." This tall face with awesome holds can be a puzzler. Stand start with your hand on a big right sidepull and climb the face above using gastons until you get to the money jug.

☐ **2f** **V8** ★
In between *Ruby Roo* and the *Mystery Machine* is this blank face. Start with thin crimps for the right hand and climb upwards using really shallow pockets and bad holds.

☐ **2g** **Mystery Machine** V3 ★★★
"Sketchy." The smooth clean scoop to the left of the arete makes for a very interesting slab problem. Start on the right side of the scoop and move up into shallow holds in a vertical seam before making a long span left to an obvious ridge.

☐ **2h** **Shaggy** V1 ★
"Sketchy." The tall arete is a nice warm-up. Start on large pink jugs and climb up using many large sidepulls around left of the arete.

☐ **2i** **V2** ★
Slightly contrived, but fun. Start right of the arete on the pink nipple jug and climb face up shallow edge pockets to the right of the arete to incut flake jugs at the top.

☐ **2j** **The Shrine** V2 ★
Squat start right of the tree on a left-facing flake. Climb face above via obvious pocket and long moves to crimpy top out.

☐ **2k** **Wide Wet Crack** V1
Not sure why you would want to climb this, so wet and mossy.

☐ **2l** **Pinch the Loaf** V3 ★★
This face is harder than it looks. Climbs just to the left of the arete. Sit start low on flake crimpers and make big moves straight up the face on crimps and cool pinches and scoops.

2. MYSTERY MACHINE BOULDER

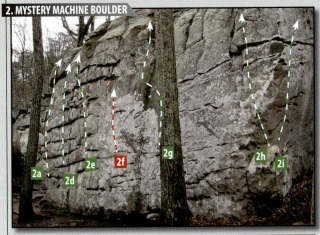

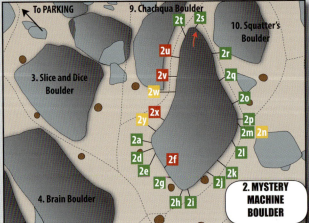

☐ **2m** **The Boogie Man-tle** V3 ★★
The clean blunt prow may be holding a slabby surprise for you. Stand start on a sloper rail at chest height and climb up blunt prow arete via balancey moves.

  ☐ **2n** **Sit Start** V4 ★★
Sit start on low crimper flake the same as for *Pinch the Loaf*. Do a move up and right to starting sloper, then follow the problem to top.

☐ **2o** **Booger** V0 ★
The slabby crack five feet right of the arete on the face.

  ☐ **2p** **V1**
Start on the sloper rail the same as for the *Boogie Man-tle* and traverse the crimpy seam into the start of *Booger*. Contrived.

☐ **2q** **V0-** ★
The middle of the slabby face has lots of good holds and ledges. Can also be used as a downclimb.

☐ **2r** **V0-** ★
Climb the hand crack on the right side of the face a few feet left of *Easy Does It*.

☐ **2s** **Easy Does It** V0-
The low angle slab on the uphill side of the boulder has some cool holds and is the easiest downclimb.

☐ **2t** **Mutiny** V2 ★
A contrived but fun problem on clean rock. Stand start on edges and climb the vertical face just to the right of the arete.

☐ **2u** **I Think I Can** V9 ★★
"Sketchy." If your dream climb is a ladder of very tiny crimps, this may be the line for you! Stand start on small crimps in the middle of the face and grab more tiny holds on your way to the top.

☐ **2v** **Reflections** V10 ★
"Sketchy." Climbs the jigsaw face just to the left of the right-facing corner on small holds. Stand start on thin crimps in horizontal seam. Lock off between bad holds.

☐ **2w** **Dirty Sanchez** V7 ★★
"Sketchy." This problem climbs the seam and arete-type feature that is in the middle of the face, just right of *Reflections*. Start at a low sidepull.

☐ **2x** **Tommy Boy** V9 ★
"Sketchy." Sit start on the left side of a long low rail which goes across most of this side of the face. Climb the face straight up, staying just right of the corner of *Dirty Sanchez*.

☐ **2y** **The Eliminator** V7 ★
"Sketchy." Sit start on the same holds as for the *Incredarete Left Sit* but the holds on the arete are off for both feet and hands. Climb straight up the rock just to the left of the arete. Contrived, but cool.

2. MYSTERY MACHINE BOULDER

Liza Rands on Mutiny, V2. Andrew Kornylak photo.

3. SLICE AND DICE BOULDER

The Slice and Dice Boulder sits across the small open area from the Mystery Machine Boulder and its chalked cracks, edges, and flakes catch the eye immediately. This face holds some cool and popular moderate problems, but for something less traveled, check out some of the interesting tall problems on other sides of this boulder. **The descriptions start from the left side of the downhill face, which faces the entrance trail, and move right around the boulder.** This boulder is easy to get off, just scramble down a ramp to the boulderer's right of *Dice*.

☐ **3a** **Hot Java** V3 ⭐

Another interesting face with cool holds. Sit start on low seam and make your way upwards staying left of the tree. You can also start a bit to the left and follow the rail of rising slopers to the upper face.

☐ **3b** **Formula 1** V3 ⭐

A nice roundy arete to add to the warm-up circuit. Stand start low on sidepulls and hug your way up more sidepulls to a slightly licheny top out.

☐ **3c** **V1** ⭐

The roughly hand-sized crack to the right of *Formula 1* on the face. Easy to use face features to help you out, often a bit dirty.

☐ **3d** **Red Label** V1 ⭐

"Sketchy." This nice white face is right of the tree and left of *Black Label*. Stand start in the corridor and climb to the top.

☐ **3e** **Black Label** V1 ⭐⭐

"Sketchy." This tall face climbs like a ladder of perfectly spaced edges. Stand start to the left of the arete, in the corridor, and climb the face to the left of the arete.

☐ **3f** **Green Label** V1 ⭐

Climbs the arete just to left of *Slice* and right of *Black Label*. Start by standing up onto obvious wide shelf and climb straight up using cracks and seams, mostly as sidepulls.

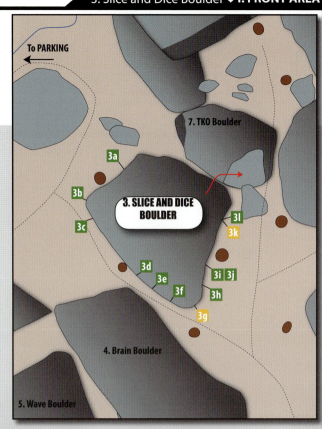

To PARKING

7. TKO Boulder

3a

3b

3c

3. SLICE AND DICE BOULDER

3l

3k

3d

3i 3j

3e

3f

3h

3g

4. Brain Boulder

5. Wave Boulder

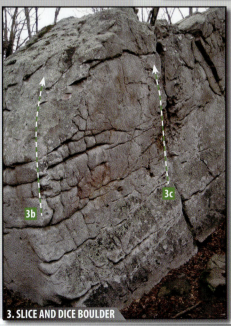

3b

3c

3. SLICE AND DICE BOULDER

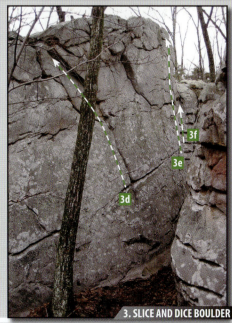

3f

3e

3d

3. SLICE AND DICE BOULDER

3. SLICE AND DICE BOULDER

☐ **3g Slice** V4 ⭐
Stand start with hands on top of detached flake on the left side of the face and climb the blunt prow using crimpy sidepulls and gastons.

☐ **3h Two Can Sam** V3 ⭐⭐
Depending on your technique, this groove can end up a lot more awkward than it looks. Start on the jug break and head up and left into the crack and groove.

☐ **3i V2** ⭐
Start on the jug rail the same as for *Two Can Sam* and move straight up to sidepulls over the lip, avoiding the crack to the right.

☐ **3j Farrah's Fawcett** V0 ⭐
Stand start in the crack. Traverse up and right behind the tree to jug flake, then up and right to top out with more jugs.

☐ **3k The Mane Event** V6 ⭐⭐
This often-tried problem can be deceptively hard. Sit start on the jug flake in the middle of the face. Previously graded a V4 the broken crimp has inceased the difficulty.

☐ **3l Dice** V2 ⭐
Sit start low on good flake the same as for the *Mane Event* and make a big move up and right to a pinch at the lip of the arete. Use this to top out straight up.

3. SLICE AND DICE BOULDER

4. BRAIN BOULDER

4. BRAIN BOULDER

4. THE BRAIN BOULDER

The Brain Boulder forms the other wall of the entrance area corridor and sits across from the Mystery Machine Boulder and the Slice and Dice Boulder. It has few worthwhile problems on it and no real classics. **The problem descriptions start with the tall problem facing the entrance, and then continuing left around the boulder.** There are many feasible ways to get off this boulder.

☐ 4a Bootleg V5 ⭐

"Sketchy." The tall red face which faces the trail as you enter the boulders is a cool problem. Stand start in the middle and follow edges and underclings up to the roundy top out.

☐ 4b Arete V0-

Climb the bulbous low angle arete on the downhill side of the boulder.

☐ 4c Crack Traverse V0

Start on the right side of the face down at the bottom in the gap and climb the sandy crack rail all the way left across the face and then top out via mossy holds into the ledgey scoop. You can downclimb from here hanging off the little sappling.

☐ 4d The Undaclink V2

Start in the middle of the face, on undercling pockets with good feet, then move up to more undercling pockets, eventually surmounting tall white bulge.

☐ 4e The Scalpel V1

Stand start in the middle of the green licheny face and climb to the top on crimps and edges. Dirty.

☐ 4f Mufassa V0

A short and mildly pointless traverse. Start on the arete on the left side of the face and traverse flakes to the right. Can finish up the *Scalpel*.

☐ 4g The Lying King V0

This problem needs a bit of traffic to clean up properly. It can also be climbed in a circle to add as many laps as you may like, if you are inclined. Start on the left side of the face and climb the cool low angle arete that arcs up and right, then climb down the center of the face via the good incut crimps and flakes of the *Scalpel*.

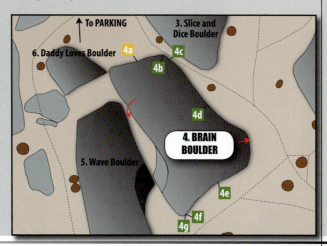

Black Carpet, V4. Dan Brayak photo.

5. THE WAVE BOULDER

The Wave Boulder hosts a very fine collection of classic problems and because of this is quite popular. Rarely will you come to the boulders and not find somebody attempting *the Wave* or *Genghis Khan*. It sits directly downhill from the Brain Boulder and on its downhill side is the express trail leading from the entrance to other areas further on. **The problems are described starting from the left on the downhill side of the boulder and continuing around to the right.** The easiest way to get off the boulder is to head for the uphill side, avoiding the prickly plants, and jumping down into a hanging corridor between the Brain Boulder and the Wave Boulder, then jumping down again right by *the Wave*.

5. WAVE BOULDER

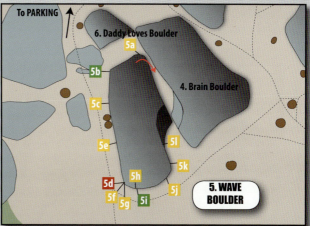

5. WAVE BOULDER

☐ **5a** **Are You Experienced?** V5 ★
The slopey arete in the back of the corner past the Daddy Loves Boulder. Squat start and climb the arete to a sloper top out. The left wall is off.

☐ **5b** **Odds My Bodkins** V2 ★★
On the arete next to the Daddy Loves Boulder. Sit start low on bad hold for the right in jigsaw type rock and good undercling for the left. Do a hard move up to a cool pinch and then follow crimps to a mantle with good jug.

☐ **5c** **Black Carpet** V4 ★★
This short problem has an interesting finish. Sit start low on good edges and sidepulls and follow the holds up to the mantle in black rock.

☐ **5d** **IDYC** V9 ★★
A cool problem with a huge finish. Sit start the same as for *Genghis Khan*. Move up and then follow a seam straight left across the face to an undercling. From here, dyno straight up to the lip of the boulder and top it out.

☐ **5e** **IDYC Stand** V5 ★
A huge move, which unfortunately is often wet. Start on holds in seam at chest height and make a giant move for the top.

5. WAVE BOULDER

5. WAVE BOULDER

☐ **5f** **Genghis Khan** V5 ★★★
A Stone Fort classic which is usually the scene of a crowd hard at work. Sit start low on the big jug and move up the arete to pebbley slopers. Aim for crimps up and left to get to the top out.

☐ **5g** **Genghis Khan Right** V6 ★
A somewhat contrived and more awkward way to finish *Genghis Khan*. Same start, but at the slopers in the middle of the face, move right using a gaston crimp and finish up the groove of *Manute Bol*.

☐ **5h** **Manute Bol** V6 ★★★
Manute Bol, from Sudan, was the second tallest player to ever play in the NBA, and was an amazing 7 ft. 7 in. tall, but only weighed a stickly 225 lbs. As you may have guessed, his reach will help you with this problem. Sit start on lowest large holds and standup to underclings. Move up and left to a water groove and top out.

☐ **5i** **V1** ★
Start on the same holds as *Manute Bol*, move up to the underclings, and then move up and right on the white and green face using gastons and crimpers to a slopey top out. Sort of a cool problem, needs to be cleaned up.

☐ **5j** **Green Machine** V4 ★★
This powerful green slab climbs to the left of the arete on *the Wave*. Start at the hole, and climb the slab above.

☐ **5k** **The Wave** V6 ★★★
Possibly one of the best problems at the Stone Fort, this arcing arete looks like a cresting wave frozen in stone. Start on the rail down and right. Make moves left to gain the arete and follow it to the rock-over top out.

☐ **5l** **The Mechanic** V7 ★★
About halfway through this problem you will understand where the name comes from. Start on the rail to the right of the beginning of *the Wave*. Engineer moves out the very steep roof and finish up the slab as smooth as the hood of a car. A large flake jug recently broke out of the very beginning of this climb, making the first move longer. However, it shouldn't change the grade.

5. WAVE BOULDER

Warren Hulsey on The Mechanic , V7 . Micah Gentry photo.

6. DADDY LOVES BOULDER

6. DADDY LOVES BOULDER

6. DADDY LOVES BOULDER

The Daddy Loves Boulder is a small detached boulder which sits next to the Brain Boulder and the Wave Boulder and is next to the express trail. It is host to four short problems which are fun but by no means classic. **The problems are described from the left to right if coming from the entrance.** It is pretty easy to just jump off this boulder.

☐ **6a Roscoe** V2 ⭐
Stand start on the left side of the boulder and climb the seam feature up the short face.

☐ **6b Roscoe Extended** V3 ⭐
A problem that climbs taller than it looks. Start the same as *Daddy Loves* on the large pink jugs and traverse left into *Roscoe*.

☐ **6c Daddy Loves** V2
Sit start on the round pink jugs. Climb straight up into an undercling and then follow the flake to the top.

☐ **6d Chicken** V0 ⭐
Sit start on big jug knob and climb the short bulbous face above.

☐ **6e Maxine** V3 ⭐
Really short and maybe a little bit pointless. Sit start right of the tree with right on sidepull and left on sloper on the arete. Do one move to obvious edge, then top out.

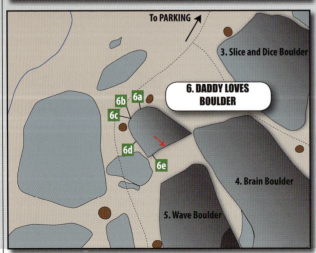

To PARKING

3. Slice and Dice Boulder

6. DADDY LOVES BOULDER

4. Brain Boulder

5. Wave Boulder

7. THE TKO BOULDER

For the purposes of this guide, the TKO Boulder is not one boulder but rather two boulders which sit next to each other and which host three problems. They are the very first problems you would encounter when coming from the entrance. **The problems are described from left to right.** After climbing these problems, you end up on flat ground, so getting off is not an issue.

7. TKO BOULDER

☐ **7a Left Blob Slab** V0- ⭐
The left blob slab. Grab the left protruding blob on the slab, mantle past it, and finish up the pink face.

☐ **7b Right Blob Slab** V0- ⭐
The right blob slab. Mantle onto the right protruding blob and follow jugs to the top.

☐ **7c TKO** V3 ⭐
This one is plenty steep, but has huge holds. Sit start on your back on incut flakes under the lip and move out holds along the lip of the roof.

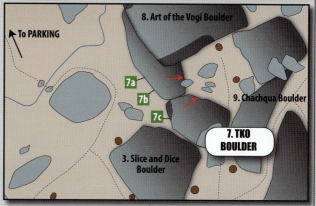

8. Art of the Vogi Boulder

To PARKING

9. Chachqua Boulder

7. TKO BOULDER

3. Slice and Dice Boulder

BOB CORMANY

In 1985 I was bouldering at Boatrock in Atlanta with Marvin Webb, who I had seen often at Sunset Rock on Lookout Mountain. He told me about LRC and how to get there. My friend Craig Stannard was living in Chattanooga, so we went there the next weekend. We met Sam Adams' aunt at the pay booth at the water tower, she allowed us to park there for years. The first few years we were by ourselves, occasionally seeing some chalk but no people. In the early days most climbers were on rope, so not much traffic at LRC. Some young people started coming like Sam Adams and Ben Ditto and crew. Craig and I lead many taller cracks and top roped many tall faces all over the site. The construction on the golf course caused the parking to be in jeopardy. Also the popularity in bouldering picked up and shut down parking at the water tower pay station. We met with the preacher at the church down the road and parked there for a long time with no problems. Craig and I did an untold number of problems over the entire area. Even after the golfers and other new people were there we knew the area so well that we weren't bothered by anyone. People parked in the field across from the tower and really got the place shut down. By the late 80's and early 90's we had found many other areas that were not an access issue so we went elsewhere. But LRC is still my favorite area, mostly because of the diversity, and sheer number of problems.

Thanks to Chad and Dawson and others who got the place open, we all can now enjoy a world class bouldering area for the foreseeable near future. Hats off to all who worked to help it open. I am really pretty reclusive so I climbed in many areas and don't care much for the crowds, but am pleased others get to enjoy many of our problems. Out of hundreds of times I've been there, only a handful have been legal. I never really cared who owned the area and didn't interfere with the owners at all. Of all the places I've seen, and they are many, LRC is the coolest place I've been by far. The example the Triple Crown and SCC has set in the south is truly remarkable.

8. ART OF THE VOGI BOULDER

8. ART OF THE VOGI BOULDER

The Art of the Vogi Boulder is one of the largest boulders in the Front Area. Unfortunately, it sits on top of a massive jumble of boulders, rarely affording a decent landing. As such, there are only a few problems found on it, including the popular and fun *Art of the Vogi*. The problems are found on top of the TKO Boulder, or by walking past the Slice and Dice Boulder. **They are listed from left to right.** To get off the boulder, head for the uphill side and either downclimb the uphill side on good big holds, or downclimb a few feet around the corner and jump off onto another boulder.

☐ 8a V6

"Sketchy." Starts the same as *Art of the Vogi* but moves left on hollow flakes underneath the lip of the roof, before making big moves past the lip. Watch out for breaking holds.

☐ 8b Art of the Vogi V4 ⭐⭐

The name is a reference to Brion Voges, who did the FA. A cool problem which starts down in a hole, making it feel like you will be swallowed whole if you fall off. Start low on flat rail and make long moves out the steep roof on good holds before establishing yourself on the upper slab.

☐ 8c Offwidth V3 ⭐

Sit start the same as for *Art of the Vogi*. Move up and right and tackle the overhanging offwidth crack. A hard one to grade — it might be considered 5.10- in Yosemite, yet feels harder than *Art of the Vogi*. You decide.

☐ 8d Truth is Stranger V2 Than Friction

The slab on the detached pedestal right of the offwidth crack. Stand start and climb it to the top. A bit mossy.

☐ 8e V1

On the block which forms the right hand wall of the "pit" where these problems are found. Super sit start on small crimp rail and do one move to good hold, then on to top.

8. ART OF THE VOGI BOULDER

9. CHACHQUA BOULDER

9. CHACHQUA BOULDER

The Chachqua Boulder, while quite large, does not offer up very much premium climbing terrain. It sits right next to the Mystery Machine Boulder and the Slice and Dice Boulder. There are only a few problems on its one climbable face and they are all quite easy, making good warm-ups or beginner problems, but be careful of the scattered blocks in the landing zones. **The problems are listed from left to right.** You can just walk off from the top.

☐ **9a** **Magua's Revenge** V0 ⭐
Stand start and climb good holds up the slabby white face. Exits to the right at the top out.

☐ **9b** **Editor's Choice** V0 ⭐
Climbs the face and seam to the right of *Magua's Revenge* and left of the arete and tree.

☐ **9c** **The Puzzler** V1 ⭐
Climb the very slabby white arete behind the tree.

☐ **9d** **Chachqua** V1 ⭐
Climb the short white face to the right of the tree.

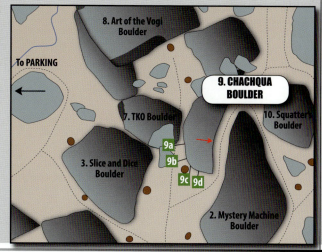

Warren Hulsey on The Wave, V6. Micah Gentry photo.

10. SQUATTER'S BOULDER

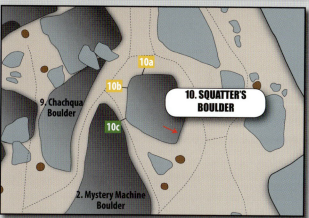

10. SQUATTER'S BOULDER

A candidate for the shortest boulder in the field (although I don't think it would win), the Squatter's Boulder is the round flat slab just uphill from the Mystery Machine Boulder. It has one side which is just tall enough for a couple of short problems. **They are listed left to right.** There is no problem getting off this one.

☐ 10a The Fouling V6 ⭐
Sit start super low with left on crimp and right on crimpy sidepull. Move upwards to crimps on flake and then follow more crimps to the top out, which is a little dirty.

☐ 10b One Bad Hat V4
Squat start on some brushed black slopers on the lip of the boulder behind the tree. Pull on and move up and right to more slopers and mantle.

☐ 10c Squatter's Rights V3 ⭐
The short little prow directly across from *Easy Does It*. Sit start with left on crimp and right on sidepull. Move up to lip of boulder and mantle.

11. THE BOWLING BALL

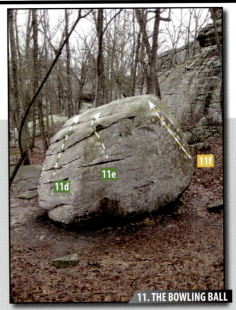

11. THE BOWLING BALL

11. THE BOWLING BALL

You will easily recognize which block is the Bowling Ball as soon as you see it. It is just uphill from the Fire Crack Boulder. The style on this boulder is reminiscent of Horse Pens 40, with sloper mantles the common theme. There are problems all the way around the boulder, except on the uphill side. **The descriptions start with the problem to the left of the tree, and follow around to the right.** To get off the Ball, downclimb the problem *Strike*, using the tree very liberally.

☐ 11a V1 ★

The arete and face to the left of the tree. Stand start on flat holds and arete and move upwards to mantle.

☐ 11b Strike V3 ★★

A good mantle problem. Start on the large rail to the right of the tree and move up to slopers over the lip of the boulder, bring up the right foot and rock over the mantle.

☐ 11c Spare V0 ★★★

The very slabby prow of the boulder. Stand start at the tip of the boulder and climb up the slab via edges for the feet, smears, and underclings to the sloper top out. A great problem!

☐ 11d Split V1 ★★

About three feet to the right of *Spare*. Stand start using underclings and slopey feet and slap your way up the egg-like slab above.

☐ 11e Gutter Ball V2 ★★

Stand start on pocket edge in the middle of the face and climb up to cool pinch, then mantle the slab above.

☐ 11f Kingpin V6 ★★★

The Font-esque egg-shaped arete certainly requires the crispest of conditions. Stand start with right hand on obvious sidepull. Slap your way up the slopers and power out the mantle. Believe in the power of the right foot.

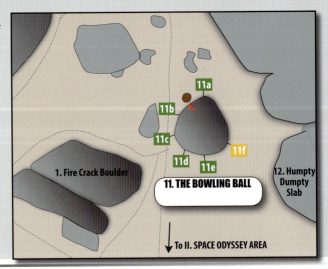

12. HUMPTY DUMPTY SLAB

The Humpty Dumpty Slab is not a boulder, but is instead a small part of the cliff line that makes up the "back wall" of the Stone Fort. It is host to four interesting slab problems and is located directly behind the Bowling Ball. **The climbs are described from left to right.** To get off can be tricky. Your options are to traverse left along the break, traverse right along the break at the top, or to keep climbing upwards until an easy walk-off presents itself.

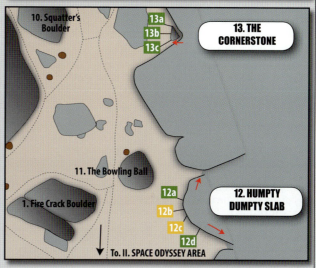

12. HUMPTY DUMPTY SLAB

☐ **12a** **Jupiter** V3 ⭐
Stand start on the left face on a flake at face height and climb straight up the steep slab using pockets to top out.

☐ **12b** **High Gravity** V5 ⭐
Stand start just to the right of the very rounded prow of the face with hands on high sloper in black face. Move up and left following faint prow to top out.

☐ **12c** **Humpty Dumpty** V4 ⭐
Stand start on slopey edges in the middle of black face. Climb upwards to sloper with high feet to surmount the face above, eventually gaining jugs.

☐ **12d** **Hog Jaw** V3 ⭐
Starts on a grouping of iron patina edges. Stand start and move right to more iron edges to surmount the slabby face above.

---

13. THE CORNERSTONE

The Cornerstone is a very small block that sits in, you guessed it, a corner of the back wall, to the right of the Spyro Gyro Wall. It is recognizable by its short stature and the shallow pockets on its face. Admittedly, it is not a classic block, and you won't regret missing it if you don't have the time. **The problems are described from left to right.** To get off, climb down one of the problems, or jump.

☐ **13a** **Left Arete** V0 ⭐
The left arete of the short triangular block in the corner. Stand start and climb the left hand arete using good holds to the top. Can make it a circular problem by climbing over to the right arete and downclimbing that.

☐ **13b** **Middle** V1
Climb the short face in the middle of the boulder via shallow pockets and sidepulls.

☐ **13c** **Right Arete** V0
Climb the right hand arete and the face to its left via lieback moves. The wall to the right is off.

13. THE CORNERSTONE

14. SPYRO GYRO WALL

14. SPYRO GYRO WALL

14. THE SPYRO GYRO WALL

The term Spyro Gyro Wall is used to describe a broad section of the back wall using the most popular problem – *Spyro Gyro* – for reference. The problems located here include a few classics of the area, as well as some excitingly tall faces and cracks and some slabby easy problems. **The problems are described from left to right and begin on the wall to the left of the obvious arete which makes up** *Spyro Gyro*, **and end about 100 feet to the right of that problem.** To get off the problems right of *Spyro Gyro*, walk right along the ledge and downclimb at its right margin, onto the Cornerstone.

☐ **14a** Pittman Face 5.12+ ⭐
Climbs the tall hanging face to the left of the next four problems. Starts up a slabby skirt, then climbs through roof and up the tall but fairly well featured face above. FA roped up and placed gear.

☐ **14b** Thin Flakes V0-
Climb cool thin flakes on the outsides of the wide crack. Stop at the obvious jug break, as the wall above is tall and dirty. Also serves as the downclimb for the wall.

☐ **14c** V0 ⭐
Climb the tall wall up the green streak on rad jugs. Downclimb the same route or traverse left and downclimb.

☐ **14d** V1 ⭐
Start on cool ghost face pockets and climb the featured wall above on cool grips. A bit dirty.

☐ **14e** V1 ⭐
The rightmost line on the face. Climb cool face past rad black grips up to jugs, then traverse left along jugs to downclimb.

☐ **14f** Spyro Gyro V7 ⭐⭐⭐
This often tried classic features some really cool holds and some hard moves. Start on the obvious jug and get your hands onto the flat shelf at the lip using either your static technique or your hops. From the shelf, follow good holds up and right before traversing off to the left.

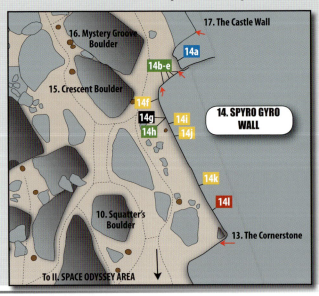

14. SPYRO GYRO WALL

☐ 14g Yin Yang Project

"Sketchy." This tall problem starts about 15 ft. right of *Spyro Gyro*, just to the right of where the rock is broken and dinner plated. Climb up and left on good white rock, eventually gaining a good incut right above the large broken area. You then have two options for passing the hard bulge above. *Yin* goes up and left, *Yang* goes up and right. They both end at the same place and supposedly neither have been climbed.

☐ 14h V3 ⭐

"Sketchy." Start the same as the *Yin Yang Project*, but after a few moves break right along a good wide edge to eventually meet up with *Train Wreck* and follow it to the top.

☐ 14i Train Wreck V4 ⭐⭐

"Sketchy." This tall crack is just to the left of the thin tree. Stand start on obvious flake crimpers about head high to the left of the crack and engineer moves up the face using sidepulls and crimps until you gain the bottom of the insipient fist crack. Follow it to the top.

☐ 14j Kaya V7 ⭐⭐⭐

"Sketchy." This fantastic tall face is a perfect candidate for lots of pads and spotters. Start on crimps and incuts just right of a thin tree. Climb upward to an obvious rock scar, then negotiate flakes up the clean white face up and right.

☐ 14k Body Glove V4 ⭐

"Sketchy." The tall offwidth crack which splits the wall to the right a ways from *Kaya*.

☐ 14l Dosey Twat V8 ⭐

Stand start and climb the reasonably tall white face on the right side of the wall, just about 10 feet left of the *Cornerstone*, which has a small capping roof over it formed by a perched boulder.

14. SPYRO GYRO WALL

Cody Averbeck on Kaya, V7 . Luke Laeser photo.

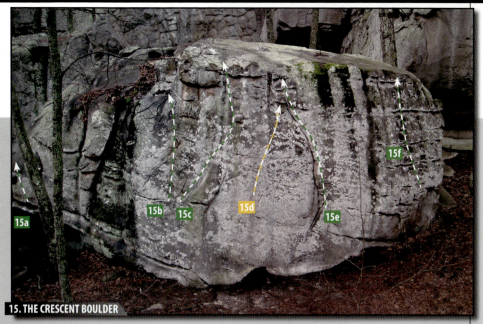

15. THE CRESCENT BOULDER

15. THE CRESCENT BOULDER

The Crescent Boulder is one of the most stacked boulders in the Front Area and is a fantastic place to warm up, or for climbers looking for easier problems. Its main face is a wide slab with good problems all the way across, while its backside bumps up against the Mystery Groove Boulder. **The problems are described from left to right.** There are many ways to get off, but the most popular is to head back and left to the point where it meets the Mystery Groove Boulder and downclimb the chimney/slot where the boulder is shortest.

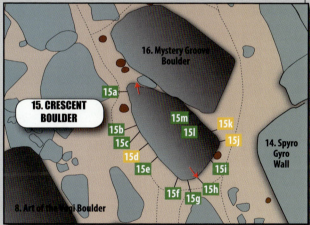

15a Hauled Ass V2 ⭐
This short problem is in the corridor between the two boulders. Start low on rail on good holds. Move up and left past slopers to top out.

15b The Little German Girl V1 ⭐
Climb the easy slab up cool edges on the left side of the face.

15c High Times V1 ⭐⭐
About six feet left of the *Crescent* is an obvious right-angling flake. Start up this, then negotiate the blankness to the large protruding head-like horn, then finish straight up.

15d Crescent Slab V7 ⭐
Start about three feet left of the *Crescent*. Start with left on sidepull crimper and right on high sidepull crimp which is a foot for the *Crescent* and climb straight up bulging white slab via interesting thin holds and long reaches.

15e The Crescent V1 ⭐⭐⭐
A really cool problem and a great warm-up. Goes straight up the middle of the Crescent boulder via the obvious arcing seam. Stand start and follow the crack to the top.

15f Hairy Underclings V3 ⭐⭐
A good fun, puzzling boulder problem. Start on molded pinches and shallow pockets about six feet right of the *Crescent* and climb up the slabby face littered with eyebrow features. Tricky.

☐ **15g** V0 ⭐

Climb the arete to the right of *Hairy Underclings* via jugs in pocket features to good jug knob top out.

☐ **15h** **Low Constitution** V0 ⭐

A couple feet right of the arete. Start low on jug rail and climb jugs up to large elephant ear flake feature and top out there. Serves as a decent downclimb option as well.

☐ **15i** **Mixer Elixir** V2 ⭐

The climb right of *Low Constitution*. Start on low pocket rail on good holds and climb up face via more pocket rails and eyeball socket undercling to top out. Avoid traversing off to the left.

☐ **15j** **Fixer** V4 ⭐

Climb rounded outside corner across from *Spyro Gyro*. Start on obvious right-handed sidepull undercling and move upwards via crimps and small feet to top out.

☐ **15k** V4

Sort of a contrived problem because you have to avoid the crack to the right, which is easily within reach, but some interesting moves none-the-less. Stand start with left hand undercling and right on chip crimp, then climb face above via slabby moves, tough feet, and long reaches.

☐ **15l** **The Feature** V1 ⭐⭐

Climb the short finger crack on the backside of the boulder, an obvious line. Despite its crack nature, there are few real jams to be found.

☐ **15m** **Puck Stick** V3 ⭐

This problem climbs the orange and brown face in the corner between the two boulders to the right of the crack climb the *Feature*. Start on a high right sidepull and move to the top.

15. THE CRESCENT BOULDER

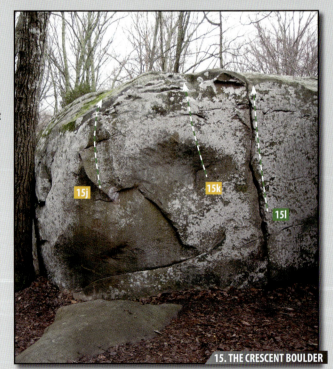

15. THE CRESCENT BOULDER

16. MYSTERY GROOVE BOULDER

16. THE MYSTERY GROOVE BOULDER

The Mystery Groove Boulder is a tall boulder which sits against and uphill of the Crescent Boulder and has problems on all sides of it. It is home to the classic *Mystery Groove,* but also has a couple of great highballs. **The problems are described from the left side of the tall face which is behind the Crescent Boulder, across from** *Spyro Gyro,* **and then to the right all the way around the boulder.** There are many ways to get off, but the easiest is to downclimb problem 16c.

☐ **16a Tall Crack** V2 ⭐⭐
"Sketchy." A highball crack climb for the trad afficionado! Due to the undulating nature of the crack, it is easily possible to climb this tall line without jamming, so boulderers fear not. Start at the bottom of the obvious crack and climb to the top. It's tall, be careful.

☐ **16b Heartbreaker** V6 ⭐⭐
A very tricky slab climb which looks a whole lot easier than it is, probably due to the benign beginning. Start up the crack in the middle of the face. When it peters out, figure out the levitation necessary to deposit you at the sloping

lip about six feet to your right.

☐ **16c Downclimb** V0-
The flake/groove just to the right of

the arete is the best downclimb off this boulder.

☐ **16d Blithering Idiot** V0
Climb the face about three feet left of *Runnel Funnel* via good holds and pockets. Also pebbly and licheny.

☐ **16e Runnel Funnel** V2 ⭐
Start about three feet left of the tree and climb the double groove features with thin feet. The rock is a bit pebbly and a little dirty, but it's still a fun problem.

☐ **16f Murfreesboro Blues** V0 ⭐
Stand start and climb the face about four feet left of *Five and Dime* via cool grips up pebbly wall.

☐ **16g Five and Dime** V0 ⭐⭐
Start standing just left of the tree on the far right side of the back side of the Mystery Groove Boulder. Climb interesting grips up wall with vertical seams and flakes to pebbly but not very hard top out.

☐ **16h Showtime** V1
Stand start, climb the arete to the right of the tree on really pebbly rock via open hand grips and jugs.

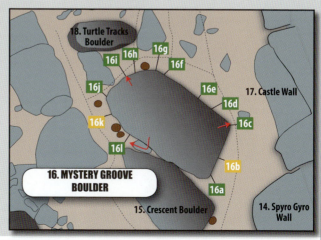

16. MYSTERY GROOVE BOULDER

18. Turtle Tracks Boulder

17. Castle Wall

15. Crescent Boulder

14. Spyro Gyro Wall

☐ **16i** V0-

The face left of *Tight Like That* has a jug break running up it. It also makes a decent downclimb.

☐ **16j** **Tight Like That** V3 ⭐

Stand start hugging the arete with your right hand in a pocket and left on vertical crimper rail. Make moves up roundy arete, maintaining the tightness.

☐ **16k** **Mystery Groove** V4 ⭐⭐⭐

Climbing this mysterious pillar of overlapping scales is like pinching your way up the backbone of a dinosaur! Start awkwardly on an ear shaped sidepull and make move out to wide pinch, then head straight up the backbone.

☐ **16l** V3

This is an interesting face climb to the right of the trees right of the *Mystery Groove* that needs some traffic to clean up. Stand start on right sidepull and left on whatever little crimps you can grab. Climb tall face past sharp crimps and slopers and sidepulls. Dirty top out on really good jugs.

16. MYSTERY GROOVE BOULDER

16. MYSTERY GROOVE BOULDER

16. MYSTERY GROOVE BOULDER

Ashley Hamilton on Mystery Groove, v4. Dan Brayak photo.

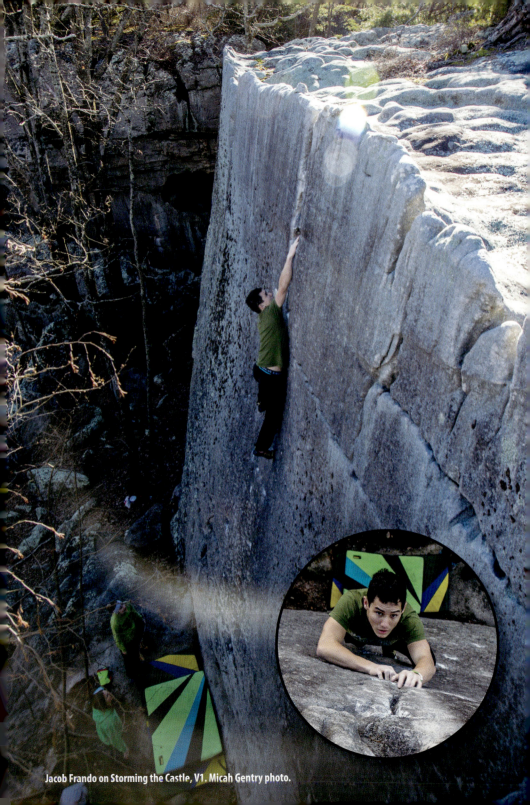

Jacob Frando on Storming the Castle, V1. Micah Gentry photo.

17. CASTLE WALL

17. THE CASTLE WALL

The Castle Wall is the part of the back wall which is directly uphill from the Mystery Groove Boulder and is easily recognizable by the battlement like fortifications at its top. The climbs on this wall are TALL, and therefore quite serious. Although injury is not guaranteed, these are not climbs you want to come peeling off of at the top, especially since the landings are on a raised platform, and if you don't "stick" the landing, you could easily roll off another 10 foot drop. To access them, scramble up the gulley on the left side of the wall to gain the ledge beneath the climbs. **They are listed from left to right.** To get down, the easiest way is to downclimb the *Corner Crack*.

☐ **17a Storming** V1 ⭐⭐⭐
the Castle
"Scary, NUTS." This classic highball slab solo might be the most aptly named boulder problem ever. If you are in doubt of your ability, then bring your grappling hook! (The parapets at the top make a great slung horn to set up a top-rope). Climb the rippled slab up some positive and some not so positive edges to the parapet ramparts at the top.

☐ **17b King of the Castle** V8 ⭐⭐
"Scary." The very blank black slab between *Storming the Castle* and the *Corner Crack*. Aim for a thin crescent hold in the middle of the face. Crux is low, but still hard way up there.

☐ **17c Corner Crack** V0
"Scary." The slabby fist crack in the corner is tall. It also serves as the downclimb for these four problems.

☐ **17d First Knight** V5 ⭐⭐
"Scary." The tall white face to the right of the crack has lots of roundy, basketball like holds, but is not often traveled. Start to the right of the crack and have yourself an adventure up there. Be wary of your landing.

18. TURTLE TRACKS BOULDER

18. TURTLE TRACKS BOULDER

19. Dos Cosanos Boulder

21. Swinger's Boulder

18. TURTLE TRACKS BOULDER

18a

18b

18c

18d

16. Mystery Groove Boulder

18. TURTLE TRACKS BOULDER

The Turtle Tracks Boulder is another candidate for shortest block in the field and sort of looks like a giant turtle. It is located right next to the Mystery Groove Boulder and has problems on two sides, the short side, and the mildly taller side, which also features some poor pebbly rock. **The problems are described from left to right.** It is easy to walk off this boulder.

☐ **18a The Cheese Grater** V5
A pretty not fun problem with rough pebbley rock — aptly named. Start awkwardly on undercling in crack for your right and left on slopers around arete. Do burly moves up arete and holds on face.

☐ **18b** V3
"Sketchy." More pebbley rock. Sit start on the wierd slide/skirt all scrunched up and make moves up the short face above, avoiding the skirt with your feet. Sort of an interesting fall due to the "slide." If you fall off you will likely tumble over backwards, so good spotters recommended.

☐ **18c V2** ⭐
The really short boulder direct. Sit and grab low holds beneath the finish of the traverse on *Turtle Tracks*. Move up to flat mantle top out.

☐ **18d Turtle Tracks** V3 ⭐
Start on the right side of this super short boulder, pretty much laying down. One move to the lip, then traverse all the way left to top it out.

19. DOS COSANOS BOULDER

19. DOS COSANOS BOULDER

19. DOS COSANOS BOULDER

The Dos Cosanos Boulder lies in the back corner of the Front Area next to the Project Wall and the passageway to the Bog of Eternal Stench (go check it out!). It has a few moderate problems on it which are fun, but not classic. **The problems are listed from left to right, starting on the downhill face.** Since the uphill side of the boulder is a very low angle slab, it is easy to walk off.

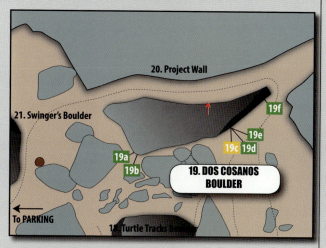

☐ **19a Dos Cosanos** V1
Stand start on the right hand side of the face and traverse the seam up and left on mildly sandy rock and top it out onto the slab up and left.

☐ **19b Worm Drink** V0
Stand start on the right hand side of the face the same as for *Dos Cosanos* and climb straight up the wall and slab above.

☐ **19c Mescal** V4 ★★
A fun low problem, although sort of contrived as this face is littered with holds. Sit start low on undercling for right and sidepull for left. Move up to good holds and follow left-trending line of holds left and then straight up via crimpers, sidepulls, and slopers.

☐ **19d Mescal Direct** V3 ★
Same start but climb straight up instead of going left, hitting sidepulls, and slopers on the way. A bit contrived.

☐ **19e Cuervo** V1 ★
Same start as the others, up to the good holds, then out right to good holds above the ramp and top out up that.

☐ **19f El Capitan** V2 ★
More bad Mexican liquor. Sit start on flake underneath the lip of the roof. Move over the roof and up to jug fin on top of the boulder.

Daniel Woods locking off on Flying High, V11, this page. Adam Johnson photo.

20. THE PROJECT WALL

The Project Wall is the tall and very smooth curving wall just behind the Dos Cosanos Boulder. It is home to some huge and very hard dyno problems, so if that is your thing, this is your spot. **The problems are described from left to right.** Topping out is not recommended. To get off, just drop off, or traverse either left or right, and then drop.

☐ **20a** V3 ⭐
The arete on the left side of the boulder doesn't climb as cool as it looks. Stand start pretty low and climb the arete feature using mostly sidepulls. Traverse off left or step off to the slab behind at about mid-height.

☐ **20b** Watch Your Back V11 ⭐⭐
An impossibly big move? Apparently not. Start on the crimps down low, then dyno a full body length up the smooth face to an incut. The first ascent traversed left to the arete and then stepped off.

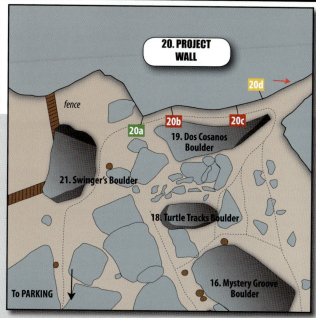

20. THE PROJECT WALL

20. THE PROJECT WALL

☐ **20c** Flying High V11 ⭐⭐⭐
A crazy huge dyno. Grab the incut in the middle of the face, paste your feet, and fly really high.

☐ **20d** Do Dat V6 ⭐
Start low on rail underneath faint arete feature on the right side of the wall and just to the left of the dark corridor. Climb the arete feature to top out into large hole, and walk off.

21. SWINGERS BOULDER

The Swingers Boulder is a rad boulder in the back of the Front Area that has classic roof problems on all accessible sides. Half the boulder is cut off from bouldering fun by a fence which marks the barrier to the grounds keeping facility for the golf course. Home to both old and new school classics, you won't want to miss it. **The problems are described from left to right, downhill to up.** Getting off the top can be a bit tricky. It is possible to jump off to the boulderer's left of *Swingers*, or to the boulderer's left of *Tennessee Thong*.

☐ 21a Swingers V3 ★★★

A cool problem – it's really steep and has a great variety of moves, and the top out is not very high up. Start in good jugs at the back of the flat roof. Climb out the roof and don't get pumped before the mantle is through.

☐ 21b Smoking Jacket V1 ★

Sit start on jugs under roof to the right of *Swingers*. Move out flat holds to the top.

☐ 21c Tennessee Thong V7 ★★★

This great problem featuring blocky rock is a classic. Sit start to the right on the large sidepull which is the lowest hold. Move up to the triangular corner hold, then left across the face past a crimp and some very flat slopers and on to a flat jug at the lip.

☐ 21d Tall Tee V13

Start the same as for *Tennessee Thong* but climb straight up into the corner using a very thin crimp, then make a huge span right to the hanging arete at the edge of the roof. Hold the swing and top out straight up. When it gets done it will be the hardest problem in the field. Many days of effort have been put into this problem, and Jimmy Webb estimates that the crux move alone could be about V13.

☐ 21e The Wedgie Project

Sit start on low good edge the same as for *On the Fence*, then move up and left and do compression moves out the roof on wide side-pulls, eventually finishing up the high slab left of *On The Fence*.

21. SWINGERS BOULDER

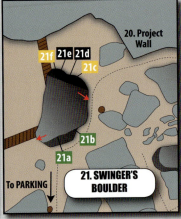

21. SWINGER'S BOULDER
20. Project Wall
To PARKING

☐ 21f On the Fence V7 ★★

"Sketchy." This cool problem was added to the boulder when the fence was moved about six ft. right. Still a little sketchy as some body parts may find themselves above the fence on the top out. Sit start on large good edge with both hands. Climb straight up and out roof to some tensiony slopers.

21. SWINGERS BOULDER

Warren Hulsey on The Glove, V5 . Micah Gentry photo.

22. THE PIT

The Pit is a small zone of problems located, yep, down in a pit. While not home to the big name classics, the problems are certainly fun and worth doing. The Pit is downhill a little bit from the Swingers Boulder towards the entrance trail. It is also on the opposite side of the large Art of the Vogi Boulder from the warm-up zone. Make a short scramble down a tree trunk to access the zone. **If you are in the Pit, looking at the problems, they are described from right to left.** Getting off is not a problem, since once you have topped out, you are back at ground level.

22a The Glove V5 ★★
Sit start awkwardly underneath the corner of the boulder on the root of a tree with right on flat jug and left on shallow pockets on face. Do moves to gain the bottom of the slopey arete and follow it to the top. Mildly reminiscent of the *Wave*.

22b Pit Fiend V3 ★★
A cool looking prow on a sunken boulder. Stand start on the shallow bowling ball grip for the right and good sidepull edge for the left. Pull feet on and work right rail to good jugs at top and mantle.

22c Tunnel Vision V5
Crawl down into tunnel on the opposite side of the same boulder as *the Glove*. Sit start low in the back of the tunnel on crimps and climb out the overhanging wall up and right, transfer to the next boulder and mantle over onto flat slab at the entrance to this area. Dark and dirty.

22d Drumm Slab V5
Start down in a pit which at times runs with water to the left of where you jump down into the Pit. Start on rail and climb up and right to cool vertically oriented iron band, then up mossy face to top out.

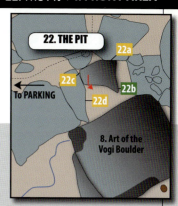

22. THE PIT

Flying High V11. Adam Johnson photo.

II. SPACE ODYSSEY AREA

The Space Odyssey Area is host to some of the hardest slab problems in the South. The twin prows of *Space* and *Odyssey* look so blank upon first glance that it's hard to believe there is chalk on them. Take a closer look, however, and you will see that these blank bulges do contain some holds (depending on how you define "hold" in *Odyssey's* case).

This is the next group of boulders that you encounter as you walk away from the Front Area, sticking close to the cliff line. The trail leads from the Fire Crack Boulder straight to the Space Odyssey Area, passing underneath the Pou Wall along the way. If you take the express trail, which leaves the front area from the problem *Genghis Khan*, you will miss these fantastic slabs.

The area is comprised of a number of boulders which are densely packed together. Most of the problems are on the faces of the boulders which point straight towards you as you walk up, but some of them must be reached by scrambling through narrow gaps or passageways. Included here are the Pou Wall (pg. 82), Space Boulder (pg. 84), Odyssey Boulder (pg. 85), Two Shoes Jack Boulder (pg. 86), Funkadelic Boulder (pg. 90), Shotgun Boulder (pg. 90), and the Chattanoogan Area (pg. 87).

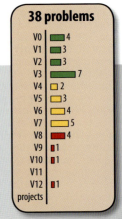

38 problems

V0		4
V1		3
V2		3
V3		7
V4		2
V5		3
V6		4
V7		5
V8		4
V9		1
V10		1
V11		
V12		1
projects		

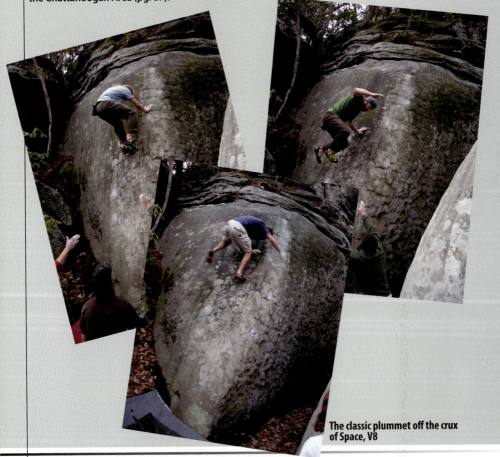

The classic plummet off the crux of Space, V8

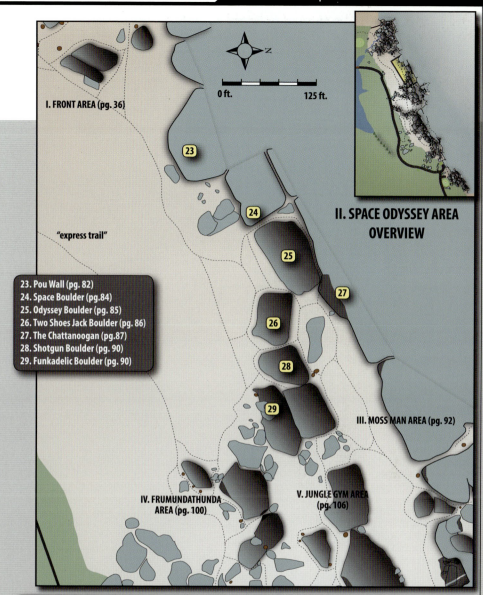

I. FRONT AREA (pg. 36)

0 ft.   125 ft.

II. SPACE ODYSSEY AREA
OVERVIEW

"express trail"

23. Pou Wall (pg. 82)
24. Space Boulder (pg.84)
25. Odyssey Boulder (pg. 85)
26. Two Shoes Jack Boulder (pg. 86)
27. The Chattanoogan (pg.87)
28. Shotgun Boulder (pg. 90)
29. Funkadelic Boulder (pg. 90)

III. MOSS MAN AREA (pg. 92)

IV. FRUMUNDATHUNDA
AREA (pg. 100)

V. JUNGLE GYM AREA
(pg. 106)

NOT TO BE MISSED:

V4 Two Shoes Jack ★★★ — I don't know who Jack is, but you will certainly need both of your shoes, and the rubber attached to them, to climb this fantastic slab.

V5 Galaxy 5000 ★★★ — Your old school Nintendo skills will not help you here. Unless all that video game playing happened to strengthen your thumbs, which might help you with the crazy molded pinches on this classic problem.

V6 Shotgun ★★★ — This problem bears no resemblance to a shotgun, so I don't have anything witty to add here. Except that this is probably the best pocket problem at the Stone Fort, so don't miss it!

V8 Space ★★★ — The quintessential slab testpiece! Space: what you feel like you're reaching for at the top of this rounded prow, or, what you will be falling through on your way back to earth. Catch it on a crisp day and bring your friends!

V9 Odyssey ★★★ — Described by many as the blankest boulder problem they've ever seen, the counterpart to *Space* has one discernable "hold" in about 12 feet of climbing. Rarely repeated, or even tried for that matter.

23. POU WALL

23. POU WALL

The Pou Wall is host to four tall problems on a bullet grey face which is a part of the back cliff line. You will walk right by it on the trail from the Front Area to *Space* and *Odyssey*. Pads and spotters are recommended here, as the problems are fairly tall and there is a large slabby boulder beneath which can make things interesting if you fall. **The problems are described from left to right.** If you are on top of the boulder, walk back and to your right to access an easy gulley to walk down.

☐ **23a Pop Rocks** V3 ⭐
"Sketchy." Stand start on arete, climb the slab skirt to jug break, then up the imposing steep arete on the left side of the face to high top out. Spotters mandatory.

☐ **23b Pou** V7 ⭐⭐
"Sketchy." Stand start just to the left of the flat boulder beneath the wall. Climb up steep rock via good holds, then surmount the overhanging bullet grey bulge above. A couple of spotters help, though you probably won't hit the boulder if you fall.

☐ **23c Two Up Two Down** V6 ⭐
Stand start to the right of *Pou* in a chossy jug break behind the low boulder. Climb up good holds, then out the roof generally following holds up the seam on the right hand side of the face. The slab boulder beneath actually provides a good landing zone for this problem.

☐ **23d Into the Owie** V4 ⭐
"Sketchy." Stand start the same as for *Two Up Two Down*. Climb up and right to jug break just out the lip of the roof and surmount the overhanging bulge above on the far right side of the wall.

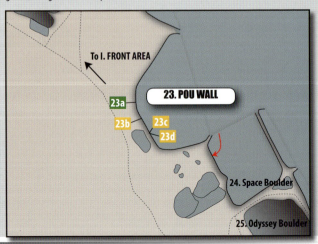

JIMMY WEBB

On a quiet day at LRC, I was finding it almost impossible to see due to the hypnotizing fall colors bouncing radiantly off the soft sandstone. It's days like this that stand out so vividly in my mind. Days where going out with close friends was not a battle for hard problems, but an almost meditating experience and a time to reflect on everything we've come to love. Days filled with good friends, world class boulders, and all around good times.

Thinking back on my most memorable times spent there I almost feel as if I've taken it for granted. Since climbing access went from closed, to open yet restricted, to paying five dollars per car, the crowds (including me) seemed to be turned off... but why? Just because we are obligated to pay five measly bucks does not change the quality of this place. In my opinion this area stands tall among the BEST in the US. Hands down.

It's honestly hard for me to speak deeply on the history of this amazing place, since I only started climbing here five years ago. Though over the past several years my knowledge of the area has grown high, and my respect for it has grown even higher. From the oldies climbing here in the 80's, to the new school generation we see today, LRC has never failed to deliver climbers of all ages and strengths with classic problems to hurl themselves at.

In the end I would like to thank the SCC for keeping the access at LRC open for all, and a HUGE dose of appreciation goes out to the Montlake Golf Course and all its employees. Please remember to be kind and courteous each and every time you visit, and climbers will be enjoying this incredible area for generations to come.

24. SPACE BOULDER | 25. ODYSSEY BOULDER

24. SPACE BOULDER

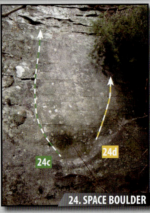

24. SPACE BOULDER

24. SPACE BOULDER

The Space Boulder is home to the ultra-classic slab problem *Space*. It is on your left, on the left side of a deep corridor just past the Pou Wall. **The problems are described from left to right, from outside of the corridor to inside of it.** To get off the boulder, scramble along the ledge to the left to gain a bushy scramble down left of *Space*.

☐ **24a** **Space** V8 ★★★
"Sketchy." One of the most classic problems at the Stone Fort, and one of the most unique slabs that you will find. Stand start with right on large sidepull pocket and left on your choice of grips. Balance and slap your way upwards and stay solid on the crux at the very top.

☐ **24b** **Spacegrass** V2 ★
In the corridor about 10 feet right of *Space*. Stand start and climb very pocketed face to easy top out. Traverse left along the shelf past the top of *Space* to get off.

The following problems are in the corridor behind the Space and Odyssey Boulders, on the back wall.

☐ **24c** **Smear Campaign** V3 ★
Right where the trail from *Space* and *Odyssey* meet the back cliff line is a clean low angle slab. This problem climbs up its left side.

☐ **24d** **Walk the Talk** V5 ★
Just to the right of *Smear Campaign* on the same brushed shield of rock. Stand start and climb up and right on the slab. At the time of writing there was a fallen pine tree blocking the top out.

☐ **24e** **Galapagos** V6
About six feet right of *Walk the Talk* is a thin brushed streak surrounded by moss and guarded at the top by a fallen tree. Climb it.

☐ **24f** **Special Agent** V7 ★
To the right of *Galapagos* is another brushed slab surrounded by moss. Stand start with your hands on twin iron crimps and climb straight up the slab above.

TRAVIS EISEMAN

I can't tell you too much about the history, but definitely we used to climb out there a lot. [This was in roughly 1985-1989.] We preferred to rope up, but we spent a lot of time bouldering. Our ethic then for routes was if you weren't falling you weren't climbing hard enough. So we went through a lot of ropes. And then whenever we trashed our climbing ropes from taking so many leader falls, we'd start bouldering at LRC since we didn't have enough money to buy new ropes as often as we went through them. Plus we viewed bouldering as the prime way to train for the harder routes we were trying to do back then. This is back when we were working out routes like Theatre of Madness (13b), The Specter (13a), and Necrophilia (13b), which are technical and have powerful and complex crux moves. So we'd take some ensolite pads, go out there to LRC and create problems. Bouldering was just like crux climbing on routes so we'd train like that and try to get strong for the day that we got a new rope. It's crazy really, some of the stuff we did ropeless and padless. Back then falling was a bigger deal, we knew the consequences were high. But we pushed it out anyway.

It was totally secluded in those days. It was rare to see other climbers at all. If we saw chalk on a problem we'd be like, "Hey look! Someone else has been out here." That's no joke. There was no golf course, no houses, just boulders in the woods, no registering, no regulations. We really loved that place. We'd bring tunes and blow bowls and just push ourselves. Whoever could put up the hardest or ballsiest problem was king for a day. We didn't really name them or rate them. This is well before the V grades came out, and we knew about Gill's system but it was disatisfying to us compared to the YDS. So we'd say, "oh that'd be like the crux of a 12+ route," etc. We didn't really think of bouldering as a sport in itself or boulder problems as routes in themselves. I remember I used to think, "man, that would be such a killer problem if it was on a route." It sounds funny to say now, but that's how we viewed it then. This is why so little is documented about problems — who did what when, etc., in the early days. For the most part we didn't care. This was just how we trained and got strong for route climbing. But definitely it was also just enjoying being kids out in the woods in our secret world that almost nobody else knew or cared about.

25. ODYSSEY BOULDER

The Odyssey Boulder is a very large boulder which forms the other side of the corridor across from the Space Boulder. It will be on your left just past the Pou Wall. **The problems are described right to left if looking at the white front face and continue back into the corridor.** The problems do not end anywhere near the very top of the boulder, but rather on ledges which can be hard to get off of. Spotting the escape before hand is recommended.

25. ODYSSEY BOULDER

☐ **25a** **Watermelon Slab** V7 ★★
Stand start with no hands. Pick a foothold, stand up on it, and grab thin iron crimp with left and knobby crimp for right. Jack your feet and go big for the watermelon hold.

☐ **25b** **Odyssey** V9 ★★★
Stand start at the base of the rounded slabby prow across from *Space*. Do your thing and make your way to the top. Rarely done.

☐ **25c** **Where's the Downclimb?** V3
In the corridor to the left of *Odyssey*. Where the smooth face ends is a shallow dihedral. Stand start in the dihedral and move up and right onto the slab above. A bit dirty.

26. TWO SHOES JACK BOULDER

26. TWO SHOES JACK BOULDER

26. TWO SHOES JACK BOULDER

The Two Shoes Jack Boulder is a large square boulder with interesting slab climbs on three sides. It will be straight in front of you if coming from the Front Area, and sits across the small open area from *Space* and *Odyssey*. **The problems are described from left to right around the boulder.** For most of the slab problems the easiest way off will be to walk along the top of the boulder to the top of problem 26l *Downclimb Arete* and downclimb that.

26a Pocket Traverse V8? ★
Starts on pocket pinch on the left side of the wall and traverses right to finish up *Slow Poke* via complex series of moves on widely spaced pockets. Guessing at V8, could not find any info about someone doing this, and couldn't do it myself.

26b Mistaken Identity V3
This pocketed face is mildly reminiscent of *Shotgun*, but not as good. Needs to be cleaned up a bit more. On the left side of the face, climb the pockets through the break to a mossy top out.

26c Jam Up V8 ★
Climbs the pockets in the middle of the face. Start matched on funky undercling pockets. Jack your foot into a small pocket out left and make a big lunge for the slot up and left. Top out above.

26d Slow Poke V1 ★★
Stand start with right hand on crimper sidepull on the arete, left on sidepull pocket. Do a couple moves to gain jugs in cool water groove feature on arete and top out.

26e Two Shoes Jack V4 ★★★
Climbs the slab to the right of the arete. Stand start using undercling pocket. Climb the slab using eyebrow overlaps to the right of the arete. Used to be an eliminate where the crack on the arete up high was considered off, someone eventually decided that since its there, it is allowed to be used. Like all of bouldering: You create your own rules. The grade is the same either way.

26f Crystal Ball V5 ★★
The slab up the middle of the face. Stand start with hands on trio of poor iron nipples. Pull onto the slab and make long moves up the slab above. Like most slabs, it's all in the feet.

26g Clarence Bowater V3 ★★ Survival
The slab to the left of the crack is really cool. Stand start two feet left of the crack and climb crimpers up the slab till it blanks out. Eventually use the vertical sidepull way up and left to get to the top.

26h High Slab Traverse V6 ★
Start by climbing up the wall the same as for *Clarence Bowater Survival*, till you reach the vertical slot hold high on the wall. From here, traverse the slab to the left, across *Crystal Ball* and eventually finishing the same as for *Two Shoes Jack*.

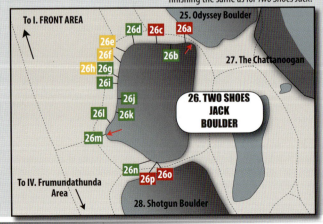

☐ 26i V0 ★
The obvious crack in the middle of the face. Mostly climbing on incut features on either side.

☐ 26j V1 ★
Start about three feet right of 26i on large jugs and climb up face on jugs to blank looking black slab above. Sort of an eliminate, don't traverse off left.

☐ 26k V2 ★
Stand start on jug rail just right of 26j. Climb up face to blank slab with twin sidepull crimpers.

☐ 26l V0 ★
A couple feet left of the arete, stand start on jugs and climb decent edges up the slab above, staying left of the arete.

☐ 26m Downclimb Arete V0-
The easiest downclimb for problems on this face. Buckets up the blunt and low angle arete.

☐ 26n Tom Jones V0 ★
A fun crack traverse. Start on pedestal underneath *Jut Strut* on jugs and traverse the seam under the roof to the left with thin feet to the arete. Can also be done in reverse.

☐ 26o Jut Strut V8 ★★
Stand start on jugs at right margin of the face and get the gaston in the blank face with your left before reaching up across the face to the right, trying to gain roundy sloper.

☐ 26p AGR V10 ★
Same start as for *Jut Strut*, but instead of grabbing the gaston, get it as a sidepull with your right and negotiate the blank white face up and left.

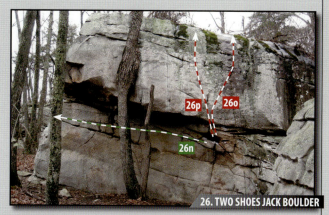

26. TWO SHOES JACK BOULDER

27. THE CHATTANOOGAN

The Chattanoogan roof is home to two good problems. It is located on the back cliff line directly behind the Odyssey Boulder. The easiest way to get there is scramble through the narrow gap between the Odyssey Boulder and the Two Shoes Jack Boulder and it will be apparent on your left. **The problems are described left to right and don't top out, except for the extension to** *Midway, Iwo Jima*, **which would require some down climbing to get off.**

☐ 27a The Chattanoogan V12 ★★
Climbs the long rightward traversing seam under the huge roof. Low, hard not to dab. Often wet. Sit start on thin crimper flake below seam in middle of wall. Follow thin crimps right out the seam. Ends once you are established on the slab at the end.

27. THE CHATTANOOGAN

☐ 27b Midway V7 ★★
Starts in the middle of the *Chattanoogan* on the largest hold (sidepull) in the seam with a bad polished foot directly underneath it. Start matched here and work right out crimpers with bad feet. Ends once you are established on the slab.

☐ 27c Iwo Jima V7 ★
"Sketchy." A direct highball finish to *Midway* has been climbed. From the end of *Midway*, where you rock onto the slab, climb straight up the face above through a scoop to eventually gain a huge jug horn. Finish straight up or traverse off and downclimb from here.

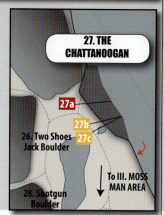

27. THE CHATTANOOGAN

26. Two Shoes Jack Boulder

To III. MOSS MAN AREA

28. Shotgun Boulder

Vikki Glinskii on Shotgun, V6. Spenser Tangsmith photo.

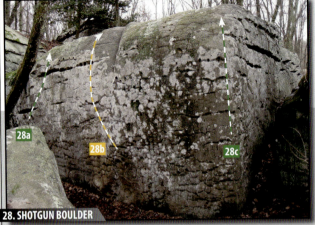

28. SHOTGUN BOULDER

☐ **28a** V2 ★★
The problem left of *Shotgun* climbs some cool pocket rails. Stand start on good rail directly underneath the tree, move up and right to another rail, then a slopey top out.

☐ **28b** Shotgun V6 ★★★
Probably the most classic pocket problem at the Stone Fort. Stand start with your hands low on a series of undercling and sidepull pockets. Move up and left to more shallow pockets, then head straight up to a brain-like top out. Originally known as *Melon Groove*, and climbed using the pocket pinch out right and topped out in the groove feature, avoiding the large rail to the left.

28. SHOTGUN BOULDER

While actually quite a big boulder, the Shotgun Boulder only has climbable problems on one side of it. It is host to one of the coolest pocket climbs at the Stone Fort. It is easily found directly across from the *Chattanoogan* and can be reached by scrambling through the narrow gap between the Odyssey Boulder and the Two Shoes Jack Boulder, or the gap on the other side of the Two Shoes Jack Boulder, and going right. **The problems are described left to right.** It is easy to walk off the backside once on top.

☐ **28c** Elephant Riders V3 ★★
Climbs the cool rippled scaled arete. Stand start using sidepulls on either side of the arete and bear hug your way up.

To the right of the Shotgun Boulder is a face littered with thin pockets and crimps, and which has a few problems on it. However, they are not described cause the are virtually always wet.

29. FUNKADELIC BOULDER

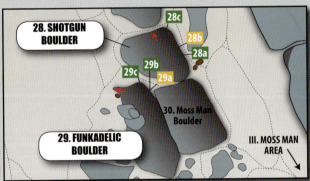

29. FUNKADELIC BOULDER

The Funkadelic Boulder is a very large boulder with not a lot of climbable terrain. The few problems on it can be found by walking to the right of the Two Shoes Jack Boulder and looking into a recess on your left. **They are described from left to right.** To get off, walk and scramble down the ramp to the right of the top outs.

☐ **29a** Galaxy 5000 V5 ★★★
AKA Funkadelic. A cool problem somewhat reminiscent of the Big Bad Boulder in Rocktown. Sit start on jug flake and climb up and right on holds under the roof until you can reach out to cool molded grips on the overhanging prow feature. Watch the boulder behind you as you make a big move to the jug.

☐ **29b** V3
A really bizarre bombay chimney type slab problem. Would feel more at home in Eldorado Canyon or Joshua Tree. Sit start same as for *Galaxy 5000* and climb the seam under the roof all the way out and around the arete. Wear a shirt!

☐ **29c** Dodge Swinger V1 ★★
Stand start on the arete with left on sidepull and right on cool fin pinch. Climb the arete above and top out straight up.

III. MOSS MAN AREA

The Moss Man Area is used to roughly describe the rest of the bouldering in the back "valley" beyond The Space Odyssey and Jungle Gym Areas. It includes the Moss Man Boulder (pg. 94), the Fish Lips Boulders (pg. 95), the Human Chew Toy Area (pg. 100), and the Now and Zen Area (pg. 96). This area is not one of the more frequently traveled areas at the Stone Fort, so it is easier to find an out of the way project to try alone. Despite having a number of fun and quite worthy problems, it is also not quite as stacked with classics as some of the more popular zones.

To get to the Moss Man Area, simply walk along trails past the Shotgun Boulder and The Chattanoogan. The Moss Man Boulder will be on your right, while the Fish Lips Boulders will be ahead of you on the left. The Now and Zen Area is accessed by climbing up through a tunnel hole beyond the Fish Lips Boulders. The Human Chew Toy Area includes all the climbing on the back wall and under the massive roof which is past the Fish Lips Boulders. There are a couple other ways to reach this area as well. You can walk through the Jungle Gym Area, towards the back wall. Coming from this direction the first boulders you encounter will be the Fish Lips Boulders straight ahead, and the Moss Man Boulder on your left. Or, you can come at them from the Glamour Block (pg. 119) or the Sternum Area, by following the back wall. From this direction you will encounter the Human Chew Toy Area first (pg. 100). If all of this has completely confused you, check the map to the right.

43 problems

V0	1
V1	2
V2	5
V3	11
V4	3
V5	5
V6	5
V7	4
V8	3
V9	
V10	1
V11	
V12	
projects	2

SAM ADAMS

My earliest memories of LRC begin in 1985 when I was about nine years old. I grew up about a half mile from there and would ride my bicycle with my brother all through the area where the golf course is now. My great grandparents owned the land above the boulders all around the water tower. My brother and I would play with our GI Joes in the main area where the boulder problems Tristar and Dragon Lady are located. We would also shoot our BB guns all around. Very rarely we would see a climber and when we did we would run and hide.

Maybe in about 1988 the golf couse opened and I decided to get golf clubs and play, mostly just so I could drive a golf cart. After a while golf was boring, so I would rally the carts up through the boulders and I eventually started climbing around the boulders in golf shoes. I soon decided I wanted to rappel, so I got about 50 feet of rope and I would put socks on my hands and go down the rope. I remember one day I was doing that and saw Chris Chesnutt climbing with his purple mohawk and tights. That same year I met Tommy Hayes at my school and he talked about climbing on those boulders. That really sparked my intrest. Soon, Tommy and I actually went climbing there. Tommy was friends with Chris and he loaned me a pair of shoes and chalk bag. That was really the beginning of climbing for me.

I spent lots of time from 1989 to 1994 bouldering there. During those years access was not really an issue. Everyone would park at my aunt's place, next to the water tower, and do whatever we wanted. I moved away to Colorado in 1995 and didn't return to LRC for years. When I did come back, it was no longer like a private hideaway and I didn't really like it. I still can't believe the national recognition the area gets and the progression that has been made. In my days, bouldering was like training for acually climbing and now it has progressed into its own sport — making LRC a destination for all types of climbers.

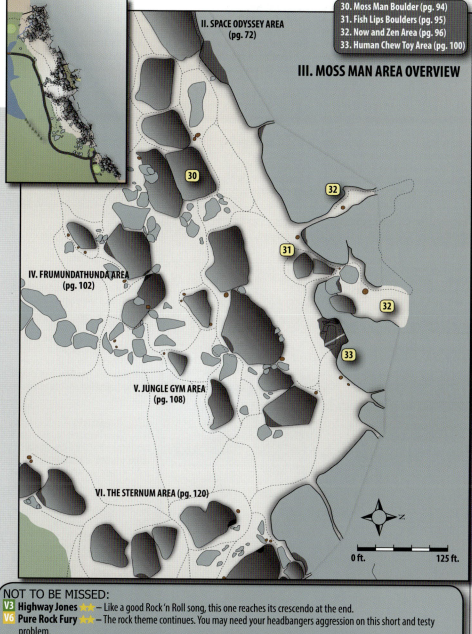

30. Moss Man Boulder (pg. 94)
31. Fish Lips Boulders (pg. 95)
32. Now and Zen Area (pg. 96)
33. Human Chew Toy Area (pg. 100)

III. MOSS MAN AREA OVERVIEW

II. SPACE ODYSSEY AREA
(pg. 72)

30

32

31

32

IV. FRUMUNDATHUNDA AREA
(pg. 102)

33

V. JUNGLE GYM AREA
(pg. 108)

VI. THE STERNUM AREA (pg. 120)

0 ft.   125 ft.

NOT TO BE MISSED:

V3 Highway Jones ★★ – Like a good Rock 'n Roll song, this one reaches its crescendo at the end.

V6 Pure Rock Fury ★★ – The rock theme continues. You may need your headbangers aggression on this short and testy problem.

V7 Now and Zen ★★★ – If a boulder problem sits in the woods and nobody climbs it, is it still a boulder problem? A perfect line of difficult to grab grips on a perfectly overhanging wall.

V8 Dr. Atkinson ★★★ – The prescription for this problem is lots of burl! Get mean, it won't come easy.

V10 The Power of Amida ★★★ – Amida was a buddhist who attained enlightenment and chose to remain in the transcendent realm. His power is that of Infinite Light. You will need to use his power to transcend gravity if you hope to conquer this tall testpiece.

30. MOSS MAN BOULDER

The Moss Man boulder is an aptly named boulder which is home to some slab problems which fit into that classic category of "should be great when they clean up." It is located to the left of the Shotgun Boulder, and is also across the way from the Jungle Gym Boulder. **The problems are described from right to left around the boulder.** To get off, walk to the left along the top of the slab, then downclimb some mossy grooves.

☐ 30a Moss Man V1 ★
Area classic? If you like pebbly rock covered in moss and lichen. Stand start in fist sized hole in middle of green face. Climb up pockets cleaned out of the moss. There are more climbs to be mined out of the moss on either side of this one, but Montlake asks that you not aggressively clean moss, and it's doubtful it would be worth it.

☐ 30b High Tide V6 ★★
The slab route on the right side of the face, just left of the arete. Stand start using underclings and large feet, then head straight up using shallow scoops on the slab.

☐ 30c Fire V7 ★★
The slab in the middle of the face, just left of *High Tide*. Stand start and aim for a pubbly knob protrusion in the middle of the face. Gain this with the left hand and finish straight up the slab above.

☐ 30d Lick the Stamp V4 ★
A variation on *Fire*. Start a couple feet further left and gain the pebbly knob with the right hand, before moving up and left to reach brushed slopers not covered in moss, then mantle over onto the lower angle slab above.

☐ 30e V3 ★
The slab problem which starts behind the small tree where the slab has gotten shorter. Stand up onto your feet and grab high small white crimps, then on to sloper mantle.

☐ 30f V2 ★
About three feet left of 30e, where the wall is quite short. Stand up onto brushed edges and reach for slopers formed by shallow water runnels, press out the mantle.

☐ 30g Surfing the High Tide V6
Start the same as for 30f, at the left side of the face. Move up to slopers, but instead of mantling, keep moving along slopers up and right to top out. Contrived.

☐ 30h Headies V8 ★
This problem is on a triangular white face to the left of the slab problems above, perched up and right from another triangular white face. Stand start with your left on crimper and right on pocket. The large foot rail beneath you is off. One long move to sloper, then mantle.

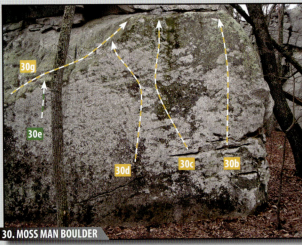

30. MOSS MAN BOULDER

28. Shotgun Boulder
29. Funkadelic Boulder
30. MOSS MAN BOULDER
30a
30b
30e
30c
30f 30d
30h
30g
35. Frumundathunda Boulder
To V. JUNGLE GYM AREA
40. Jungle Gym Boulder

30a
30. MOSS MAN BOULDER

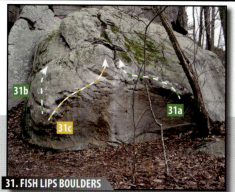

31. FISH LIPS BOULDERS

31. FISH LIPS BOULDERS

31. FISH LIPS BOULDERS

The Fish Lips Boulders are a small grouping of two boulders and a face across from them which are home to some short but good problems. These boulders also guard the entrance to the Now and Zen Area. **The problems are on all sides of the boulders, and also on separate blocks, so check the map to understand how they are described.** Getting off these boulders is not an issue, as they are all short.

☐ 31a The Ghast V3 ⭐⭐
On the right side of this short face, sit start low with hands on crimper underneath lip of small roof. Bust up and left to slopers, ride them left till you can rock over and press out the mantle.

☐ 31b Conway Twitty Twister V2 ⭐
Sit start on the left arete of the boulder with left in large hueco sidepull and right in undercling pocket. Pull on and bear hug straight up arete to sloper rockover. Short.

☐ 31c The Barrier V7
Sit start the same as for *Conway Twitty Twister*. Follow pocket holds up and right to reach water groove, then top out on slopers. Contrived.

☐ 31d Pure Rock Fury V6 ⭐⭐
This is the left hand problem on the short overhanging wall across the way from the last three problems and at the mouth of a dark, dank corridor. Sit start on undercling pockets and move out lip to slopers and crimps.

☐ 31e Slow and Low V4 ⭐
This one climbs like the crimper problem on your home woody. On the right hand side of the short overhanging face. Sit start low on crimps in hueco and move up to more crimps, finishing left at the top.

☐ 31f Slow-Fury Traverse V6
Begin on the crimps in the hueco as for *Slow and Low* and traverse across the wall to the left, encountering *Pure Rock Fury*, and finish up it.

☐ 31g Holy Roller V3 ⭐
Sort of squeezed, but still fun. Start on the crimps to the right of the hueco where *Slow and Low* starts, and move up and right to the top out.

☐ 31h Kenny Loggins Road V0 ⭐
The long low angle arete on the pointy boulder just uphill from *Conway Twitty Twister* is fun. Start at the bottom of the arete with pockets and climb up the arete.

☐ 31i Fish Lips V3 ⭐
Around the back side of the boulders is a small corridor with a roundy arete on the left side. Sit start low with your hands in a shallow black scoop on slopey lip. Bust up and right to obvious huge jug, then rock over.

31. FISH LIPS BOULDERS

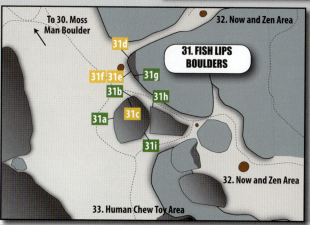

To 30. Moss Man Boulder

32. Now and Zen Area

31. FISH LIPS BOULDERS

32. Now and Zen Area

33. Human Chew Toy Area

32a

To 32. Now and Zen Area

32. NOW AND ZEN AREA

32c

32b

32. NOW AND ZEN AREA

32d

32f

32e

32. NOW AND ZEN AREA

32. NOW AND ZEN AREA

The Now and Zen Area comprises two groups of boulders that sit up on the plateau above the main wall which runs the length of the Stone Fort. They are not easy to see and you are unlikely to stumble upon them unless you are looking. That said, there are some very fine problems here indeed. To access them, crawl up through a tunnel which is in the corner behind the Fish Lips Boulders. This will bring you to the first group of boulders and problems 32a – 32f. If you follow a faint trail through this small area and stay on it as it switchbacks to the left up the hill you will eventually come to the second wall, which hosts the classic problems *Now and Zen* and *Dr. Atkinson*. **Check the map to understand the order the problems are listed.** Getting off most of these problems simply involves walking off of the top and back around to the base.

☐ 32a **Casper the Friendly** V5 ⭐⭐ **Ghost**
Start standing on jugs on the low end of the tunnel as you enter the Now and Zen Area. Make a few moves up through the tunnel on good jugs, then move out to crimps on the vertical face. Climb the face above using pockets and crimps to a long last move.

☐ 32b **Jungle Foot** V5 ⭐
At the point of the boulder above a cave/tunnel leading down towards *Human Chew Toy*, sit start with your hands on sloper rail and move out the short bulge above on slopers to a powerful mantle.

☐ 32c **Toll Gate** V3
On the face to the right of *Jungle Foot* is a left sidepull. Stand start here and climb the bulge above. The holds lie in a water streak, so it is often wet.

☐ 32d **The Eyes Have It** V5 ⭐
A tougher than it looks one-move wonder. In the middle of the white face are twin slopers under "eye"-brows. Stand start on these and go for the lip.

☐ 32e V3
Laydown start awkwardly on a jug flake very low at the base of the blunt arete and make your way up the arete to the break. Very lowball.

☐ 32f **Minerva** V5 ⭐
The blank open scoop. Stand start with your right hand on the flat edge and left on undercling crimps and make a big move to a pocket in the seam under the roof, then climb out the roof above.

32g

32i

32j **32h**

32k

31. Fish Lips Boulders

40. Jungle Gym Boulder

32a

32. NOW AND ZEN AREA

trail

32e

32f **32d**

32c

32b

39. Jerry's Kids Boulder

33. Human Chew Toy Area

Ben Case, Now and Zen V7, see below. Adam Johnson photo

32. NOW AND ZEN AREA

32. NOW AND ZEN AREA

The following problems are found along a steep wall in a separate gulley. To reach them, walk past the above problems and follow a trail which doubles back to the left and comes down into the gulley from above. The problems are listed right to left.

☐ **32g Pussy Patrol** V6 ⭐
To the right of the overhanging wall which holds *Now and Zen* is a left-leaning ramp/rail. Sit start at the bottom of the rail and climb crimps and slopers up and left to slopey top out. Often wet and a bit mossy.

☐ **32h Highway Jones** V3 ⭐⭐
The overhanging arete which forms the right side of the steep wall. Sit start low on the boulder with hands on crimps. Bust up and left following the rail and arete to a slopey top out.

☐ **32i Now and Zen** V7 ⭐⭐⭐
Climbs the right hand side of the 40 degree overhanging wall. Sit down low on trio of interesting grips, choose your start. Then move up out the steep wall on cool holds and bullet stone. Pinches, crimps, incuts, and then right to horns for the top.

☐ **32j Dr. Atkinson** V8 ⭐⭐⭐
The slightly less steep line left of *Now and Zen* is burly. Sit start on obvious pocket jugs. Immediately throw down the hammer up the underclings and thin pinches to gain jugs. Some crimp moves guard the slopey top out.

☐ **32k Injury Free Guarantee** V4
"Sketchy." Left of *Dr. Atkinson* and above the crazy laying down tree and jumbled boulders. Stand start on weird horn for right and nipple horn for left. Climb the wall above with big moves. Dirty.

Michael Lacour on Simply Irresistible.
Adam Johnson photo.

33. HUMAN CHEW TOY AREA

The Human Chew Toy is a massive roof with a roughly one-foot wide offwidth crack running the entire length. It is one of the few routes worth leading at the Stone Fort - as long as you like this sort of climbing. The Human Chew Toy Area describes the problems which are in the cave formed by the massive overhang as well as on the walls to the right and left of the cave. There are some not very often traveled slabs in this area, as well as a couple very difficult problems. In general this is a quiet and peaceful area, where you are almost guaranteed to be climbing alone. **The problems are described from left to right along the back wall.** Each problem has a different way to get off which are described below.

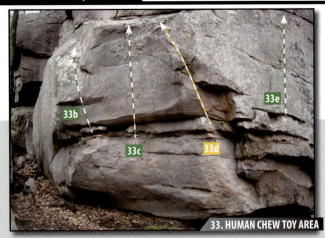

33. HUMAN CHEW TOY AREA

☐ 33a Project?
On the bullet white face directly across from the problem *Fish Lips* are some very thin brushed crimps above head height. Pull on these and stand up to the crack edge and mantle. May have been climbed.

☐ 33b Corn Grinder V2 ⭐
Stand start on jug flakes in crack and move up to the undercling flake on a ramp. Follow it to the top out and walk off left to get off.

☐ 33c Cling-On V3
Sort of a contrived problem located in between *Corn Grinder* and *Drumm Arete*, as holds from both of these problems are within reach. Grab the high undercling and stand up to the jug far above. Mantle and move left to get off.

☐ 33d Drumm Arete V5 ⭐⭐
Just to the right of *Cling-On* is a blunt arete. Stand start on the corner with hands on decent holds in crack break. Move up via a series of very thin crimps and sidepulls on thin flake to mantle. Walk off left to get off.

☐ 33e V3 ⭐
"Scary." A few feet right of the *Drumm Arete* is a slabby white face. Stand start on decent holds and move up to arching rail to get a horn. Slab it out above all the way up to the ledge up and right.

☐ 33f Project?
"Scary." A few feet right of 33e and left of *Diatribe*. Climb the very tall slabby white face straight up to the ledge 20 feet up. May not be super hard, but definitely serious.

☐ 33g Diatribe V3 ⭐
"Sketchy." Just to the right of the tree is an obvious red dihedral. Stand start matched on crimp beneath dihedral. Move up and climb the arete which forms the left side of the dihedral on iron patina crimps. At the top, traverse rail right and then downclimb the jumbled boulders to get off.

33. HUMAN CHEW TOY AREA

☐ 33h T-bone V2 ⭐
Just to the right of *Diatribe* is a pointy triangular boulder which looks like a T-bone (I guess). Start on the flat edge with both hands and squeeze up to the jug fin at the top. Step off.

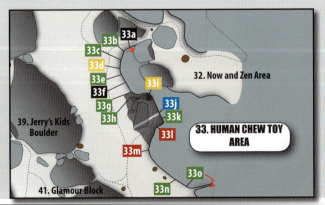

33. HUMAN CHEW TOY AREA

33. HUMAN CHEW TOY AREA

33. HUMAN CHEW TOY AREA

33. HUMAN CHEW TOY AREA

☐ **33l Simply Irresistable** V8 ★★
"Sketchy." Climbs the improbable arete on the right hand side of the cave. Stand start on giant bread loaf pinch slopers. Move up the overhanging arete, mantling onto the starting holds, then jump for triangle pinch hold under the roof and drop to get off.

☐ **33m The Power of** V10 ★★★
Amida
"Sketchy." This tall, cryptic, and blank looking arete is a neo-classic. First done by James Litz. Sit start on jugs underneath a small roof on the arete that forms the right hand side of the cave. Climb up to obvious large blocky sidepull and then trend right on the high slab to top out.

☐ **33n EFD Slab** V3 ★
About 20 feet right of *The Power of Amida* on the outside wall is a clean black and grey slab. On the left hand side of the slab is a black streak. Climb it to slopers and eventually jugs. Traverse right to get off.

☐ **33o Farmer Slab** V2 ★
Starts at a large hole undercling. A stand up problem – stand onto the slab and reach for slopers, then on to the jugs.

☐ **33i Webb Problem** V7
"Sketchy." An improbable problem with a rectal impaler flake right beneath it, located in the back of the cave. Sit start on small crimps right above the impaler and get your left foot up around the corner. Toe in and reach slopers then crimps at the top of the boulder. Watch your back.

☐ **33j Human Chew Toy** 5.11d ★★
The huge imposing offwidth roof crack. You'll want to put on the harness and bring the big cams for this one. Starts in the back of the cave and climbs outward by chimneying, groveling, and using a fair amount of face holds.

☐ **33k V1** ★
The low angle slab in the back of the cave. Stand start and climb thin flakes up the slab. Traverse left to get off.

IV. FRUMUNDATHUNDA AREA

The Frumundathunda Area is comprised of a couple of large boulders which sit right along the "express trail" through the boulders, and as such are very hard to miss. Although there are only two boulders here, there are many popular and a few classic problems, and it can be hard for a first-timer to the Stone Fort to walk by these jigsawed faces and overhanging aretes without stopping for a session. Sadly, moss and vegetation on the tops of the boulders often store water long after the last rain and slowly drain over many of the problems, making them wet or dirty at times.

To reach the Frumundathunda Area, simply walk along the "express trail" from the Front Area, which leaves those boulders by *Genghis Khan*. The first two boulders that you come to will be the Blind Spot Boulder (pg. 104) and the Frumundathunda Boulder (pg. 105) on your left. You can also reach them from the Space Odyssey Area by following the trail which skirts the boulders heading downhill to the right. Approaching this way will deposit you at *Diesel Power*.

32 problems

V0		3
V1		8
V2		2
V3		2
V4		3
V5		5
V6		3
V7		2
V8		
V9		2
V10		1
V11		
V12		
projects		1

NOT TO BE MISSED:

V4 Thundafrumunda ★★ – A cool arete that can't be missed. A long reach for some, a dynamic move for others, just don't blow the top out.

V5 Diesel Power ★★ w– Drop the clutch, but keep it low gear. One of the coolest overhanging aretes at the Fort. Slap and squeeze your way up this burly rig.

V5 Fat Cat ★★ – Someone's got it easy. See if this one comes easy for you. Cool moves on good stone.

V7 Blind Spot ★★ – Overhanging pockets, what more could you ask for.

V9 Robbing the Tooth Fairy ★★ – A good lowball traverse for people who like these types of problems. Popular for the grade.

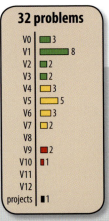

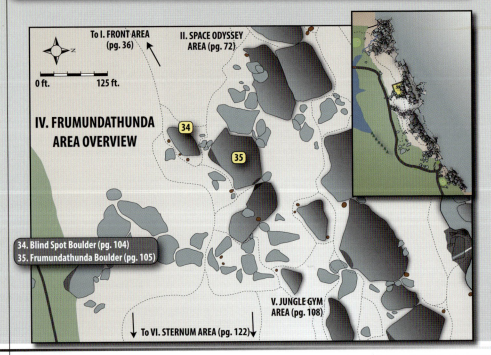

To I. FRONT AREA (pg. 36)

II. SPACE ODYSSEY AREA (pg. 72)

0 ft.   125 ft.

IV. FRUMUNDATHUNDA AREA OVERVIEW

34

35

34. Blind Spot Boulder (pg. 104)
35. Frumundathunda Boulder (pg. 105)

V. JUNGLE GYM AREA (pg. 108)

To VI. STERNUM AREA (pg. 122)

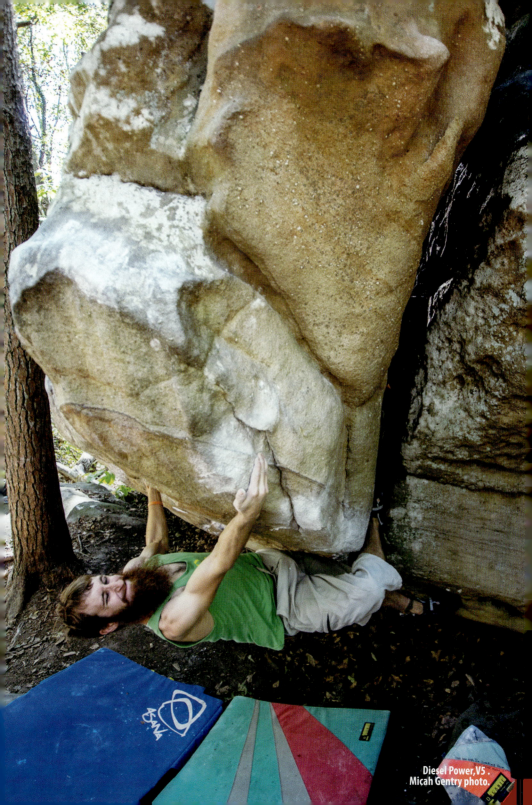

Diesel Power, V5 .
Micah Gentry photo.

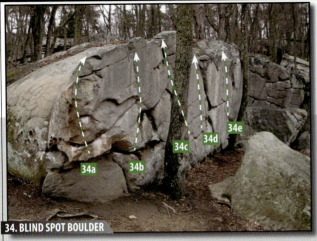

34. BLIND SPOT BOULDER

34. BLIND SPOT BOULDER

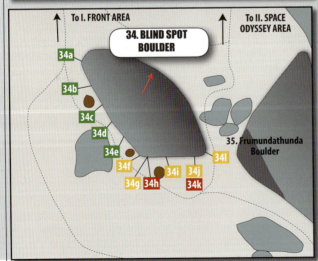

34. BLIND SPOT BOULDER

The Blind Spot Boulder is the smallest of the boulders in the Frumundathunda Area and sits right next to the "express trail." It has climbing on two sides of it. The left side is a vertical white face laced with jugs and cracks which will suit the first time climber. The right side of the boulder is host to a number of high-quality harder climbs. **The problems are listed from left to right.** Getting off this boulder is easy, just walk off.

☐ 34a Dis V2 ★★
The left arete of the boulder looks sort of like the backbone of an eaten carcass (or not). Sit start on jugs at the base of the arete, move up to slopey pocket and follow holds up arete to juggy top out. Can also start on the problem to the right and traverse into the start.

☐ 34b V1 ★
Just to the left of the tree and right of *Dis*. Sit start low on jugs, make a big move to good jugs in pod, then make moves to top of the face.

☐ 34c V0-
Just to the right of the large tree on the left side of the face, stand start and climb obvious jugs and cool horns which form jigsaw cracks. Good first time boulder problem.

☐ 34d V1
Climbs the left hand shield of rock left of the wide crack. Stand start in low underclings and good really low feet, make move into middle of face and climb above using edge of crack on right. Not very tall, a bit contrived.

☐ 34e V1 ★
Stand start in pockets in middle of shield left of tree in the middle of the face with thin feet. Climb the shield using the sidepull rail on the right. Short, a bit contrived, and slightly dirty due to run-off.

☐ 34f Bear Hug Arete V5 ★★
The super rounded and polished arete. Stand start with right hand in the black water groove and pull onto the wall with a high foot. Hug your way to the top.

34g Get Your Groove On V6 ⭐

Sit start the same as for *Robbing the Tooth Fairy* on good holds on the right side of a low block. Move up and left into the black groove and follow it to the top. Often dirty as it runs with water.

34h Robbing the V9 ⭐⭐
Tooth Fairy

A lowball traverse problem which is quite popular for the grade. Sit start on the block same as for *Get Your Groove On*. Move up to sidepull and then out right, squeezing between the rock and the tree to the start of *Tooth Fairy*. Finish on it.

34i Tooth Fairy V7 ⭐⭐

Starts just to the right of a large tree on flat shelf. Start matched, then traverse right using shallow pockets and a heel-hook to gain the pockets of *Blind Spot*. Finish up using shallow brushed sloper and holds on *Blind Spot*.

34j Blind Spot V7 ⭐⭐

A cool problem. Sit start left of *Diesel Power* matched on crimper pockets. Pull on and climb decent pockets on steep wall to gain obvious flake, finish straight up. Avoid using holds on the arete to the right.

34. BLIND SPOT BOULDER

34k Blind Spot V9 ⭐⭐
(original)

The original version of this cool pocket problem was done more as an eliminate. It's simple – don't use the crack beneath *Diesel Power* for your feet, instead use a small slippery edge for your foot directly beneath the starting holds.

34l Diesel Power V5 ⭐⭐⭐

The classic overhanging squeeze arete on the right side of the boulder. Sit start matched with your hands in the crack or liebacking the edge of the crack. Slap up the burly bulge above, eventually moving up and right on rounded holds to finish.

35. FRUMUNDATHUNDA BOULDER

The Frumundathunda Boulder is named after its most prominent and striking line, which also happens to be a mouthful of a name. This is a great boulder for climbers in the V4 - V5 range, with a number of worthy problems at that grade. Unfortunately, if it has rained recently, then water may be seeping over most of the best lines. And, even if they are not wet, they may be dirty from runoff, so be prepared to do a little brushing. The top is easily reached by walking around the left side, so it may not be a bad idea to check out your intended top out beforehand if you are in doubt. **The problems are described from left to right,** and you just walk off to the left to get down.

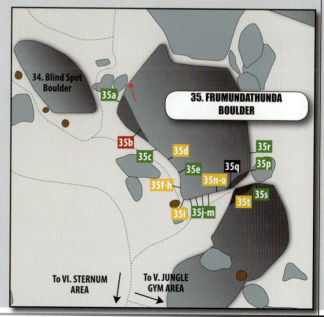

35. FRUMUNDATHUNDA BOULDER

35. FRUMUNDATHUNDA BOULDER

35. FRUMUNDATHUNDA BOULDER

☐ **35a Nutrageous** V3
Stand start on the far left side of the boulder with hands above your head on pebbly sloper. Climb up and right out the prow. Cool position, but not so great rock, watch out for breakage.

☐ **35b Disparate Impact** V10 ⭐
On the right side of the overhanging face which makes up the left side of the boulder. Stand start on thin crimpers formed by iron patina in the middle of the face. Put on a foot and do a large move to small pocket in seam/overlap straight up, then top out.

☐ **35c Karmageddon** V3 ⭐
About 10 feet left of the water groove. Stand start on good jug pocket in crack and climb up the face on more pockets, jugs, pinches and slopers.

☐ **35d Black Hat** V4 ⭐
Just to the left of the water groove is a line of holds straight up the face. Start in a slot and climb up using mostly crimp edges.

☐ **35e V0** ⭐
Sit start in the crack about five feet left of the beginning of *Fat Cat*. Climb the ledgy slopers up the water groove to top out same as *Fat Cat*.

☐ **35f The Curse** V4 ⭐
Sit start low the same as for *Fat Cat* and *Olive's Oil*. Traverse left on the low crack on mostly good holds. Continue until the crack starts to rise on the face. Finish straight up on large jugs just right of the large tree. Used to start to the left of the water groove when a tree stump was in the way. The stump has been removed, adding more moves to this fun traverse.

☐ 35g Fat Cat V5 ★★

This cool problem is often wet and dirty due to run-off. Sit start low on big jugs left of the arete. Move up to obvious pocket and sidepull and then make moves to gain the break up and left, topping out by the horn left of the tree.

☐ 35h Olive's Oil V6 ★

Sit start on big jugs left of the arete, same as for *Fat Cat*. Climb the holds up and rightward underneath the tree, avoiding the holds to the right on the arete, to top out just right of the tree. Cool holds, but definitely an eliminate.

☐ 35i Thundafrumunda V4 ★★

The sharp overhanging arete is probably the best climb on the boulder. Stand start on the obvious large block just right of the arete. Can also be started on the jugs down and right to add a couple moves but doesn't change the grade. Pull on and bear hug up the overhanging arete using positive sidepulls.

☐ 35j Full Moon V1

Climbs the circular hole just right of the arete. Sit start on obvious jugs and move up and right on good holds into the hole and top out above. Suffers from runoff.

☐ 35k Vlad the Inhaler V1 ☆

Sit start on low rail left of the *Shining* on jugs. Climb up good holds to right-facing dihedral and crack feature to easy top out. Fairly dirty.

35. FRUMUNDATHUNDA BOULDER

☐ 35l The Shining V2 ★

Sit start on jugs on low rail and move up the face on pockets in the middle of the wall to a slopey top out. Dirty.

☐ 35m V1

The crack and face. Pretty dirty to a mossy top out.

☐ 35n Frumundathunda V5 ★★

Starts on the right side of the wall, just left of the cave and above a seasonal stream. Begin on jugs and move up the face on slopers, then angle to the right on better slopers to a not too bad top.

☐ 35o Thundatathunda V5 ★

This problem traverses the wall from right to left and finishes up the arete. Start the same as for *Frumundathunda* on the low jugs. Traverse the low break

all the way to the left and finish up *Thundafrumunda*.

The following problems are found through the small cave to the right of Frumundathunda. Scramble through the cave, turn around to look back at the problems, and you will find 35p, 35q, and 35r on the right side and 35s and 35t on the left side.

☐ 35p Baby, One More Time V0

The arete on the right wall of the cave. Sit start on jugs in crack break. Climb the arete above on good holds.

☐ 35q Project?

Traverse the seam into *Baby, One More Time*. Stand start on crimpers in seam in the back of the cave and traverse the seam right to finish the same as *Baby, One More Time*.

☐ 35r Oops, I Did It Again V1

To the right of *Baby, One More Time*, on the dirty face. Sit start and climb jug rails upwards.

☐ 35s V1 ★

The arete on the left boulder. Sit start on large conglomerated jug just above a low slab and climb mossy arete on big holds.

☐ 35t Stretch Armstrong V6 ★

Sit start on crimpers in the back of the cave on the left wall formed by orange iron patina. Move left out the cave on slopey rails and tensiony moves to finish the same as for 35s.

35. FRUMUNDATHUNDA BOULDER

V. JUNGLE GYM AREA

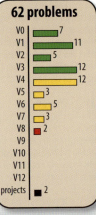

62 problems

V0		7
V1		11
V2		5
V3		12
V4		12
V5		3
V6		5
V7		3
V8		2
V9		
V10		
V11		
V12		
projects		2

The Jungle Gym Area is an area of large boulders with many great problems. In general the boulders here are tall and have problems on multiple sides. Here you will find some not to be missed classics, as well as a number of quality problems that don't quite make classic status, but are of course worthy of your time. The bright orange rock on the face of Jerry's Kids is like a magnet to the seasoned boulderer, and if there are people in the boulders, then there will probably be some people in this area.

The boulders found here are the Castaway Boulder (pg. 110), Funhouse Boulder (pg. 111), Fish Market Boulder (pg. 112), Jerry's Kids Boulder (pg. 113), Jungle Gym Boulder (pg. 117), and The Glamour Block (pg. 119). These boulders fill the large area of space on your left after walking on the trail past the Frumundathunda Area, or downhill if you are in the Moss Man Area.

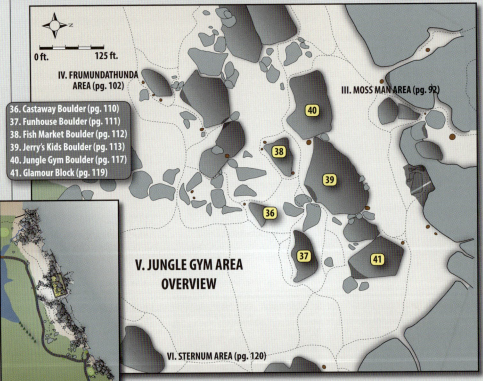

IV. FRUMUNDATHUNDA AREA (pg. 102)

III. MOSS MAN AREA (pg. 92)

36. Castaway Boulder (pg. 110)
37. Funhouse Boulder (pg. 111)
38. Fish Market Boulder (pg. 112)
39. Jerry's Kids Boulder (pg. 113)
40. Jungle Gym Boulder (pg. 117)
41. Glamour Block (pg. 119)

V. JUNGLE GYM AREA OVERVIEW

VI. STERNUM AREA (pg. 120)

0 ft.   125 ft.

NOT TO BE MISSED:

V1 **Mizzen Mast** ★★ – Arrrr! Climb the *Mizzen Mast* and don't fall off or you'll land on the poop deck. Arrrr! A good warm-up and one of the longest rail traverses at the Fort.

V4 **The Fish Market** ★★ – A cool short problem which is a great place to work on your mantling skills without the terrifying consequences of sliding off the top of a taller problem.

V7 **Castaway** ★★★ – A cool dyno with a very literal name. If you were cast away on a desert island with only one boulder problem, which one would it be?

V7 **Jerry's Kids** ★★★ – A fantastic boulder problem. Cool moves, a great variety of grips, perfect orange rock, awesome landing, what more could you ask?

Taylor Mason on Castaway.
Adam Johnson photo.

36. CASTAWAY BOULDER

36. CASTAWAY BOULDER

The Castaway Boulder is a relatively small boulder which is recognizable for its smooth white prow. It only has two faces, and they both rise to meet in the middle at this monolithic point, home to the classic dyno problem *Castaway*. **The problems are described from left to right.** It is very easy to walk off the back side of this boulder.

☐ **36a** **Mizzen Mast** V1 ⭐

This rail traverse is a great warm-up or endurance problem for the beginner. Squat start on low jugs at left side of the boulder and traverse the jugs along the lip to right until the highest point is reached, then rock over mantle.

☐ **36b** **Castaway** V7 ⭐⭐⭐

A great dyno problem up the prow of the boulder. Stand start on obvious crimper with both hands, use a black polished bad foot to dyno to jugs over lip of boulder.

☐ **36c** **High Five V11**

Sit start with hands on sloping seam edge about three feet off the ground and foot on large edge. A longstanding project that saw its first ascent in 2011 by Jimmy Webb

☐ **36d** **V0**

A shorter version of *Mizzen Mast* on the other side of the boulder. Great jugs, easy warm-up. Start on the lower right hand side of the boulder, traverse the lip left along jugs for about 15 feet until bushes, mantle.

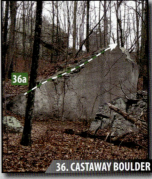

36. CASTAWAY BOULDER

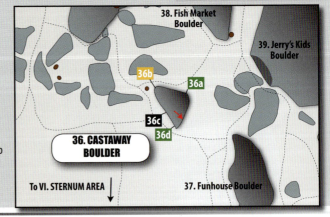

38. Fish Market Boulder

39. Jerry's Kids Boulder

36. CASTAWAY BOULDER

To VI. STERNUM AREA

37. Funhouse Boulder

37. FUNHOUSE BOULDER

37. FUNHOUSE BOULDER

The Funhouse Boulder is a fairly non-descript boulder with no super quality problems to bump its status. It is basically a tall and bright white face which faces downhill, just right of the Castaway Boulder, or just downhill of the right side of the Jerry's Kids Boulder. Despite the mediocre quality, the grades of these problems make it worth a stop some day to switch up the warm-up circuit. **The problems are listed from left to right,** and it is easy to walk off the back side of the boulder.

☐ **37a** Farmhand V2 ⭐
The left-hand arete is the coolest line on the boulder, despite the pebbly rock. Squat start on large jug on arete and move up the arete via crimpers and decent holds on arete to jugs at top.

☐ **37b** Funhouse V1
The left line of two chossy looking pod lines. Stand start with hands in pod and climb up steeper-than-it-looks rock via huge jugs, then traverse right along pebbly seam to top out in the notch shelf.

☐ **37c** V0
In the middle of the boulder, stand start and climb the rightmost of two lines of chossy looking pods and broken up rock. Finish in notch ledge.

☐ **37d** V0
Climbs the thin seam through white rock on the middle of the boulder. Stand start on jugs and climb seam via good jugs to top out at notch shelf.

☐ **37e** The Swollen Goat V1 ⭐
Start the same as for 37d on jugs at the base of seam, but instead of climbing thin seam branch off to the right and climb crack shaped with pods up to angling seam underneath overhang, head right to jugs at lip of boulder. Top out on dirty pebbly rock or traverse right on jugs. An eliminate.

☐ **37f** V0-
On the right hand side of the face the wall deteriorates into a jumbled mess of cracks and pods and holes. Climb the left hand side of the pods and jugs.

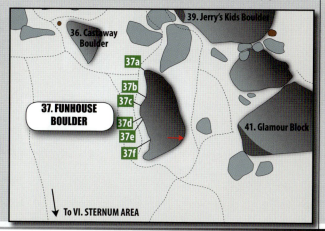

38. FISH MARKET BOULDER

The Fish Market Boulder is a short boulder with many problems on it that sits across the "courtyard" from the Jerry's Kids Boulder and the Jungle Gym Boulder. The problems here are short in stature, although generally worthwhile. This is a great place to work on some low to the ground mantle problems without the fear of a large fall if you fail. **The problems are described in a circle, left to right, all the way around the boulder, starting on the downhill side.** To get off the boulder, walk to the uphill side and downclimb a short face or jump off.

☐ **38a** **Red Tape** V0 ⭐
Start on jugs in rail at the left end of the face, just to right of tree. Climb the bulging face above via good holds in pods and cracks, beware of somewhat licheny top out.

☐ **38b** **The Fish Market** V3 ⭐ **Traverse**
An interesting traverse with the crux at the end. Start the same as for *Red Tape* on jugs at left end of seam rail. Traverse right along crack via decent holds all the way until you encounter the top out of 38d and follow it up via roundy slopers.

☐ **38c** **Unusual Suspect** V4 ⭐
Start in the middle of the traverse crack on good jugs. Move right along crack and up onto slopey edge and slopey pinch just above seam in white rock, then climb face above via good holds in eyebrows. Could also start the same place as the traverse, but wouldn't add any points.

☐ **38d** **V3**
Sit start awkwardly in large pocket in shattered looking rock on the right side of the face. Move up and right via decent holds to eventually gain large round sloper and finish above on licheny slab.

☐ **38e** **The Fish Market** V4 ⭐⭐
This problem may not be very tall, but sure takes a lot of effort. Sit start low on big sloper rail. Do moves upwards towards slopey pockets and then make desperate slopey mantle to top out.

☐ **38f** **Soapmakers** V2 ⭐⭐
A very low and safe problem to practice your sloper mantles. Start in obvious jugs just to right of *the Fish Market*. Move up and right to good flat shelf and then follow holds up and right to another desperate slopey mantle.

☐ **38g** **Big Wheel** V5 ⭐
A slopey lip traverse. Start on *Soapmakers* and climb up to the slopers over the lip of the boulder. Then traverse left along slopers till you are at the top out for *the Fish Market*, and finish up that.

☐ **38h** **V0-** ⭐
Stand start on right side of arete and climb sculpted holds up the cool turtle head looking feature.

☐ **38i** **Fish Tank** V1 ⭐
Sit start in low pocket jugs in the middle of the face, just right of ramp and crack. Climb straight up over bulge via pocket and interesting holds and up featured wall to slopey but clean top out.

To the left and right of problem Fish Tank are many places to climb in the V0 to V1 range which are not described. Fun climbing, but not very descript or obvious lines.

38. FISH MARKET BOULDER

38. FISH MARKET BOULDER

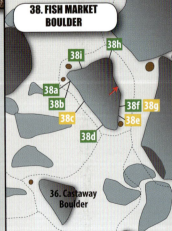

38. FISH MARKET BOULDER

36. Castaway Boulder

39. JERRY'S KIDS BOULDER

39. JERRY'S KIDS BOULDER

The Jerry's Kids Boulder is a large, wide, and tall boulder stacked with fun problems. Although home to only one genuine classic – *Jerry's Kids* – almost every problem on this boulder is worth climbing. The main attraction is the beautiful orange face. These problems are tall, so it may be a good idea to run around the backside and check out the top outs to make sure you know what you are grabbing, and find out whether the holds are free of water, moss, lichen, and leaves, all of which can be found on top. **Descriptions are from left to right.** Walk down the backside to get off.

☐ **39a** **Clarice** V4 ★
Starts in the tunnel between the Jerry's Kids Boulder and the Jungle Gym Boulder. Sit start low on a left-facing sidepull. Move up to a break, then top out up and left over the bulge. A bit dirty.

☐ **39b** **Warm-Up Traverse** V1 ★
"Sketchy." A pumpy and airy traverse. Start behind the tree in the cave on the left side of the boulder. Pull on and move to chicken head jugs, then traverse the break to the right as it slowly rises all the way across the face to where it becomes easy to top out without mantling.

☐ **39c** **The Big Much** V4 ★★
"Sketchy." Sit start really low in the dirt with right on crimper horn and left on textured sloper. Do a hard move to get off the ground, then follow the good edges in the orange jigsaw rock up to jug rail. Make a couple long moves slightly up and left to mantle top out.

☐ **39d** **The Merovingian** V6 ★
"Sketchy." Begin as for the *Big Much*, but after a couple moves, traverse holds to the right to finish up on *Jerry's Kids*.

☐ **39e** **Jerry's Kids** V7
★★★ "Sketchy." The center line up the orange jigsaw face is a Stone Fort classic with small holds. Sit start in the middle of the low cave with right on slopey pinch and left on sloper edge. Move up to divot pinch, then follow crimpers and slopey edges up the face above to mantle top out.

☐ **39f** **Sink 'Em Low** V6 ★★
"Sketchy." Problem right of *Jerry's Kids*. Sit start very low, almost laying down, with left on chalked crimp flake on right side of low cave and right hand on gaston right above it. Do a pretty hard move straight up to sloping edge, then right to large ledge. A couple of good holds lead to cryptic moves on roundy bulges up orange face.

☐ **39g** **Jerry Rigged** V8 ★★
Start on the very low holds of *Sink 'Em Low* and do moves to reach the starting holds of *Jerry's Kids*, then finish up that.

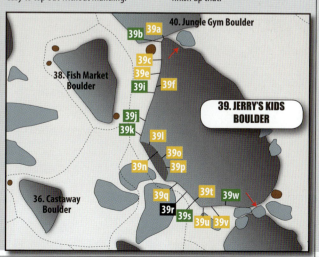

39h Fussili Jerry V8 ★★
Start on *Sink 'Em Low*, same as *Jerry Rigged* and do moves into the beginning of *Jerry's Kids*. From there, climb up and left to finish on the *Big Much*.

39i V3 ★
"Sketchy." Good rock, but a nebulous line. Sit start about four feet right of *Sink 'Em Low* with right on eye socket type pocket and left on sloping edge a foot left of that. Pull on and do a big move a crimp, then a pinch for your left, then up and right into black water groove, climb it to the top.

39j V1
On the right hand side of the face about 10 feet right of the last route. Stand start on obvious pointy horn jug at the base of water groove/crack. Climb interesting holds up the water groove.

39k V2 ★
"Sketchy." Short and sort of contrived. Stand start on jug horns about four feet right of the last problem, sort of at the arete of the boulder. Paste feet and go up to slopey pinch on edge of red rock, then up to crown horn and more jugs.

39l Oracle V4 ★★
"Sketchy." This route is the first route on the left side of the chossy looking cave. Sit down start very low on the lowest incut flake and move up via open hand sidepulls and pinches to jug rail and continue following crack break up with long moves on pretty good holds on steep wall to steep top out. Watch your back.

39m Stand Start V3 ★
Start the problem standing on obvious jug rail at face height.

39n Long Day Traverse V3 ★
Just to the right of *Oracle*, stand start with your back against the boulder on the lowest biggest jug. Climb up and right via good holds through the chossy looking but solid rock to eventually gain huge undercling pockets, then out horizontal roof to huge jugs and rock over.

39o V3 ★
This really steep roof problem starts by lying flat on your back on the slab. Start on huge jugs under roof. Pull off the slab and climb out the roof via crimper to huge jugs and top out.

39p V4 ★
The rightmost line in the chossy looking cave. Stand start in the pit on chalked sidepulls to the right of the low slab. Do moves up and left out steep bulge to eventual jugs. Top out via easy holds, or just step off to rock behind you.

39. JERRY'S KIDS BOULDER

39. JERRY'S KIDS BOULDER

Carolyn Coffey Jerrys Kids.
Adam Johnson photo.

39m

39n

39l

39n

39o

39p

39. JERRY'S KIDS BOULDER

39. JERRY'S KIDS BOULDER

39. JERRY'S KIDS BOULDER

☐ **39q** **V6** ⭐
On the blank shield of white rock to the right of the cave. Start matched on slopey crimp on the left hand side of the face, move up to ripple crack crimp and finish up and left around the bulge.

☐ **39r** **Project**
The right-hand line on the blank face to the left of the crack. This one needs someone with some serious crimp strength and hops. Start left hand on ripple of texture and right foot on little ripple edge and jump for huge pocket.

☐ **39s** **Snipe Hunt** V0 ⭐
The obvious crack on the right hand side of the face. Stand start with your hand in the crack wherever you want and climb the crack. Walk off right to get off.

☐ **39t** **The Blast Tyrant** V7 ⭐
Start on the crack of *Snipe Hunt* and traverse right across the face fairly low, past *Watermark*, to eventually finish up the slab of *Boob Fight*.

☐ **39u** **Watermark** V4 ⭐
"Sketchy." This cool slab climbs up the rippled face to the right of *Snipe Hunt*. Stand start on the curved crimp and climb up and slightly left on the black and mildly licheny face. Not such a great landing.

☐ **39v** **Boob Fight** V4 ⭐
"Sketchy." The slab to the right of *Watermark* starts at a sloping jug which looks like a smiley face. Stand start and climb up more slopers and edges above.

☐ **39w** **Two Thumbs Up** V3 ⭐⭐
A cool slab which climbs very interesting holds up wierdly sculpted rock on eyebrows and similar holds. Sit start low with both hands on right-facing jug sidepull and climb slabby face above via underclings.

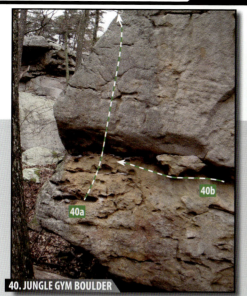

40. JUNGLE GYM BOULDER

40. JUNGLE GYM BOULDER

40. JUNGLE GYM BOULDER

The Jungle Gym Boulder is the tall, white boulder which sits left of the Jerry's Kids Boulder and often has a seasonal stream bubbling out from beneath it. It is host to many traverses and variations, and some very tall highballs. **The problems are described from left to right.** To get off this boulder, downclimb a vertical white face with large jug break running up and down it right next to the Jerry's Kids Boulder.

☐ **40a** **V1** ⭐

Stand start on jugs on the left side of the face and climb the arete and face straight up using holds on the face and the pebbly arete. Rock over left when you reach the second break. Mossy slab traverse to the left to get off.

☐ **40b** **Tombstone Traverse** V1 ⭐

Stand start on the right side of the face on jugs and traverse to the left on the jug rail. Finish at the arete. Can also be reversed.

☐ **40c** **The Tombstone** V3 ⭐

Stand start with hands above your head on decent edges at the base of the hanging tombstone feature on the arete. Pull on and climb up the tombstone feature to jugs at its top. Move to left and downclimb ramp feature on jugs to get off.

☐ **40d** **Mayor for a Day** V5 ⭐⭐

"Scary." The very tall arete above the *Tombstone*. Move up to a positive crimp and then carry on up the rounded arete above.

☐ **40e** **The High Traverse** V3 ⭐

Start with *the Tombstone*. From the finishing jugs traverse the high crack/seam straight left with positive feet. Downclimb juggy break 2/3 way across face.

The scooped face in the middle of the boulder hosts any number of very tall problems on flakes which are not described here. Beware of rock quality, and make sure your top out is not mossy, wet, or covered in poison ivy.

The Ditto Traverse, V6. Dan Brayak photo.

40h **The Crush of Love** V4 ⭐
"Scary." The middle line on the tall orange and brown face roughly follows a vertical seam feature. Sit start in the low sloper hole, then climb straight up the tall face using patina edge crimpers.

40i **Finish Your Homework** V5 ⭐⭐
"Sketchy." Sit start on good jugs on break on the right side of the boulder. Do cool moves up good holds to break at 10 feet, then make long move through blank section and up more jugs to top.

40f **V3** ⭐
"Scary." The blunt arete left of the *Cardinal Sin*. Stand start on holds above head level and climb up the blunt prow arete using big moves.

40g **The Cardinal Sin** V3 ⭐
"Scary." This one climbs the tall orange face just left of center on this face. It is to the right of the arete, and to the left of the *Crush of Love*.

40j **The Ditto Traverse** V6 ⭐
This problem traverses the face from right to left between the two aretes. Start the same as for *Finish Your Homework* and head left on the lower of the two seams. Follow holds in the lower seam left across the face, finishing on the higher seam on the arete. You can continue to follow this around the corner and across the face as far as you like before jumping off.

40. JUNGLE GYM BOULDER

41. GLAMOUR BLOCK

Despite its name, the Glamour Block is probably not the best place to be seen looking glamorous. Situated on the uphill side of the Jerry's Kids Boulder, it has quality problems on both uphill and downhill sides, but no classics. Here you will find some worthy tall moderates, a pumpy traverse, and some cool roof problems at a mellower grade. **The problems are described from right to left, starting on the uphill side of the boulder.** Getting off can be tricky, and involves some down climbing. From the uphill problems, move right a short ways and then downclimb a short wall onto a slab, and make your way down that.

41. GLAMOUR BLOCK

41a The Bulge V6 ⭐
This problem is on a very short boulder to the right of the Glamour Block if you are on the uphill side. Sit start on crimper rail and move straight up to a hard rockover mantle.

41b V1 ⭐
This problem boils down to one reach. Start on the far right side of the boulder with hands in the jug rail. Put feet on and make a long reach to a flat edge. Move up to rock over mantle.

41c Line of Scrimmage V5 ⭐
Starts on the right side of the boulder same as for 41b. Traverse the break left with mostly good holds and long reaches. When you get to the end, pull over onto the obvious shelf and finish up the arete. Pumpy.

41d Milk Money V2
"Sketchy." Pretty contrived with some questionable holds high on the face. Start on jugs just left of the large X-marked block. Do a dyno move three feet up to a flat edge, then continue up and right to tall top out.

41e Blow by Blow V1 ⭐
"Sketchy." A more natural line up the face just left of *Milk Money* and just right of the tree. Stand start on jugs under the roof. Climb straight up the face above.

41f ABC's V2 ⭐
"Sketchy." The bulge left of the tree and just right of the arete. Stand start on pinchy jug horn in traverse crack and climb out the steep bulge above via burly moves.

41g Moonminer V1 ⭐⭐
"Sketchy." The best problem on this side of the boulder. Stand start on obvious shelf at face height and climb up the obvious arete above.

41h Glamour Boy V3 ⭐⭐
"Sketchy." This and the following problem are found on the downhill side of the boulder under a fairly large roof. Stand start on the ledge on the right side under the roof. Move out the roof on cool pinch grips to the lip. Pull over and follow the flat ledges up and left to top out. The top out is not very hard, but tall and feels a bit insecure.

41i Glamour Girl V4 ⭐
"Sketchy." Sit start awkwardly underneath the roof on the far left side of the boulder where a large hold has broken off in the past. Move out the roof on crimper flakes to gain right facing corner at the lip, straight up from there.

41j V4 ⭐
Link the beginning of *Glamour Girl* into the top out of *Glamour Boy*.

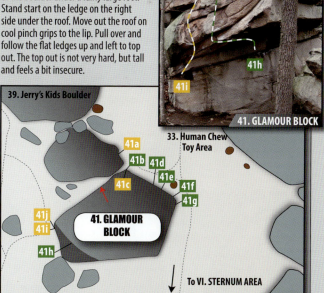

41. GLAMOUR BLOCK

39. Jerry's Kids Boulder

33. Human Chew Toy Area

41a
41b
41d
41c
41e
41f
41g
41j
41i
41h

41. GLAMOUR BLOCK

To VI. STERNUM AREA

VI. THE STERNUM AREA

The Sternum Area is the next group of boulders that you come to after walking past either the Frumundathunda Area or the Jungle Gym Area. It includes the Sternum Boulder, the Crack of Doom Area and a few boulders strung out in a line down towards the golf course – the Chronic Boulders and the Bonesaw Area. There is something for everyone in this area, as the variety of problems runs the gamut from moderate classics to hard classics to obscurities that are virtually never climbed. There are cracks as well as faces, and even a slab or two thrown in for good measure. One thing this area does lack is easy problems suitable for warming up on, making it probably not the first area you would want to hit up for the day.

To get there, follow any number of trails uphill past the Frumundathunda Area or the Jungle Gym Area. All trails seem to lead to the Sternum Boulder.

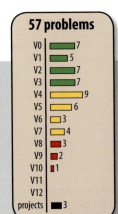

57 problems

V0		7
V1		5
V2		7
V3		7
V4		9
V5		6
V6		3
V7		4
V8		3
V9		2
V10		1
V11		
V12		
projects		3

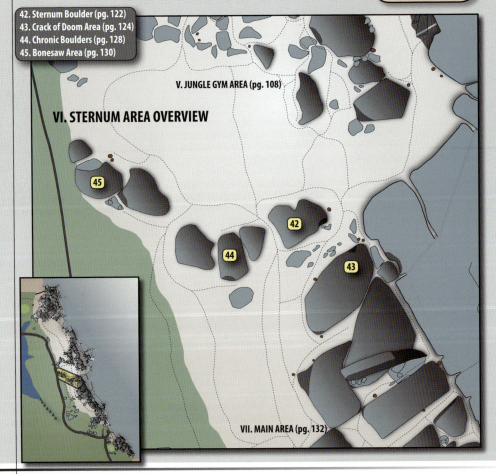

V. JUNGLE GYM AREA (pg. 108)

VI. STERNUM AREA OVERVIEW

45

42

44

43

VII. MAIN AREA (pg. 132)

NOT TO BE MISSED:

V2 **Mousetrap** ★★★ — A tall finger crack which is one of the best cracks at the Fort, and at a moderate grade!

V3 **The Ribcage** ★★★ — The undulating grooves which form the holds on this testy mantle sort of look like the ribcage of a corpse. Hopefully this is the closest you will ever get to climbing over a corpse.

V5 **The Sternum** ★★★ — Right next to *the Ribcage*, this awesome problem uses its namesake hold, which does look just like a Sternum.

V5 **Crack of Doom** ★★★ — Is it easy, is it hard? Depends on your crack climbing skills. If you are a master of the ringlock, it will probably be a piece of cake.

V7 **A Face in the Crowd** ★★★ — If crimping is your forte, find this problem! Complex ticky tack moves on sometimes painfully small crimps. Love it!

V8 **Grimace** ★★★ — Ascending rails of perfect slopers, this one is the anti-crimp! The often feared top out is not that bad, you can climb around and see where to go.

V10 **White Face** ★★★ — A desperate crimp problem authored by the one and only James Litz — what a surprise! Hit it in the winter, it bakes in the sun.

JODY EVANS

The drive time from my home in Cleveland, TN to LRC was about 1 hour and 10 minutes. I made that journey on average four times a week and each time couldn't wait to get there. Cresting the hill near the parking area (the old parking in the field across from the water tower), I could tell from the cars who had arrived early and beaten me there. A short walk down a twisting path, and then a scramble down a corner over by Dragon Lady, and you were in the center of one of the primo bouldering areas in the South/ Southeast. This is a place where I spent too many days to count and still not enough to do everything I wanted. It was also a place where friends met, talked shit, climbed until our fingers bled and we could hardly lift our arms, then do it all again the next day. Some of the most beautiful fall days with absolutely perfect temps, to some of the hottest, stickiest days of the year when you couldn't hold on to anything, we were there. Be it climbing classic problems that LRC has plenty of, or working tirelessly to clean and establish new ones on boulders covered in moss and leaves, we always had a smile on our face. Of all the problems that we established, some of them we named and graded. Most we didn't. We just climbed it and moved on to the next project.

A boulder that I named "The Fish Market" was completely covered with moss. The moss took me days to scrub and scrape off the boulder, and smelled just like fish. I did at least four great problems on it and a traverse linking those problems. Being many years removed from climbing now, and having not been to LRC in as many years, I think about it often. I have no idea if "The Fish Market" is being climbed today, and if it is, what it's called, but I hope someone is enjoying it as much as we did.

Over the years I climbed all over the country and many places abroad and think of the phases in my climbing life as chapters in a big story. LRC is the binding to that story. It was always there and was always a place that I felt so at home. I hope climbers now, young and old, have similar experiences there because it's just that special of a place. I've been living in Salt Lake City for the past eleven years, and while I rarely get out climbing these days, climbing will always be a part of me and LRC is a big part of that.

I wouldn't trade anything in the world for all those days spent hanging out with "the gang" at LRC. Some days on the walk out we would climb the water tower (but don't tell anyone), watch the sunset and imagine where our climbing adventures would take us next. Cheers and keep an eye out. There's still plenty of unclimbed rock out there.

42. STERNUM BOULDER

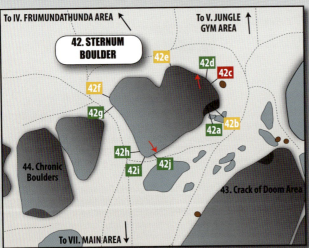

To IV. FRUMUNDATHUNDA AREA

To V. JUNGLE GYM AREA

42. STERNUM BOULDER

42e
42f
42d
42c
42g
42b
42a
42h
42i
42j

44. Chronic Boulders

43. Crack of Doom Area

To VII. MAIN AREA

42e

42e

42. STERNUM BOULDER

42. THE STERNUM BOULDER

The Sternum Boulder has problems on all sides of it, but is really known for two classic problems that climb out of a small little cave on its uphill side – *the Sternum* and *the Ribcage*. Due to their grades, low height, and friendly grips, these are two of the most popular problems at the Fort. **The problems are described starting with these problems and move from there around the boulder to the right.** There are a number of ways to get off of this boulder, depending on the route that you climbed, but for the *Sternum* and *Ribcage*, it is fairly simple to just head down the slab over the top of the boulder.

☐ **42a The Ribcage** V3 ★★★
A classic and popular short problem. Sit start in the small cave on the corner of the boulder with hands on your choice of a bunch of chalked holds. Move up and left to slopers out the lip of the roof and press out the mantle.

☐ **42b The Sternum** V5 ★★★
A somewhat puzzling problem which may make more sense after you see somebody do it. Sit start the same as for the *Ribcage*. Move up and right to the "sternum" pinch and on to holds in water groove. Head straight right along lip of roof, eventually gaining decent holds around the corner and top out.

☐ **42c Ace of Spades** V9 ★★
On the tall smooth triangular face to the right of the *Sternum*. Start with very low undercling pocket for right and left on slopey dish. Climb directly up the face using a toehook right around the corner.

☐ **42d** V0 ★
The really short and contrived arete to the right of *Ace of Spades*. Sit start on pocket rail on arete and make moves up the arete.

☐ **42e Candy Corn** V4 ★
Climbs the short, blunt, and slabby arete to the left of the gash in boulder. Sit start with right on good sidepulls and left on holds to the left. Make moves up the power slab with good right handholds and mantle the top out.

JEFF DRUMM

Little Rock City is the big kid's playground. As it is slowly becoming recognized as a world class bouldering area, my memories are triggered back to the days when it was somewhat undeveloped, access was sketchy at best, and people were finding out about the best bouldering close to Chattanooga. These were the days when rednecks roamed the 'rock maze' as they liked to call it and left trash, beer cans, and other novelties for us to find in the beautiful crystal corridors. It's a stark contrast to the pristine beauty climbers see today in the boulderfield.

I first started climbing at Little Rock City in 1996. Many of the people I climbed with during this era are no longer in the climbing game, but it was a revolutionary time in Chattanooga's climbing history. Most of us preferred climbing on the numerous quality sandstone cliffs surrounding the Chattanooga area, and the idea of bouldering was regarded mainly as a training tool or a way to get a good session in when either there was not enough time in the day to make it to the cliff or a partner just wasn't available. This was also back in the day when crash pads were beginning to transform bouldering into a sport of its own. Bouldering became much easier because you only needed yourself, your pad, and some psyche to have a great afternoon. As we spent more time in the safety zone of our pad, our perspective of what was possible began to change. I'll admit that some days we spent more time lounging on our new found friend, the crash pad, than climbing, but as we dialed in the classic problems like Tristar, Dragon Lady, Celestial Mechanics, & Spanky, our sights evolved to see new ascents like Blind Spot, The Pinch, The Law, Bedwetters, Heroin, Junkie and more. LRC has always been an inspiration for my climbing and even more so now that climbers have access and are being integrated into a greater and more diverse community. I believe climbers are still creating a transformation today in those beautiful corridors, not only in the ascents that await the new breed of climbers, but also in the respect and awe that climbers show and share for Mother Nature and her wonderful gift, the Boulder.

☐ **42f Cable Route** V4 ★★
"Sketchy." The tall arete on the downhill side of the boulder which is usually chalked. Stand start on lowest holds and move up decent edges and blocks to obvious pocket. Surpass the blankness above to top out.

☐ **42g** V2
About eight feet to the right of the *Cable Route* above an obvious red rock scar on the corner. Stand start with hands on slopers and climb up the blunt white prow using sloper edges in cracks to rockover mantle. Move right and downclimb to get off.

☐ **42h Scully** V2 ★★ Climbs the scoop and ledge to the left of the arete. Stand start using handholds on the low ledge. Mantle onto it and stand up, following incuts to the top.

☐ **42i** V0 ★
The low angle arete right of *Scully*. Stand start with hands on thin crimps on right side of arete. Move up slabby arete to good jug top out.

☐ **42j Downclimb Slab** V0- ★
The low angle and short slab a few feet right of the arete to break. Not recommended finishing to the top due to height and dirtiness. Downclimb it to get off. Also serves as downclimb for the couple problems to the left.

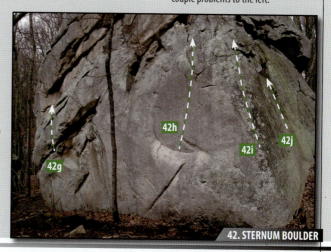

42g
42h
42i
42j

42. STERNUM BOULDER

43. CRACK OF DOOM AREA

43. CRACK OF DOOM AREA

43. CRACK OF DOOM AREA

The Crack of Doom Area is named after it's most recognizable problem – *the Crack of Doom* – which splits the tall white face that points directly at the Sternum Boulder. However, there are a number of other totally classic problems on this block. The area extends from the deep alcove which is host to many problems left of the *Crack of Doom*, to around the corner in the wide corridor behind. Most of the problems do not top out this huge block, and there is usually some downclimbing involved to get off. **The problem descriptions start in the deepest recess to the left and continue around the boulder to the right.** The easiest way to get off most problems is to traverse ledges to end up above *A Face in the Crowd*. From here you can step across to a smaller pointy boulder and downclimb a low angle slab on it.

☐ **43a** One Man Stand V6 ★
Go through the tunnel at the end of the corridor beyond the following routes. When you get to the back, turn around, and this problem is directly behind you. Stand start on sloper rail above head height, slap up to more slopers and mantle. Gets the award for the most confined problem in the boulders.

☐ **43b** Thinner V4 ★
The slab to the right of the corner hand crack is often wet. Stand start and climb the slab using incuts and pockets, avoiding the crack to the left. To get off, walk off back and then right till you can find a place to descend back into the boulders.

☐ **43c** Dihedral V0 ★
If you follow the trad persuasion, jam your way up this short corner hand crack. If you write off all hand jams as not real bouldering technique, then you can just lieback up it instead. To get off, walk off back and then right till you can find a place to descend back into the boulders.

☐ **43d** South America V3 ★
"Sketchy." Stand start on good holds in break. Move up and left on good holds to the trunk feature (Argentina) of the South America. Climb this feature to jug break up high. Top out straight up on dirty slab. Walk off to the right.

☐ **43e** South Pacific V3 ★
"Sketchy." Problem immediately left of *South America*. Stand start in underclings in break. Climb out to large roundy holds above roof, mantle your way onto the slabby face above via shallow pockets and sidepulls. To get off traverse right and top out same as *South America*, or use the tree behind you to shimmy down.

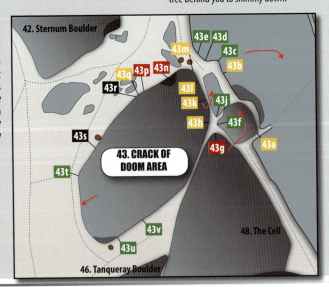

43g

43i

43h

43j

The following five problems are found in a small room accessed by ducking through a tunnel to the right of the downclimb boulder.

☐ **43f** **V0** ⭐⭐
The low angled scaled, backbone like arete just left of *Grimace* in the back of the corridor. Stand start and climb right up, not dabbing.

☐ **43g** **Grimace** V8 ⭐⭐⭐
Rad slopers with endless superlatives to describe them. How about climbing out the fat rolls of Roseanne's belly? That will make you *Grimace*. Sit start on lowest rail of slopers and climb up many more rails of slopers to roundy top out. Classic!

☐ **43h** **A Face in the Crowd** V7 ⭐⭐⭐
This sharp but classic problem is a must do for the crimper aficionado. On the smooth patina face directly behind *Grimace*. Sit start on lowest sharp edges and climb up and right on many more crimps to jug flakes top out. Watch the dab. AKA Out of Africa.
  ☐ **43i** **Stand Start** V3 ⭐⭐
  Stand start the problem on holds in the middle of the face.

☐ **43j** **V1** ⭐
The last piece of climbable stone not yet described in the back of the corridor. Slabby arete left of the entrance. Stand start.

☐ **43k** **Symmetry** V7 ⭐⭐
In the corridor just before you duck through the hole to get to *Grimace*, on the right side. Sit start very low on undercling pockets. Burl onto the wall and follow more pockets up the steep wall to eventual jugs.

☐ **43l** **Pocket Pool** V4 ⭐⭐
On the right hand wall of the corridor, to the right of *Symmetry*. Start in the middle of the face on lowest incuts. Climb straight up the wall on shallow pockets and incuts. To get off, traverse left and step off above *A Face in the Crowd*.

☐ **43m** **Meeks Traverse** V5 ⭐
Stand start on high rail behind the tree on the right side of the face and traverse edges and pockets left through *Pocket Pool* and eventually top out straight up same as for *Symmetry*.

43m

43l

43k

43. CRACK OF DOOM AREA

☐ **43n Tyrone Biggums** V9 ⭐⭐
Climbs out the small cave on the left side of the broad white face. Sit start in the cave sideways on undercling seam. Reach out the roof and gain a shallow pocket/edge hold. Lock off and move up to incut flake. A crack head character of comedian Dave Chappelle was named Tyrone Biggums.

☐ **43o Undertow** V6 ⭐
Stand start on the shallow pocket/ edge and just do the last move.

☐ **43p White Face** V10 ⭐⭐⭐
AKA Scarecrow. Stand start on crimper edges to the left of the *Crack of Doom*. Move left to series of thin crimps, then on to a very thin crimp up the face and rock up to top out. A great problem for a very cold day as the face bakes in the sun.

☐ **43q Crack of Doom** V5 ⭐⭐⭐
The best crack problem at the Stone Fort is harder than it looks. If you've never been to Indian Creek but always wanted to master the ring-lock, then this is the problem for you. Stand start on jugs in hole, its pretty easy to guess where to go from here. Walk left on the ledge to step off above *A Face in the Crowd*.

☐ **43r Project**
Starts on the *Crack of Doom*. From about half way up, trend right onto crimp seam and then up the face.

☐ **43s Project**
The tall blank face to the left of the arete. Stand start on underclings, gain the thin seam in middle of the face and follow more thin seams upward.

☐ **43t V0**
"Sketchy." The tall arete on the right hand side of the face. Climb up and into the corner crack. Tall, and with some questionable holds, be careful. The best way off is to downclimb this problem.

☐ **43u Moustrap** V2 ⭐⭐⭐
"Sketchy." The obvious zagging finger crack on the back side of the boulder. Is this the same crack that makes up the *Crack of Doom*? Stand start and find the finger locks. To get off, move left on the vegetated ledge and downclimb tall face around the corner. Pads recommended.

☐ **43v Traverse Start** V2 ⭐⭐
This problem can be started about 15 feet to the right. Traverse the holds left into the crack. Sort of fun, but doesn't add to the grade, the feet are too big.

43. CRACK OF DOOM AREA

Sarah Grimace, V8. Corey Wentz photo.

44. THE CHRONIC BOULDERS

44. THE CHRONIC BOULDERS

The Chronic Boulders are a group of three boulders right next to each other which are just across the trail from the Sternum Boulder, towards the golf course. There are problems on all sides of these boulders. The most popular problems in the area are the *Chronic* and *Fatigue Syndrome*. **The descriptions start with the problems right across the trail from the Sternum Boulder and continue to the right around the boulders.** To get off of these problems, climb up the slab and then down-climb along a crack to the left. Most of the other problems are easy to get off of.

☐ 44a V2 ⭐
A shorty squat problem. Start on jug really low. Pull off the ground and immediately start topping out.

☐ 44b V3
About 10 feet to the right of 44a. Lay-down start on low sloper rail. Awkwardly pull on and move up more sloper rails to top out.

The next four problems climb the white face which is on top of the boulder where the previous two lines were found. To get to them, scramble up onto the flat boulder.

☐ 44c Chorizo V5 ⭐
Located about 10 feet right of the left arete of the face. Stand start standing on the slabby boulder with left in shallow pocket crimp and right on undercling block with crimp on top and climb directly up the face above to mantle top out.

☐ 44d Blood Sausage V5 ⭐
Stand start standing on the slabby boulder with hands on crimper sidepulls and pinches beneath shallow arete type feature in the middle of the face. Climb straight up using incut sidepulls to dirty top out.

☐ 44e Fight Club V4 ⭐
Squat start on the slab on the right hand side of the boulder with hands on a triangular shaped crimp block. Move up and left on more crimps to dirty top out.

☐ 44f Project
There is a project that has been tried which starts standing on the ground beneath the boulder with back against the slab on double undercling feature in broken rock. Move up and right to thin shallow crimper sidepulls, eventually meeting up with *Fight Club*, and finish up that line.

☐ 44g V2 ⭐
"Sketchy." This problem starts on the ground and climbs up the tall overhanging arete. Stand start in the gash between two boulders on jugs and follow the left-trending crack/seam, eventually climbing above the other boulder, where you can throw a pad. Top out on jugs.

☐ **44h** Snoop V1 ⭐
This line climbs the rounded black bulge
and slab to the right of the arete in the
gap. Stand start with your hands on
good slopers and move straight up the
slab, which gets lower angled the higher
you go. Finish at the angling crack and
downclimb it left to get off.

☐ **44i** The Chronic V7 ⭐⭐
Climbs the left hand side of the slabby
prow. Sit start to the left of the prow on
large sloper with ripples of texture and
climb the face straight up using slopers
on the arete. Top out on slab and downclimb to the left along angling crack.

☐ **44j** Fatigue Syndrome V8 ⭐⭐
Start the same as for the *Chronic*. Move
right to slopers and edges on the prow,
then rockover to the right using thin
holds and establish yourself on the slab.
Scamper to the top and downclimb the
same as the *Chronic*.

☐ **44k** Black Belt Jones V4 ⭐
On a separate short boulder to the right
of the *Chronic* and *Fatigue Syndrome*.
Sit start on decent holds in seam
underneath slightly overhanging wall.
Move up and left to edges, then straight
up to top out.

☐ **44l** Left Wing V6 ⭐⭐
The left hand line coming out the short
but steeply overhanging "breadloaf" wall
on the opposite side of the boulder from
the *Chronic*. Sit start with left on incut
jug left of the overhanging wall and right
on crimper in orange rock on the steep
face. Follow the lip to the right until the
apex and go straight up.

☐ **44m** Right Wing V7 ⭐⭐
The right hand line coming out the short
steep wall. Sit start with right on crimper
edge on the lip of the roof and left on
crimper under the lip. Move left out the
lip to top out at apex as well.

44. THE CHRONIC BOULDERS

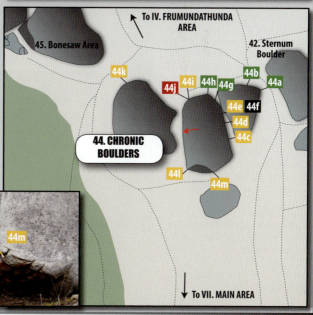
44. THE CHRONIC BOULDERS

45. THE BONESAW AREA

45d Between the Trees V1
This and the next problem climb a non-descript section of the boulder directly across from *Black Belt Jones*. Stand start and climb the slabby face which is, you guessed it, between two large trees.

45e Old Maid V0 ⭐
Stand start on crown featured jugs to the right of *Between the Trees*. Move up and left using sidepulls and vertical seam to top out on slopers.

45f Jersey Turnpike V1 ⭐
The arete left of *Geez-Us*. Climb the arete and face staying mostly on the left side.

45g Geez-Us V4 ⭐
"Sketchy." The not-very-pretty face to the left of the hole/gap in boulder. Start by climbing up smooth low angle face into juggy rotten roof to a good break, then surmount the blank face straight above.

45h Skeleton Crew V4 ⭐
"Sketchy." Starts on the left side of the face at a shallow left-facing dihedral. Sit start and climb straight up to decent holds in break. Carry on to the tall but featured face.

45. THE BONESAW AREA

The Bonesaw Area is made up of three closely nestled boulders, much like the Chronic Boulders. They reside just downhill, towards the golf course, from the Chronic Boulders. While not home to any bona fide classics, there are in fact many good and worthy problems found here. **The descriptions begin with the slab to the left of the cave where *Bonesaw* is and continue around the boulders to the right.** Getting off these boulders does involve some down climbing, look for the arrows on the map.

45a V2 ⭐
The slab problem on the boulder to the left of the *Bonesaw* roof. The hardest part is not dabbing the tree. Start matched on sickle shaped hold, stand up and slab upwards. Needs to clean up a little.

45b Bonesaw V5 ⭐⭐
A great problem which suffers a bit from conglomerated rock. Stand start on the left side of the cave on chalked pedestal. Move out the roof on flakes, hold your feet on as you bump up to progressively higher and better holds.

45c Jolly Roger V3 ⭐
Stand start on the broad flat flake. Move up to good holds under the roof, traverse them to the right, and then climb straight up the conglomerated face above the roof.

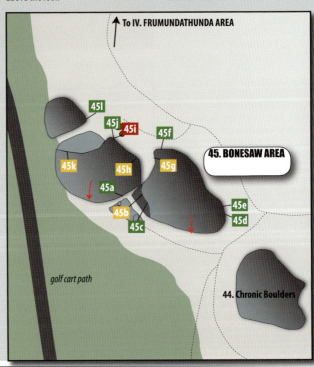

To IV. FRUMUNDATHUNDA AREA

45. BONESAW AREA

golf cart path

44. Chronic Boulders

45i Man Hands V8 ⭐

The problem which traverses the face from right to left. Sit start low on holds on the arete. Move left into underclings above seam, then up to narrow pockets in seam, traverse it left to finish same as for *Skeleton Crew*.

45j The Bronco Arete V3 ⭐

"Sketchy." The tall overhanging arete on the right side of the face. Stand start at the bottom of the arete, climb up jugs in somewhat flakey rock. Higher up the rock gets more bomber. A long reach or thin crimps guard the top.

45k All In V4 ⭐

"Sketchy." To the right of the *Bronco Arete* is a wall with a skirt slab beneath it. This problem climbs out the wall on the right side of the boulder. Start by moving up the slab to obvious big underclings. Make a long reach to pockets at the lip of the face and follow them up over the roundy top out.

45l V1 ⭐

Sits by itself on small boulder to the right of the *Bronco Arete*. Sit start on obvious jugs and climb up the short overhanging arete on jugs. Easiest way to get off is to jump, or downclimb the face which points towards the golf course.

45f   45g

45h   45i   45j

45. THE BONESAW AREA

Carolyn Coffey, Bonesaw, opposite page.
Adam Johnson photo.

VII. MAIN AREA

The Main Area is a densely nestled group of huge boulders which form lots of sheer tall walls and corridors. Along with the Front Area, it is the most popular area at the Stone Fort – and rightly so! This area is stacked with classics of all grades. It is a rare day that you will walk up to *Tristar* or the Dragon Boulder and have the place to yourself. The list of classics includes the famous and popular *Tristar*, *Dragon Lady*, and *Celestial Mechanics*. There is also quite a concentration of hard problems as well, with area test-pieces *Dragon Man*, *King James*, and *the Law* seeing lots of attention. This area is also home to the largest concentration of traverses at the Fort, so if you like adding distance by going sideways, you will love this area. Although it's not as stacked as the Front Area for easy problems, there are a few good ones to be found, and this area is probably the second most favored zone to hit for a warm-up.

To get here, follow the trails that continue past the Sternum Area. The Tanqueray Boulder will be the first thing you see on your left, across from the back of the Crack of Doom Area. Beyond this you will follow the main trail as it wraps around the Phillip's Fury Boulder, after which you will want to head left into an open "courtyard" of sorts which forms the center of the Main Area.

76 problems

V0	▬	5
V1	▬▬	9
V2	▬▬	9
V3	▬	7
V4	▬▬	10
V5	▬▬▬	13
V6	▬	8
V7	▬	5
V8	▪	1
V9	▪	2
V10	▪	1
V11	▪	3
V12		
projects	▪	1

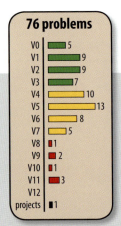

VI. STERNUM AREA (pg. 120)

48

48

46

49

51

52

VII. MAIN AREA OVERVIEW

47

50

IX. THE HIDDEN AREA (pg. 160)

46. Tanqueray Boulder (pg. 134)
47. Phillip's Fury Boulder (pg. 136)
48. The Cell (pg. 139)
49. Tristar Boulder (pg. 142)
50. The Frontside (pg. 144)
51. Dragon Boulder (pg. 145)
52. The Backside (pg. 147)

N

0 ft.   125 ft.

VIII. THE FAIRWAYS (pg. 148)

The Mystery of the F.A. of Celestial Mechanics AKA 'Behind the Barndoor'

Early 1990s
John Sherman suggests a personal First Ascent of the problem, dubbing it 'Behind the Barndoor'

↓

Late 1980s
Travis Eiseman refutes Sherman, claiming an ascent of the problem years earlier

↓

Mid 1980s
Eiseman acknowledges that there was chalk on the problem pre-dating his own ascent

↓

Paleo Age
Ancient pine resin and magnisium carbonate residue carbon dated to 750 BCE leading to the prevailing theory of the existence of an ancient tribe of Vertically inclined Chattanoogans...

Matthew Gant, Celestial Machanics V7, previous page.
Micah Gentry photo.

46. TANQUERAY BOULDER

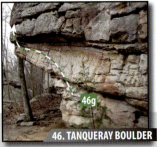

46. TANQUERAY BOULDER

46. TANQUERAY BOULDER

The Tanqueray Boulder is the large white block which sits across the open corridor from the Crack of Doom Area and the obvious finger crack *Mousetrap*. It is recognized by a large orange and black overhang which is easily visible from the trail. There are problems on this face, as well as on the tall orange face which faces the "courtyard" of the Main Area. **The problems are described from left to right around the boulder, starting in the back of the wide corridor across from *Mousetrap*.** The easiest way to get off this boulder is to carefully make your way to the lowest corner closest to the golf course and jump or scootch from here onto the top of the Phillip's Fury Boulder. Then jump off or downclimb the groove on that boulder's uphill side.

☐ **46a Pennzoil Arete** V7 ☆
"Sketchy." The tall leaning arete on the left side of the boulder, just right of the narrow corridor. Stand start at base of arete on some incut holds, stand on a high foot, and continue up the licheny face.

☐ **46b Project**
About 15 feet right of the arete is this blank slab. Stand up on ledge with underclings and reach for pair of thin seams. Use these to get to the top somehow.

Between these two problems are opportunities for numerous slab problems with cool holds. However, there is a bit of a ledge beneath, and the wall seems to be coated in a powdery form of lichen, so it may not be worth it.

☐ **46c V0**
The fist and hand crack which is often wet.

☐ **46d Short Long** V4 ☆☆
"Sketchy." Start on the left side of the overhang, left of the swirly orange rock, on jugs. Work up jugs to a big move to incut pocket, then out to positive slopers over lip and finish up and right.

☐ **46e Traverse Start** V5 ☆
"Sketchy." Start on large jug flake and traverse flakes right for eight ft. to *Short Long* and finish up it.

☐ **46f Tanqueray** V4
"Sketchy." A good climb which is not recommended to be climbed at all due to large x-marked flake in the middle of the roof which WILL pull off on top of someone who decides to hang off it. Grabbing it is sort of unavoidable.

☐ **46g V3** ☆
"Sketchy." Stand start on good holds in white rock to right of large overhang. Move up and left above the lip of the overhang, eventually gaining jugs at apex of roof. Not recommended to finish up from here, traverse jugs right till you can downclimb.

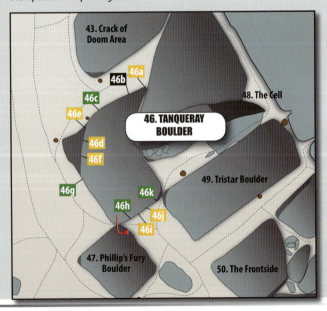

46. TANQUERAY BOULDER

The next four problems are found on the opposite side of the boulder. To reach them, walk past 46g and duck through a tunnel on your left. They are on the left wall.

46h Paper Dragon V2
"Sketchy." On the left side of the wall just right of the tunnel. Squat start on crimps in break and follow good holds up the tallish, dirty face.

46i The Relic V4 ⭐
"Sketchy." Sit start low with undercling and crimp. Make big moves upwards to thin patina crimps. Make a few more moves to right-facing sickle hold. Move right and follow dirty pockets to top.

46j Old Scratch V5 ⭐
"Sketchy." Climbs a series of very thin crimps through blank orange wall. Sit start on tiny crimps. Move up past move painfully tiny crimps, and a bigger hold out right. Top out straight up.

46k Crackerjack V1 ⭐
"Sketchy." The face just left of the tunnel leading to the Cell. Stand start on jugs and climb the tall face on incut patina.

NOT TO BE MISSED:

V1 Brian's Brain ⭐⭐⭐ – A classic easy problem or warm-up littered with cool and varied holds.

V4 Dragon Lady ⭐⭐⭐ – A very popular and cool problem which surmounts a horizontal roof. Core tension and a positive reach will help you here.

V4 Tristar ⭐⭐⭐ – Probably the most often tried problem at the Stone Fort. According to Marvin Webb, this was tried the first day anyone ever climbed here, and sent very shortly afterwards. Powerful, techy, dynamic, and with many different ways of solving it – none of which make it any easier!

V5 Latin For Dagger ⭐⭐⭐ – A cool tall face for those who like to grab those small orange crimpers.

V7 Celestial Mechanics ⭐⭐⭐ – Supposedly "the last great problem," at the fort when John Sherman scrubbed and climbed it, dubbing it *Behind the Barndoor*. He has heard that someone else may have done it first, and the name which has stuck seems to be *Celestial Mechanics*. No matter the name or history, this is one of the best boulder problems anywhere!

V8 Spanky ⭐⭐⭐ – Similar to *Grimace*, but with thinner holds. Climbs an amazingly orange face on just good enough edges. If this is your first time up *Spanky*, you must top out *Spanky*! Them's the rules.

V9 Psychosomatic ⭐⭐⭐ – Another stop on the hard slab tour. Psychosomatic means referring to both the body and mind. If this is a clue to you, it may take more than just brawn to solve this friction puzzle.

V10 King James ⭐⭐⭐ – An awesome tall problem with many long and interesting moves. Becoming very popular for the grade.

V11 The Law ⭐⭐⭐ – One of the simplest and most pure hard problems at the Fort. A horizontal wall with an obvious series of similarly bad crimps.

47. PHILLIP'S FURY BOULDER

47. PHILLIP'S FURY BOULDER

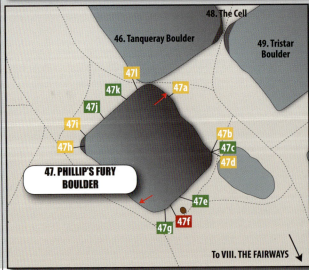

47. PHILLIP'S FURY BOULDER

The Phillip's Fury Boulder is a large square block made up of orange and white stone which rests against the Tanqueray Boulder at one of its corners. It is home to a wide variety of problems on all sides of it, from traverses to slabs to a finger crack and even a cool dyno. **The problems are described starting on the right side of the uphill face of the boulder, next to the tunnel, and continue around the boulder to the left.** To get off of the problems on the uphill side of the block, make your way to the corner nearest the Tanqueray Boulder and either jump off or downclimb at a groove. To get off of the slabs, move either right, or left around the corner, and downclimb the lower angled faces.

☐ **47a** **Main Area Reverse** V6 ★★
Traverse
Start on the right side of the wall on a shelf left of tunnel. Traverse the holds in the seam to the left across the wall and finish with the *Trailer Hitch* at the end.

☐ **47b** **Main Area Traverse** V6 ★★
Start on the left side of the wall on jugs just right of the arete and traverse right to the shelf at the end.

☐ **47c** **Trailer Ball** V1 ★
The arete which is across from *King James*. Stand start on good jugs just right of the arete and climb straight up, no holds barred.

☐ **47d** **Trailer Hitch** V5 ★★
Start the same as the *Trailer Ball* and dyno to the jug at the very apex of the boulder.

☐ **47e** **Phillip's Fury** V3 ★★
A cool slab problem in the middle of the face which ascends black ripples to break at about 12 ft. Finish straight up or move right to downclimb.

☐ **47f** **Psychosomatic** V9 ★★★
A cool and popular hard slab, just left of *Phillip's Fury*. Start up a very faint left-facing corner and figure out how to gain the thin mono pocket high on the face. Finish straight up from the break or move right to downclimb.

King James, V10. Spenser Tangsmith photo.

ANA BURGOS

In the days before LRC was open to the public, I learned to climb there with friends like Andrew Gross and the Drumm brothers and later with Luis Rodriquez, Eric Pittman, and Andrew Traylor. I found myself climbing there almost daily with these friends. Back in these days you rarely saw climbers there that you didn't know.

Over the years LRC has undergone many changes. It would be hard to explain my experience of climbing at LRC without bringing up the subject of sneakiness. Not only did we have to find low profile parking, we had to hide from golfers as well. The helicopter hanger added to these complications by adding construction workers to sneak past. One memory that sticks out in particular was the day Andrew Traylor put up "The Law". After trying to sneak in undetected but being caught and being told by surly construction workers that he was going to "call the law" on us, Andrew sent his project and appropriately named it, "The Law".

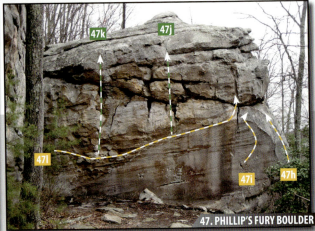

47. PHILLIP'S FURY BOULDER

47. PHILLIP'S FURY BOULDER

47g High on Crack V1 ⭐⭐
"Sketchy." The right-leaning finger crack on the left side of the face is not as straightforward as it seems. Traverse left around the corner and downclimb that face to get off.

47h Clutch V5 ⭐⭐
Sit start at the base of the short overhanging arete. Make a couple moves out the steep part and then make your way up the rounded slab above on edges and slopers.

47i Sidewinder V4 ⭐
Stand start using the obvious left hand sidepull pocket in smooth face. Climb up the face using a series of edges close to *Clutch* for the right, eventually gaining the vertical crack.

47j Boardwalk V1 ⭐
The next weakness in the face to the left of *Sidewinder*. Stand start matched on a high incut flake above head height and climb straight up the juggy wall above.

47k Jug Head V1 ⭐⭐
Short but sweet. Sit start on lowest pockets and other cool molded grips. Climbs straight up more cool holds to top out.

47l Boro Traverse V6 ⭐
A cool lowball traverse on interesting incut holds. Sit start to the left of *Jug Head* and traverse across the face to the right, eventually finishing up the same place as *Sidewinder*.

Zach Bopp, Boro Traverse V6, above.
Corey Wentz photo.

48. THE CELL

The Cell is a secretive zone made up of two corridors with tall walls, making it feel like you're in a cell. It's one of the better places to run to if the sun is out and the temps are a little hot, as most of the walls and problems in this area stay in the shade and receive air conditioning from the many tunnels underneath the boulders. To get to the Cell, duck through a tunnel to the left of *Melon Theory*, on the Tristar Boulder, or right of *Cracker Jack* on the Tanqueray Boulder. **The problem descriptions start with *Stimey*, on the wall left of the tunnel if you are looking at it, and continue right around the walls.** Topping out many of these problems means you will have to find a way down. The ways differ, but you can't go wrong by hopping boulders back towards the level ground, and then finding a groove to worm your way back into the boulders.

☐ 48a Stimey V1 ⭐

"Sketchy." The face directly across from *Spanky*. Climb the patina edges, crimps, and pinches all the way up the 20 foot tall face.

☐ 48b Spanky V8 ⭐⭐⭐

"Sketchy." Climbs the overhanging orange wall in the tunnel. Sit start on positive edges at bottom of the wall. Climb up more edges, some ok, some bad, to jug flake in the middle of the wall. Finish up the tall top section. Not the original name, but the one that's stuck.

☐ 48c Latin for Dagger V5 ⭐⭐

"Sketchy." Climbs up the cool patina crimps on the face right of *Spanky*. Stand start on crimper edges and climb up knifeblade edges to the top. At the top, move right on large incut flakes and step off to other boulder.

48. THE CELL

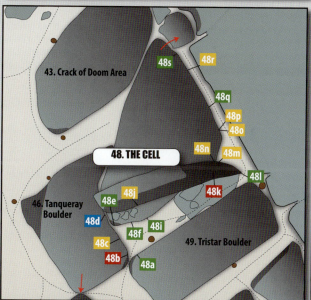

43. Crack of Doom Area

48s 48r
48q
48p
48o
48n 48m
48l
48. THE CELL
48j 48k
46. Tanqueray Boulder 48e
48d 48f 48i
48c 49. Tristar Boulder
48b 48a

☐ 48d Big Fat Momma V? ⭐

An offwidth roof. Crawl about 18 feet back into the dark and constricting hole and climb out the dead horizontal offwidth crack. I have no idea how you would attach a V-grade to this. Finish up *Green Lantern*.

☐ 48e Green Lantern V3 ⭐

Climbs the arete to the left of the scoop. Squat start with hands at the lip of the roof. Pull on and climb the mossy arete above.

48. THE CELL

48. THE CELL

Jump. Sit start with your back against the perched boulder on incut edges. Climb up the steeply overhanging face above on more good edges, eventually topping it out. Most of it is protected well with a pad on the boulder beneath, but be very careful on the top out.

☐ **48k The Law** V11 ★★★
A classic overhanging line. Climbs out the horizontal roof of the crazy boulder perched above the Cell. Scramble up the ledge beyond the last problems to find it. Stand start matched on crimp. Big move to two more crimps, then repeat.

☐ **48l** V2
The arete to the right of *the Law*. Sit start on low holds, pull on, and move up. Dirty.

☐ **48m Drumm Problem** V7 ★
On the same overhanging spike as *the Law*, but on the opposite side. Stand start on the low slab beneath the boulder. Make a massive move out left onto the horizontal roof to gaston, match as an undercling, and bump to a crimp edge with your feet on the slab. Bust straight up and left beneath the tree to top out.

☐ **48n Webb Problem 2** V7 ★
"Sketchy." Just to the right of the *Drumm Problem*. Start with right on edge in black rock and left on good edge to the left. Using a heel hook, and not the slab beneath you, pull on and bust a long move to a jug at the lip of the boulder, mantle.

The following problems are located in a corridor behind the Law, *to the left. It has one overhanging wall and stays fairly*

shaded and cool on hot days. However, these problems also suffer from runoff and are often wet or dirty. But, you can stem up the opposite wall to clean off any dirt or leaves before climbing. The easiest way to get off is to stem across the corridor and downclimb the slabby side.

☐ **48o The Cutpurse** V5 ★
Start on the left side of the left wall of the corridor at an obvious brushed pinch. Start with this for the left and climb straight up the wall and slab on cool iron crimps.

☐ **48p Iron Man Traverse** V7 ★★
Not nearly as classic as its more popular brethren in the Buttermilks, this traverse is still fun and provides a good workout. Start on the pinch on the left side of the wall and traverse right for about 30 ft. using any holds to eventually finish up *By Jove*.

☐ **48q The Prison Planet** V3 ★
About 10 feet right of *the Cutpurse* at a vague vertical crack feature. Sit start on undercling and pocket and climb the wall and slab above.

☐ **48r Pockets of Resistence** V6 ★
About 10 feet left of the end of the corridor. Sit start low with pinch pockets. Move up the wall on shallow edges and pinches to gain flat holds, carry on up to the mantle.

☐ **48s By Jove** V2 ★
Just to the left of the end of the corridor. Stand start on an undercling in the middle of the face and do a big move to jugs.

☐ **48f Butt's Up** V2 ★★
Sit start on low flake at the base of the scoop. Pull on and mantle into the scoop. Finish up the slab to the left, eventually gaining holds under perched block.

  ☐ **48g Stand Start** V1 ★
  Climb the slab scoop from a standing start.

☐ **48h** V5 ★
Start as for *Butt's Up* and get yourself established in the scoop. Then stem and lean right to gain holds on a faint roundy arete. Stem higher to reach jugs straight up. Sorta contrived, but cool. Easier if you're tall.

☐ **48i Jump** V3 ★
The slab to the right of the scoop. Stand start on obvious rail for feet. Jump to gain jug at the top of the boulder. Height dependent.

☐ **48j Superman** V5 ★
"Scary." On the same boulder as *the Law*, but way to the left, above the problem

Joey Stamenkovich on The Prison Planet.
Micah Gentry photo.

49. TRISTAR BOULDER

49. TRISTAR BOULDER

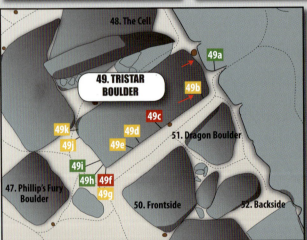

49. TRISTAR BOULDER

The Tristar Boulder is a massive boulder which is home to some of the most classic, famous, and often tried problems at the Stone Fort. It has a very tall face which faces the Phillip's Fury Boulder and is home to a few highballs, and a long, sheer, grey face which has a ledge on it at about half height. This face is stacked with classics, check it out. **The descriptions start on the up-hill end, the far end, of the corridor, and proceed left.** To get off the top of the boulder, walk back till you can down-climb on the uphill side. To get off of the problems in the corridor, simply walk along the ledge to the right to get off.

☐ **49a** **Amen** V0 ⭐
On a seperate boulder, just to the left of the break in the cliff band. Sit start really low on good jugs and move up on more good jugs.

☐ **49b** **Slap Happy** V5 ⭐⭐
On the far right side of the boulder is a shallow and short left-facing corner. Stand start here and slap, like the name implies, along the brushed slopers on the lip left about 15 feet till the holds improve and you can throw up a heel and rock over to mantle.

☐ **49c** **Made in France** V11 ⭐
Just left of the tree. Start on a crimper about three feet up and move up to another thin crimp, then to the top.

☐ **49d** **Tristar** V4 ⭐⭐⭐
One of the ultra-classics of the field and tried just about every day of the year. Stand start with hands in a vertical crack and follow face holds up the surprisingly powerful and technical face above, following the seam. Mantle onto the ledge at top and walk right to get off.

☐ **49e** **Celestial Mechanics** V7 ⭐⭐⭐
AKA *Behind the Barn Door*. The big brother of *Tristar* and just as good, if not better. It is common practice to stack many pads for added height to start this problem, which makes pulling onto the wall easier. Some may frown, either way, you create your own rules. Stand start with right on undercling and left gastoning the triangle pinch. Pull on and have at it. Walk off right from the ledge at top.

49. TRISTAR BOULDER

☐ **49f King James** V10 ★★★
"Sketchy." The hits just keep coming!
A neo-classic. Many pads and spotters
advised for the last couple moves. Stand
start on the arete. Do a few moves before
moving out right at a scoop to undercling
block and continue further right to crux
at round belly type bulge. Finish next to
Celestial Mechanics.

☐ **49g The High Arete** V5 ★
"Scary." The complete arete which forms
the start of *King James*. Very tall and
committing, be careful of the solidity of
holds up high. Usually top-roped.

☐ **49h Low Traverse** V2 ★
Start just left of the right arete and
traverse the wall left for about 25 feet to
where it blanks out and becomes mossy,
never getting more than a foot or two
above the ground.

☐ **49i Block and Tackle** V2 ★★
"Scary." Climbs straight up the tall slabby
face. Start in a hole on the right side a
few feet left of the arete. Climb straight
up past a slab crux, then easy jugs to the
top. Be careful what you pull on up there.

☐ **49j V5** ★
"Sketchy." On the left side of the tall face
is a shallow left-facing corner which
starts about half way up. Climb up the
smooth face beneath and then top out
using the corner.

☐ **49k Melon Theory** V4 ★
On the left margin of the wall, just right
of the tunnel leading to the Cell. Sit start
on good jugs in the tunnel, move right
out the overhang, then straight up the
face past shallow finger pockets to a
brushed sloper. Drop from here, or top it
out for more points.

49. TRISTAR BOULDER

50. THE FRONTSIDE

50. THE FRONTSIDE

50. THE FRONTSIDE

The Frontside is a loose term used to describe the boulder problems on the face which point towards the Main Area. Here you will find a couple of easy problems which can be used as warm-ups, or just climbed for the fun of it, as well as some taller problems and a pretty good traverse. **The descriptions start on the left corner of the face and proceed to the right.** To get off of this boulder is easy, just climb down the low angle slab around the corner to the left.

☐ 50a Slabatical V0- ⭐
To the left of the downclimb slab is a low angle black friction slab. Pad your way up it.

☐ 50b Warm Up Arete V2 ⭐⭐
On the left-hand side of the face is a low angle arete with a slab to its left. Sit start low on wide sloper and lieback up the arete. When you reach jugs where the arete levels out, rockover and mantle. You can also take it all the way to the top of *Brian's Brain* before topping out.

☐ 50c Brian's Brian V1 ⭐⭐⭐
This popular climb is a great warm-up and features some cool grips. Stand start with hands on the lowest chalked holds and ascend up and left to a long reach before the top out.

☐ 50d Life is Goodlett V6 ⭐
Sit start on the lowest holds on the right hand corner of the boulder. Pull on and follow the large flat rail up and left. Keep traversing left to the starting holds of *Brian's Brain*, negotiating some thin crimps on the way. Finish up *Brian's Brain*.

☐ 50e Keel Hauled V3 ⭐
"Sketchy." Climbs steeply upward just left of the right arete. Sit start the same as for the traverse, but climb straight up on juggy holds, eventually gaining large incut flakes to a surprisingly slopey top out.

☐ 50f Decidous Enima V4 ⭐
"Sketchy." This is a good problem which unfortunately suffers from the very close tree, which simultaneously makes it hard not to dab, and offers the "enema" as a consequence of failure. Sit start same as the last two, but climb up and right, then out the roof just left of the tree.

☐ 50g V6 ⭐
Stand start in holds in crack underneath roof in the corridor to the right of the tree. Move out the bulge above on slopers and thin pockets. Watch your back on the opposing wall.

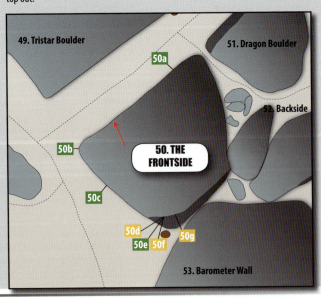

51. DRAGON BOULDER

51. DRAGON BOULDER

51. THE DRAGON BOULDER

The Dragon Boulder is one of the most popular boulders at the Stone Fort, and has fun problems to climb no matter what grade you are looking for. It is easily recognizable by the long flat roof which nearly every problem on the boulder attempts to surmount. A long reach, some core tension, and the ability to hold a swing will all serve you well on these fun problems. **The problems are described from left to right across the face.** Most of the problems traverse a jug break high on the wall to the left and then involve a short down-climb to get off.

☐ **51a** **V0** ⭐
The far left arete of the Dragon face. Stand start on decent holds and climb the short arete above.

☐ **51b** **Smog** V2 ⭐⭐
Stand start with hands in leftmost side of horizontal crack jug/pocket underneath the roof. Make big moves around the roof to the left to good holds in a right-angling crack. Hold the tension and finish up the crack to good break.

☐ **51c** **Dragon Lady** V4 ⭐⭐⭐
This is a classic problem that couldn't be any more different than *Tristar*, the other classic V4 in the corridor. Start the same as for *Smog*. Make a long move out the roof to a right-facing sideull. Depending on your height, jump or lock off and reach to slopers and good holds up under the next small roof. Move up to higher break and traverse left to downclimb and jump off at *Smog*.

☐ **51d** **Dragon Traverse** V0 ⭐⭐
A decent warm-up to get the blood flowing. Stand start the same as the last two problems on the left margin of the crack. Traverse good holds in crack straight right to the right arete. Drop off, or finish up the arete.

☐ **51e** **Dragon Traverse** V2 ⭐⭐
Loop
"Sketchy." Do the *Dragon Traverse*, but from the right hand arete move up about six feet and then traverse the higher break back left above the lip of the roof. Downclimb *Smog* to the starting holds and start all over if you want.

☐ **51f** **Dragon Man** V9 ⭐⭐
Got core tension? Stand start in the middle of the roof in the crack. Move out the roof using holds in the roof to a flat left-facing sidepull. Jack your left foot up and reach for a small pocket underneath the next overlap. Move up to jugs, then traverse left to get off.

☐ **51g** **Dragon Slayer** V11 ⭐⭐
Just to the right of *Dragon Man* is this harder version. Stand start in the crack and climb out the roof using flakes and underclings to sloper at the lip for right and the left-facing sidepull for left. Use them and a sloping edge in the middle of the face to reach a small pocket underneath the next lip.

☐ **51h** **Dragon Ballz** V6 ⭐
Contrived and height dependent. On the right side of the wall, just left of the arete. Stand up onto the slab, move out to sloper at the lip of the roof and move up and right to pocket in seam at the base of the vertical crack. Finish up the arete.

☐ **51i** **Dragon Back** V1 ⭐⭐
This arete with unique rock cut like fish scales will test your footwork. Stand start on the left side of the arete. Stand up on the slab and reach for the jug. Drop off, or finish straight up on jugs. Eventually walk off right.

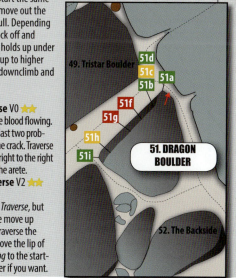

51. DRAGON BOULDER

49. Tristar Boulder

52. The Backside

ADAM HENRY

Like sands through the hourglass so are the Days of Our Lives… The sentiment echoes from the TV as I flip channels on another sultry, summer day trapped in the deep south. The daytime TV soap echoes the sentiment of the drama that has unfolded at Little Rock City. The "Back in the Day" experience has been replaced by ease of access and crowds swarming the bullet white sandstone gems hoping to glean from the rock features another jewel send in the boulderfield. Not too far in the distant past, this experience was available only for those special few willing to hide behind the cloak of stone from landowners and golfers who knew we were there, but had better things to do than worry about a few rogues.

As the years have progressed, the true Chatt local has become a rare find. The majority that claim this status are infiltrates from areas outside of the deep south, bringing their ideals and helping to create a meld of cultures that forms the "outdoorsman paradise" we know today. The Boulder of the South, with its endless amount of stone, has enticed many useless bums, but also a fair amount of movers and shakers of the game to the area.

The names of early "true local" artists such as Robinson, Eiseman, Rymer, and Hayes have weathered from the stone with time and history that is only passed by word of mouth. My experiences there started around 1990 with a small band of true locals including Sam Adams, Jody Evans, and Ben Ditto. We would park at the water tower where Sammy's relative worked and proceed into our ninja-like effort upon entering the boulders. The area was still fairly open on the upper end of the single digit grade, but most of the obvious lines under V5 hinted at previous ascents with a faint scrub or perhaps a caking of chalk. Many problems went up at the time as these climbing bums would just stroll up the mountain from the valley below to spend an entire day or a session between sport climbing. Jody was a bit more serious about it claiming many of the area classics in the upper range of the single digit V range. A good bit of the 600+ problems are the results of their efforts. A couple of the more notable lines that would go up at the time are now known as Deception, Castaway, and Spanky. Like most full time climbers at that time, these guys moved on to other things or presumed better places. These days Jody is a fairly successful businessman in SLC and triathlete, Sam stays busy with his landscape company in Chatt, and Ben now jumps the globe seeking inspiration in exotic stone and cultures. Their ascents provided the impetus for transplants to take it to the next level. There were many that helped shape the boulderfields, but Andrew Traylor would put his blue collar ethic to the stone creating the majority of the difficult lines in the park.

In the late 90's, the massive amount of stone in the region along with potential higher education enticed a young Andrew Traylor to Chattanooga. Having spent his high school years dominating the Alabama scene, single-handedly putting up 90% of the double digit lines, we knew that Chattanooga would not be the same upon his arrival.

Lines such as The Law, The Chattanoogan, Biggie Shorty, Bedwetters, and many more are attributed to his drive to put up the hardest in the area. Whether it was Hueco, Flagstaff, or home at Rocktown, his intent was to crush, and the first ascent was even better. He was usually the best, but on occasion the style wouldn't fit him and his outbursts were legend-

ary. There wasn't anyone better than James Litz to force Traylor into high gear. Their friendly rivalry resulted in one, two's on the hardest at the time with James dominating on the crimps such as Scarecrow, and Traylor when pure power and tension were requisite. These days Andrew lives on a lake back home in Alabama – still crushing, but preferring the safety of a rope. His impact on Little Rock City was massive, but just like the early artists, his history will pass with time just as he would want it.

I have spent countless days in the field as a trespasser and later as a paying customer. The efforts of the true locals and transplants have made LRC a special place. Along with HP40 and Rocktown, it has created a stretch of sandstone bouldering that's hard to beat. But be warned, a sojourn may result in a stay.

52. THE BACKSIDE

The Backside is the area behind the Dragon Boulder. There are problems back here on a few different boulders and the back wall. This area is not super-popular, or very well traveled, as there are no classics in this zone. The easiest way to get here is to walk around the Dragon Lady Boulder. On your right you will see the *Font Arete* and to the left is a corridor against the back wall where the rest of the problems can be found. **They are described from the furthest back, and then moving out towards the Dragon Boulder.** To get off of these boulders is usually a walk off, although if the problem is on the back wall, you may need to top out or jump off, just follow the descriptions.

52. THE BACKSIDE

☐ **52a** **Rise to Rebellion** V4
"Sketchy." Walk through a corridor along the rear wall past a large scoop and look for a cave on your left. Stand start on two crimps under the lip of a roof to the left of the cave. Move right out seam and straight up conglomerated and mossy face above.

☐ **52b** **The Tempest** V3 ★
"Scary." Stand start on good edges on the right side of the obvious large scoop on the back wall in a corridor. Climb the smooth face up and left past incuts and crimps to gain jugs out right at about 20 feet. Step off onto the top of the boulder behind. Tall, not a good landing, and no way to spot really, but fun climbing.

☐ **52c** **V6** ★
Located on an overhanging but mildly chossy boulder across from *the Tempest*. Sit start low with right on black pinch and left in vertical mail slot pocket. Cross right to angling crimp and make long move to finger bucket up and left, top out straight up on some choss.

☐ **52d** **V4**
Start same as for 52c. Make a big move up and right to jug on right margin of wall, then straight up to hole. Top out on mossy and chossy rock.

☐ **52e** **Gross Mantle** V?
On the low flat boulder about 15 ft. left of the *Font Arete* is a mantle problem on the low roof. Lay down beneath the roof, throw up a heel and press out the mantle. Unrepeated?

☐ **52f** **Font Arete** V5 ★★
Climbs the short but smooth and clean arete to the right when coming from the Dragon Boulder. Squat start with left in pocket and right on pinch. There is chalk on really low holds, but you may get more than you bargained for if you start here. Burl your way up the arete.

☐ **52g** **Font Right** V5 ★
Start the same as for the *Font Arete*, but move right into groove and slap right to slopers. Power your way up the slopey bulge.

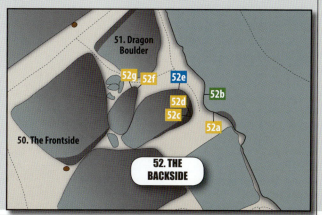

VIII. THE FAIRWAYS

The Fairways Area describes the boulders which face downhill towards the golf course and line up one after the other in a row after walking past the Main Area. The trail goes downhill slightly at this point, and the boulders will for the most part form a wall on your left. This area includes the Barometer Wall, the Hoops Boulder, the Pancake Boulder, The Pinch and Cleopatra Boulders, the Super Crack Wall, and Your Sister's Boulder, which sits below the Super Crack Boulder, separate from the others.

There is a lot of variety and grades in this section, as well as a few classics that should not be missed. Always popular are the trifecta of harder classics right next to each other – *The Pinch*, *Cinderella*, and *Cleopatra*. *The Pancake Mantle* is a popular V2, and Your Sister's Boulder holds many great easy problems and is a little out of the way.

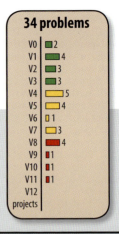

34 problems

Grade	Count
V0	2
V1	4
V2	3
V3	3
V4	5
V5	4
V6	1
V7	3
V8	4
V9	1
V10	1
V11	1
V12	
projects	

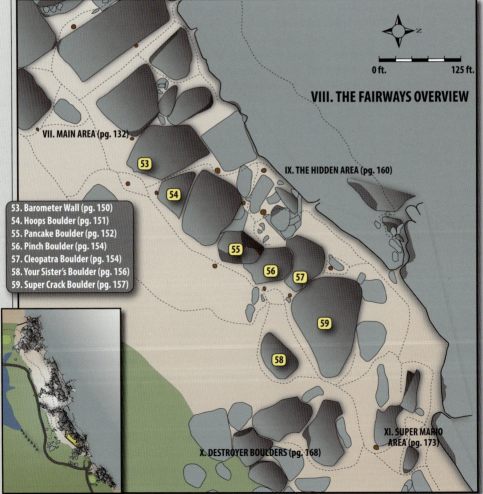

VIII. THE FAIRWAYS OVERVIEW

VII. MAIN AREA (pg. 132)

IX. THE HIDDEN AREA (pg. 160)

53. Barometer Wall (pg. 150)
54. Hoops Boulder (pg. 151)
55. Pancake Boulder (pg. 152)
56. Pinch Boulder (pg. 154)
57. Cleopatra Boulder (pg. 154)
58. Your Sister's Boulder (pg. 156)
59. Super Crack Boulder (pg. 157)

0 ft.   125 ft.

X. DESTROYER BOULDERS (pg. 168)

XI. SUPER MARIO AREA (pg. 173)

LUIS RODRIGUEZ

It's open... it's closed. It's open... it's closed! And so the story went when we first began visiting Little Rock City back in the early nineties. The local repelling tactic worked for several decades, warding off many climbers from arguably the best boulderfield in the Deep South. But these tactics were not enough to repel us from the hardest sandstone in the South. Dreams of micro-edges, waves of stone, and stone crescents abound. Week in, week out we made the pilgrimage to Soddy-Daisy, TN to wear out our skin on this gritty sandstone bluff/boulderfield. When we finally took the leap of faith and made the move to Chattanooga (circa 1999), part of the Atlanta climbers contingency (Eric Pittman, John Guin, and I) and the B'ham contingency (Andrew Traylor), met the Chattanooga locals (Sam Adams, Chris Chesnutt, Jerry Roberts, Travis Eiseman, Andrew Gross, Jeff Drumm, Shan Webb, etc.), and like peas in a pod the game was on! The entire Southern climbing scene coalesced into one movement of sending in Chattanooga. In the first couple years we climbed right through the summers. The question was not whether you were going climbing, but more so, with whom. Every morning the phone would ring several times over with climbers on the other end of the line begging to get out and climb, and the locale of choice was more often than not Little Rock City. Climbers would load into vans, carpooling by necessity, or else risk "being towed," making the ride up Mowbray Mtn. to park by the water tower, or making a drive-by drop-off of climbers on the side of the road, like a special training unit on a recon mission.

Once in the woods, you were safe to frolic in the corridors surrounded by the grayish hues of God's own stone. The silence was extraordinary, only broken by the occasional swoosh of a wayward golf ball, or the thud of another failed attempt on the latest testpiece. Yes, we felt special to partake in this endeavor, as special as all those that came before us. As a matter of fact, it was difficult to claim any first ascent at LRC, as there had been such a strong contingency of climbers generations before. As always, Bob Cormany led the way in pointing out the goings on of the past, and Jerry Roberts and Sam Adams further enhanced those recollections. But there was always a sense that you were not treading on such virgin grounds, even when you were assured that no one had ever topped out unsaid boulder. "Team '87" came to be the code name for those that came before us. You could never rest assured that "Team '87" had not climbed your project long before. And so it came to be time and time again, that even though you may claim your FA and call it by your little heart-warming name, someone was sure to clarify that it had been done many ages ago by "Team '87," and there was little you could argue against that.

In the end it was humbling, and climbing at Little Rock City became an end in itself, not the means to an end. The way it rightly aught to be. Keep the faith!

NOT TO BE MISSED:

V2 The Pancake Mantle ★★★ – A fun short mantle problem onto a giant pancake. You can't miss it.

V7 Cinderella ★★★ – Done as a dyno or done statically, its about the same grade. A cool blunt arete with apposing crimps.

V7 The Pinch ★★★ – A short and burly bulge on cool shallow pockets and slopers. The pinch hold is obvious, although it is easier for most to reach past it.

V8 Cleopatra ★★★ – On the right side of the grey wall is this line of shallow divots and crimpers. The start can be a bit awkward, especially if there is water coming out from under the boulder. A classic face.

53. BAROMETER WALL

53. BAROMETER WALL

53d **53d** Cormany Wall 4 V1 ⭐
Sit start on low break on the arete and climb up to water groove on good holds.

53e **53e** Low Traverse V6 ⭐
Start on the very left side of the Barometer Wall on a low rail and traverse it right all the way across the wall to the far side.

53f **53f** Crack of Pain V4 ⭐
On the left side of the face is an obvious jagged crack in a shallow dihedral. Sit start low on break and climb upwards into the overhanging crack, making sure your skin isn't eaten off, to higher break.

53g **53g** V5 ⭐
About six ft. to the right of *Crack of Pain*, sit start on flat edges and move upwards to large pocket, then up the blank shield above using sidepulls to the break.

53h **53h** Mother Thrutch V4 ⭐
Stand start matched on the higher crimp edge in the middle of the red face and climb straight up the wall to the break.

53i **53i** Gross Sit V8 ⭐
Sit start on sloping crimp to the left of the *Mother Thrutch* low start, and directly beneath the stand start. Climbs straight up into a shallow roof, and then straight up the face above, finishing same as *Mother Thrutch*.

53j **53j** Mother Thrutch V5 ⭐⭐ Right Sit
Sit start on shelf directly under obvious crimp flake. Move up right hand to crimp, then head left to sidepulls and crimpers in the blank face and climb to the break.

53k **53k** Mother Trucker V4 ⭐
Starts the same as *Mother Thrutch Right Sit*, but move up to the crimp with your left hand and climb the white face above using edges in rippled rock.

53l **53l** V3 ⭐
The rightmost line on the face. Sit start on shelf about six ft. left of the tree. Climb the white face above.

53. THE BAROMETER WALL
The Barometer Wall is a smooth plate of grey and red rock which hangs over the trail just past the Main Area. These are the first problems you encounter as you leave the Main Area, and they are on the left. The climbs here are fun and worth the effort if you have already climbed the classics for the grade. **The problems are described from left to right.** To get off of these problems, simply jump off, or traverse jugs to the right margin of the wall.

53a **53a** Cormany Wall 1 V0 ⭐
Starts between the trees on the left side of the face. Squat start on incut flakes and climb up the well featured wall above to break and jump off.

53b **53b** Cormany Wall 2 V1 ⭐
Start just right of 53a on sidepulls and underclings at face height. Climb up a water groove feature using slopers and pockets to break, traverse left to get off.

53c **53c** Cormany Wall 3 V2 ⭐
Stand start left of the arete and climb the blankish slab on pockets and slopers to the large pointy horn, jump off to get off.

54. THE HOOPS BOULDER

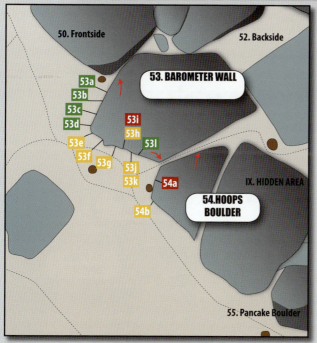

54. THE HOOPS BOULDER

The Hoops Boulder is a relatively small boulder with two problems on it, on the smooth short face and arete which face the trail. To the left of this boulder is the easiest access for The Hidden Area. **The problems are described from left to right.** It is easy to get off this boulder.

☐ **54a Hoops** V8 ⭐
To the left of the tree on the smooth vertical face. Sit start on twin crimps, then use crimper gastons and sidepulls to climb the short but hard wall above.

☐ **54b Profits of Doom** V5 ⭐
Climbs the left-angling lip of the boulder to the right of the tree. Sit start on low slopers and move upwards. The water groove to the right is not part of the problem.

55. PANCAKE BOULDER

55. PANCAKE BOULDER

55. THE PANCAKE BOULDER

The Pancake Boulder is a large boulder with a tunnel underneath it big enough to crawl through. The problems described here are on the front side of the boulder next to the trail. The other problems on this boulder are described in the Bedwetters Area of the Hidden Section. *The Pancake Mantle* is exactly what its name says, and is good fun. **The problems are described from left to right.** To get off this boulder move across the face to the right or left and climb down on the adjacent slabs.

☐ **55a Steamroller** V5 ⭐⭐
To the left of the *Pancake Mantle*, sit start on underclings underneath the roof, struggling to keep off the slab below. Power out the roof, then make moves up and right around corner to top out.

☐ **55b White Chili** V8 ⭐
A link-up of sorts. Sit start on the starting holds of *Steamroller*, and climb underneath the roof towards the *Pancake Mantle*, and top it out on that problem.

☐ **55c The Pancake** V2 ⭐⭐⭐
Mantle
Above the cave which you can tunnel through to get to *Bedwetters*. Stand start on horns in break above the lip of the boulder. Pull feet on and move up to the pancake shelf. Mantle onto it. Short and sweet.

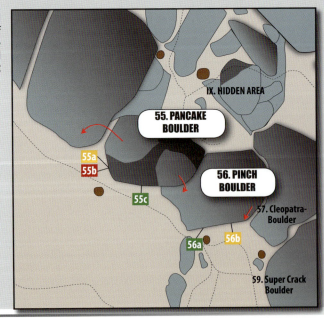

THE CHATTANOOGANS

The Chattanooga Bouldering Crew
with James Litz (center)

TBA Halloween Parties
with Chris Chestnutt (left)

Adam Henry's Sandrock
Bouldering Comp

Jason Young (Center)
1970-2015

Battling for the First Ascent of Instinct

56. THE PINCH BOULDER

The Pinch Boulder is home to a classic problem – *The Pinch*. It is the next steep boulder along the trail from the Pancake Boulder, and sits to the left of the Cleopatra Boulder in a nice open area on the trail. **The problems are listed from left to right.** To get off this boulder, shimmy down next to *Cinderella*.

☐ **56a Burgos Problem** V3 ⭐
Sit start on low rail behind tree with your right on crimp and left on sloper. Move up and left into shallow pockets and then into better holds further left and up.

☐ **56b The Pinch** V7 ⭐⭐⭐
This classic is short in height but not on quality moves and holds. Sit start on a large flat rail on the boulder left of *Cinderella*. Move up to a broad sloper/

56. THE PINCH BOULDER

sidepull and then move right on pockets to the rockover above on black rock. AKA *Behind the Eye* (check out the tree next to the problem).

57. THE CLEOPATRA BOULDER

The Cleopatra Boulder is a vertical white face which forms one wall of an open area next to *the Pinch*. It is home to some classic harder problems that should not be missed. This is a boulder for someone who likes to crimp. **The problems are described from left to right.** To get off this boulder, you can either down climb over towards *the Pinch*, or walk straight back and down climb or jump off the uphill end and walk back around.

☐ **57a Cinderella** V7 ⭐⭐⭐
A classic problem commonly done using a couple different methods. Climbs the overhanging left arete of the boulder. Sit start on left-facing corner. Move up, eventually choosing whether to test your lock-off skills or to dyno. Finish straight up.

☐ **57b Cleopatra – V9** ⭐⭐
Cinderella Traverse
Sit start same as for *Cleopatra* on the right and move left across the face to encounter the holds on the arete and finish straight up as for *Cinderella*.

☐ **57c Cleopatra** V8 ⭐⭐⭐
This classic line climbs the cool grips up the right side of the white face. Sit start on the right side of the boulder on a low flat ledge. Awkwardly move straight up the face. Top out straight up, "It's not over till it's over."

☐ **57d** V4 ⭐
The not often done line right of *Cleopatra*. Sit start on flat holds right of *Cleopatra* and climb up the face on decent edges to break. Top out not recommended due to dirtiness.

57. THE CLEOPATRA BOULDER

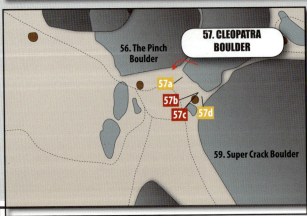

57. CLEOPATRA BOULDER

56. The Pinch Boulder

59. Super Crack Boulder

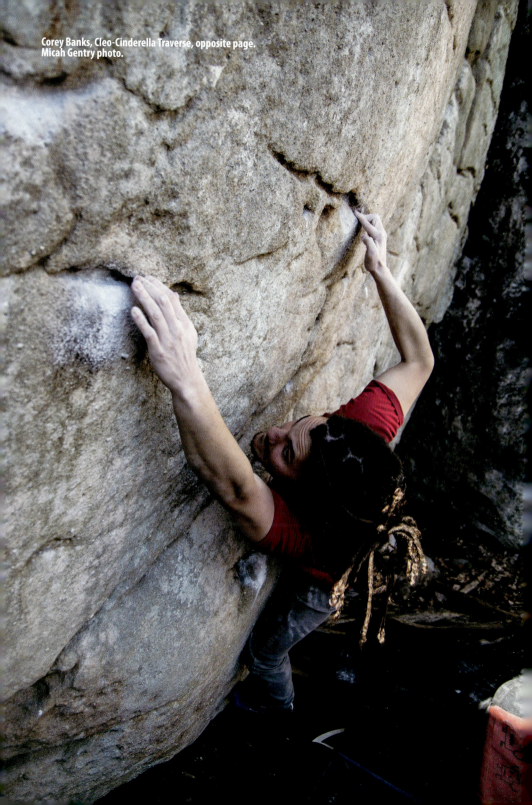

Corey Banks, Cleo-Cinderella Traverse, opposite page.
Micah Gentry photo.

58. YOUR SISTER'S BOULDER

58. YOUR SISTER'S BOULDER

Your Sister's Boulder is a separate boulder which is just downhill from the Cleopatra Boulder. It has a number of nice lines on its downhill side; from above it is covered with vegetation and leaves. Look for some cool flakes, a good traverse, and of course a pair of rounded slopers. **The problems are described from the right side of the face to the left.** To get off this boulder is an easy walk off.

☐ **58a Shits and Giggles** V0
On the right hand side of the boulder is the easiest warm-up. Stand start and climb the bulbous feature.

☐ **58b High Traverse** V2 ⭐
Stand start on the far right side of the boulder and traverse the high break all the way to the left, finishing up *These Feel Like Your Sister's*, or just stepping off.

☐ **58c Drag Me Down** V1 ⭐⭐
The best problem on the boulder. On the right side of the boulder is a cool line of pockets. Sit start at an undercling and climb straight up.

☐ **58d Uncle Punchy** V1 ⭐⭐
On the left side of the boulder are lots of flakes. Sit start on the lowest flakes and move straight up the wall to top out at highest point.

☐ **58e These Feel Like** V3 ⭐⭐
       Your Sister's
Sit start on flakes just left of the start of *Uncle Punchy*. Move straight up and left, then left along break to top out with sloper mantle on "your sister's."

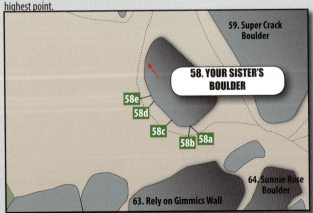

59. Super Crack Boulder

58. YOUR SISTER'S BOULDER

64. Sunnie Rose Boulder

63. Rely on Gimmics Wall

59. SUPER CRACK BOULDER

59. SUPER CRACK BOULDER

The Super Crack Boulder is a very large and tall boulder which is of course home to a problem named *Super Crack*. It is next to the Cinderella Boulder and uphill from Your Sister's Boulder. Tall is the keyword when discussing the problems on this block, and you should treat these problems with respect. Some roped prep work should be considered mandatory, as it is very common for top outs to get really dirty from the weather. Be smart, an injury means your trip, or season, is over. **The problems are described from the left to right around the boulder.** To get off this boulder, down climb over onto the Hulk Boulder and jump off or down climb easily off its uphill side.

☐ **59a** Neurotica 5.10 ⭐
"Scary." The tall face covered in flakes and incut holds. This is the left line up the face. Probably wise to top-rope.

☐ **59b** Exotica 5.10 ⭐
"Scary." The right line on the tall face covered in flakes and incuts, just a few feet right of *Neurotica*.

☐ **59c** Don't Tell My Daddy V7 ⭐⭐
"Scary." This line is on the arete which overhangs the trail and climbs the scoop and tall smooth face above via the crack line in the center. Stand start in the scoop and climb friable looking black rock to a thin crack on the headwall. A very serious highball.

☐ **59d** Super Crack V4 ⭐⭐
"Sketchy." Stand start at the base of the crack and climb it about 15 ft. to a break. Then move up and right on a gaston crimper rail before making a big reach left to another gaston crimp, then to jugs. Very tall.

☐ **59e** Clarien's Cherry V11 ⭐⭐
"Scary." The blank face about 10 ft. to the right of *Super Crack*. Probably a wise idea to toss down a rope on this one to clean and brush it before you attempt it from the ground.

☐ **59f** Lurod/Gross V10 ⭐
Undercling
On the short boulder perched right behind *Clarien's Cherry*, in the cave, stand start matched on the left side of the large undercling flake and feet on little chips. Pull on and bust long move to incut holds at the lip, mantle.

To the right of the Undercling Boulder is another tall face on the Super Crack Boulder. There are multiple tall lines which have been brushed out of the moss. There are at least three vertical lines and possibly a traverse along the base. No information on these is known except that they are tall, sketchy, and setting up a top rope would be a very good idea.

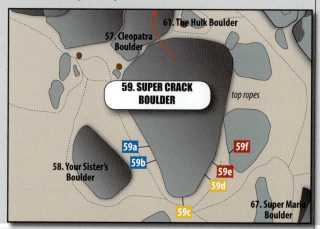

CHAD WYKLE

In the mid to late 90's I made countless trips to the Deep South... Foster Falls, the Obed, Horse Pens 40, T-Wall, Buzzard Point, Rock Town, Laurel Falls and also a few visits to 'Little Rock City'(LRC). Partners on those trips were my wife Rebecca, Robert and Lisa Semple, Jim Horton, Travis Tweed, Tonya Owens, Sean Barb, and others.

I was truly inspired by LRC...tons of fantastic boulders along a beautiful, wooded hillside. Despite the setting and perfect boulders, I could never fully relax knowing that I was climbing in an area with no legal access. I'd heard a few horror stories of encounters with land managers, and I didn't particularly care for hiding in the corridors. Very simply, any climbing there during that time was trespassing; we were climbing without permission.

The fantastic boulderfield that is now known as the Stone Fort would remain a Holy Grail for the climbing community for many years... immortalized by the insightful words of John Sherman in his 1994 climbing 'bible' the "Stone Crusade:" "The southeast's best sandstone boulderfield is Little Rock City. Little Rock City is closed to climbing, it's loss a tragedy. Hopefully local efforts to re-open the area will succeed."

The Southeastern Climbers Coalition made several attempts in the 90's to open a dialogue with Montlake Golf Club (proprietor of the boulderfield property)... all had been unsuccessful. And while clandestine climbing was certainly ongoing there, the outlook for legitimate climbing access was considered bleak and fleeting as the Montlake golf course continued to develop.

My wife Rebecca and I moved to Chattanooga in May of 2001... both fully taken with the sport of rock climbing. We were born, raised and proudly 'cut our climbing teeth' in the High Country of North Carolina. But, we had fallen in love with the Deep South's 'Sandstone Belt' on our frequent and extended trips.

I was hired in June of 2001 by Rock/Creek, and spent much of the following year climbing around Chattanooga, but also traveling back frequently to NC. I was spending many climbing days with Jim Horton on those trips 'back home'. We did lots of brainstorming about his now legendary bouldering event, Hound Ears, and we talked about the potential of a series of outdoor comps that would benefit climbing access. Ironically, Jim had talked to Adam Henry, author of the Horse Pens 40 Bouldering Competition about the same thing.

We got together for several meetings in 2002, and with very strong support from Rock/Creek, the concept of the Triple Crown Bouldering Series was born. Obviously, both Hound Ears and Horse Pens 40 would provide two excellent venues for the event. Initially, our plan was to include Rock Town as the third leg, but as both Jim and I brainstormed on a gloomy February afternoon in 2003, we happened upon an idea... literally at the same time.

With strong motivation from Jim and co-owner of Rock/Creek Dawson Wheeler, I took the opportunity to visit the Montlake Golf Club and meet with the superintendant. In the meeting, I talked hopefully about the concept and goals of the bouldering series... and the prospect of LRC as one of the venues. After a long-winded (on my part) meeting, the superintendent agreed to forward the information on to the landowner, Henry Luken, a very well-known, well-respected and successful entrepreneur. I subsequently had several positive discussions with Mr. Luken by phone and eventually met with him at Rock/Creek. He liked the idea of the competition, but was concerned about liability. With his help, we restructured a long-standing climbing liability waiver that had been created for Hound Ears by Sean Coburn (climbing activist and former president of the Carolina Climbers' Coalition). The re-vamp of the waiver led to discussions about year-round climbing access to the boulderfield. Mr. Luken wanted assurance that we could create a system that would require all climbers to sign the liability waiver, and that there would be clear signage in place to support compliance with a short list of regulations. With the help of the climbing community, a unique system of visitation was created and climbers were given legal access to one of the best boulderfields in the eastern US.

Since 2003, the climbing community has enjoyed year-round access to this wonderful resource... and the Triple Crown Bouldering Series (with Stone Fort/LRC as a venue) has donated well over $100,000 in support of non-profit organizations including the Southeastern Climbers Coalition, the Carolina Climbers Coalition, the Access Fund, Friends of the Cumberland Trail, Land Trust for Tennessee, Habitat for Humanity, the Alabama Bouldering Fund, and the Wilderness Trail Association.

The relationships developed with Stone Fort have opened doors with private and public land managers that have been closed to the climbing community in the past. While no other region of the US faces more climbing access issues, a massive and growing list of access successes have been accumulated by the Southeastern Climbers Coalition and the Carolina Climbers Coalition. I am both humbled and proud to have had the opportunity to support both of these organizations in their ongoing effort to gain and maintain access to climbing resources in the Southeast.

We are very fortunate in the South to have many wonderful climbing areas... Stone Fort is simply one of the best. It is my hope that as our community grows, that we will continue to respect and take care of this wonderful resource.

TRIPLE CROWN BOULDERING SERIES

Photo by Andrew Kornylak

Triple Crown has donated over
$100,000 to support climbing access

Learn more at www.triplecrownbouldering.org

IX. THE HIDDEN AREA

The Hidden Area is a narrow valley which lies behind the line of large square blocks which forms the Fairways. Half of it is a small and tightly nestled maze of boulders which choke the valley, while the other half is open and easily navigated. Here you will find a nice mix of lines, most of which are infrequently climbed. Not to be missed is the classic *Bedwetters*, one of the longest and most overhanging problems at an area known more for its faces than its roofs. Also be sure to hit up the mega-classic *Hulk*, a problem which anyone climbing the grade should try. You can also expect to find some worthwhile faces and slabs, as well as some moss.

There are two entrances to the Hidden Area, on either end of the little valley. Or you could always get there by crawling through the tunnel underneath the *Pancake Mantle* as well. The recommended way has you taking a left through a narrow gap in between the Barometer Wall and the Hoops Boulder. This way will take you to the Back Wall as well as the Bedwetters Area. The problems are described in the order that you encounter them if coming from this direction. You can also get there by following a trail as it wraps around the Super Crack Boulder, and enters the valley from the other side.

Sitting above the Hidden Area on top of the tall back wall is the Crypt. This area has a few problems that you may want to check out if you have done most everything else. To get there, you actually need to head back to the Main Area, walk to the end of the corridor past the Dragon Boulder, and climb up through a short break in the wall. From here, follow a trail as it goes right and eventually ends at a grouping of boulders perched next to a couple of large roofs.

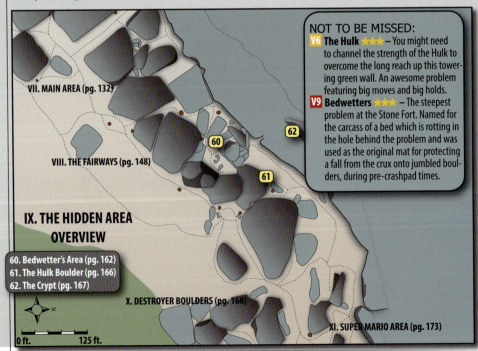

VII. MAIN AREA (pg. 132)

VIII. THE FAIRWAYS (pg. 148)

IX. THE HIDDEN AREA OVERVIEW

60. Bedwetter's Area (pg. 162)
61. The Hulk Boulder (pg. 166)
62. The Crypt (pg. 167)

X. DESTROYER BOULDERS (pg. 168)

XI. SUPER MARIO AREA (pg. 173)

NOT TO BE MISSED:

V6 The Hulk ★★★ — You might need to channel the strength of the Hulk to overcome the long reach up this towering green wall. An awesome problem featuring big moves and big holds.

V9 Bedwetters ★★★ — The steepest problem at the Stone Fort. Named for the carcass of a bed which is rotting in the hole behind the problem and was used as the original mat for protecting a fall from the crux onto jumbled boulders, during pre-crashpad times.

RONNIE JENKINS

Born and raised in Chattanooga, TN, I thought it was a dirty old town with nothing to do besides get into trouble. In 1998 I found climbing by breaking my hand in a gymnastics meet. After school one day my friend Evan Anderson ask me if I wanted to go to Little Rock City. I said you mean Rock City. He said no this boulderfield on a golf course. We drove up the mountain and parked at a water tower. Walked down a trail that led us to the main area, the Dragon Lady area. I was blown away by the rock formations and quantity of problems. That's where bouldering took over my life.

When you parked at the tower you could see who was all there. You had to stay very low key from the golfers and you did not dare to go past the Wave Boulder. All the old schoolers would sandbag the hell out of us. I remember one time when Jon Woodruff, aka Special Agent Utah, said, "try this problem, it's like V5." It was Spanky which gets V8 now. People like Andrew Traylor, Shan Webb, Eric Pittman, Luis Rodriguez, Justin and Josh Goodlett, Jon Woodruff, Andrew Gross, Jon Deerdorf, Jeff Drum, and many others were putting up many of the classics problems at LRC.

Access started to get real bad in the early 2000's. They blocked off the water tower parking, so people started to park on the side of the road. Then signs were posted and cars were getting ticketed or towed. Things did not look good for LRC and people were going other places to boulder around Chattanooga. Only a few people would stay and keep it a secret. If anybody asked about LRC, you would make up some crazy story that you had a gun pulled on you and your car got broken into. Then in a weeks time a Helicopter landing pad was installed right on the trail to get into LRC. This really freaked us out and we were wondering what is going on. Then one day I parked down the road and a silver Benz with a big UT Vols sticker on the door came to a stop right by me, rolled down the window, and a the man in the Benz said he owns this property (LRC) and could you just park at the golf course to go bouldering. I was blown away that this man just invited me to park at the golf course.

The place was still considered closed to the public but for the small community that was in the know it was open. Then the Triple Crown started up which gave better access to everyone and for the longevity of keeping this place open. If there was one season that sticks out the most at LRC, it was when the French invasion came. Tony Lamiche, Julien Nadiras, Stephan Denys, and Isa Carrier came over from France for a month. All the major projects got done by these boys. The Shield, Dragon Slayer, New Sensations, Flying High, Clarien's Cherry, and many others. They stayed with me and my roommates at the Dirty Mansion where they drank tons of coffee and played many games of foosball. If you go to this website you can view a taste of what it was like when they were here. Click on the link for Sandstone Cookies:

http://www.eider.tv/home.asp?l=1#61-429-ESCALADE-Scrabble-Berb%C3%A8re

One of the problems that Julien Nadiras put up was Clarien's Cherry. He named it after my roommate Clarien. She is the one walking around in the towel in the above video. LRC will always be the place where climbing evolved into a lifestyle for me.

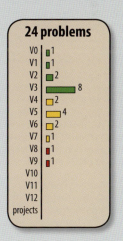

24 problems

V0	1
V1	1
V2	2
V3	8
V4	2
V5	4
V6	2
V7	1
V8	1
V9	1
V10	
V11	
V12	
projects	

60. BEDWETTERS AREA

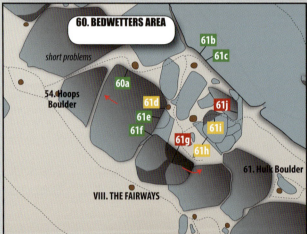

60. BEDWETTERS AREA

short problems

54. Hoops Boulder

61b
61c
60a
61d
61e
61f
61g
61h
61i
61j

61. Hulk Boulder

VIII. THE FAIRWAYS

60. BEDWETTERS AREA

The Bedwetters Area is the jumbled mess of boulders which all lie one on top of each other as soon as you enter the Hidden Area from next to the Barometer Wall. Here you will find problems on the tall walls which enclose the area, as well as on the myriad of perched boulders found within. There is a good variety of slabs, but the main attraction is *Bedwetters* – a steep cave problem that climbs out a near-horizontal prow. **The problems are described as you come to them.** The problems are on many different blocks, but in most cases you can walk off or down climb easily.

On the left wall as soon as you enter the Bedwetters Area are a few short straight up problems with sit starts of varying difficulty which are not described here.

☐ 60a Myrmidon V3
Low and on your right is this rising lip traverse which you have to walk around to see. Sit start on the rail at its lowest point and traverse slopers up and left to mantle at the top.

☐ 60b The Horn V1 ⭐
On the face which forms the back wall of the Hidden Area are the next two problems. This one is the left one. Stand start on two flat edges and move up to underclings, then long move to the penis shaped horn. The grade is a bit height dependant.

☐ 60c Boxing Your Shadow V3 ⭐
Stand start about 10 ft. right of *the Horn*, just left of a crack. Stand start on left-facing sidepull. Move up and right on cool sculpted incuts, then up to jugs in break. Face right of crack is off.

☐ 60d Mosquito Deleto V4 ⭐
On the super mossy slabby face on the right as you are descending towards *Bedwetters*. Stand start matched on thin crimp between two trees. Pull onto the slab, up left to another crimp, then on to top. Super mossy, but still quality. Everything you need to use is brushed.

60g

60. BEDWETTERS AREA

Doug Lanuario on Bedwetters, V9.
Adam Johnson photo.

60h

60i

60. BEDWETTERS AREA

60e Hocus Pocus V3 ⭐
To the left of the large tree, about eight ft. left of *Mosquito Deleto*. Stand start on right-facing flake. Move up and right up the slab using thin crimp in white rock.

60f Pittman 1 V3 ⭐
"Sketchy." On the right side of the large *Bedwetters* block, just left of *Hocus Pocus*. Climbs the white arete and smooth white face to the right of it. Sit start on jugs underneath roof, move up to the arete and climb the face above to tall and mildly dirty top out with not a great landing.

60g Bedwetters V9 ⭐⭐⭐
"Sketchy." Named for the old rusty bed frame which fills the "pee spot" in the hole near this problem, and which protected the first ascensionists from breaking their backs on the jumbled boulders beneath the crux, this classic is the longest overhanging problem at the Fort. Stand start on pedestal in the back of the cave. Move out the horizontal roof to incuts and edges, trend leftward till the crux sequence which involves smaller holds, more tension, and an exciting finish. Step off left at finish. Lots of pads recommended due to uneven landing.

60h Acid Drop V7 ⭐
"Sketchy." Directly behind *Bedwetters* behind two trees, stand start this problem on a slab and move onto slightly overhanging boulder above. Climb it up shallow pockets and divots.

60i Rodriguez Problem V5
In the corridor directly behind *Bedwetters*, on the right hand side, is a smooth white face with a roof boulder perched above it. In the middle of this face stand start with your right hand in a pocket/divot and left foot on slopey rail. Move up to crimp gaston and then to the crack.

Drop from there.

60j Riddim Warfare V8
"Sketchy." On a perched overhanging boulder in the corridor leading to *the Hulk* is this steep problem on not so amazing rock. Sit start and follow pockets and underclings to top out. Precarious.

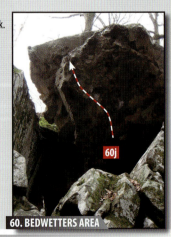

60j

60. BEDWETTERS AREA

John Sherman, The Hulk V6. Micah Gentry photo.

61. HULK BOULDER

61. THE HULK BOULDER

The Hulk is actually located on the same amazing boulder which is home to *Cleopatra* and *Cinderella*, but because it is located on the far side, we will refer to it here as the Hulk Boulder. *The Hulk* is one of the best problems of its grade at the Fort. Access it by following the trail around the Super Crack Boulder, or by following the trail through the maze of boulders in the Bedwetters Area and then downclimbing a 10 ft. wall. **The problems are described from left to right, starting at *the Hulk*.** To get off of this boulder, move right from the top out and walk along until you can downclimb the short face.

☐ 61a The Hulk V6 ★★★
A super classic of the area. Stand start in huecos. Move left to more heucos, get established, and make a long move straight up to flat edge. Match and move up and right to finish.

☐ 61b The Conformist V2 ★
Requires certain atmospheric conditions in order to be climbable, do to all the moss. Starts about 15 ft. right of *the Hulk* on an incut flake. Climb straight up the face above on rails to a sloper top out.

☐ 61c Swimming Pools, V3 ★ Movie Stars
Just a few feet right of the *Conformist* is a very similar line. Start on pockets at the base of the face and climb upwards to a slopey top out.

☐ 61d Baxter Traverse 5.12+ ★
Start on the right hand side of the face on a sidepull, same as for *Swimming Pools*... Move up to sloper rail and traverse straight left across sloper rails, eventually dropping down to start of *the Hulk*, then finish up that.

The following problems are not located on the Hulk Boulder, but along the back wall of the Hidden Area, right next to the climb up/down from the Bedwetters Area. Look for a tall clean pillar with a large tree growing right on top of it.

☐ 61e Pittman Face V3
"Sketchy." To the left of the corner, stand start on obvious sidepull flake, move up to good edges, and climb up the face to an off balance move up and left to finish. Angled slab beneath the landing.

☐ 61f Eiseman Corner V5 ★
"Sketchy." The shallow corner on the tall pillar right next to the climb up or down from the Bedwetters Area. Stand start at the base and climb it upwards, eventually moving around the arete and finishing on *Pop Top*.

☐ 61g Pop Top V5 ★
"Sketchy." The tall white face which has been cleaned up on the right side of the pillar. Stand start at the bottom and climb crimps and edges in white rock up to the tree stump.

61. HULK BOULDER

62. THE CRYPT

Six Feet Under and the few problems near it are included in this area because they sit right next to it on the map. However, to approach these problems, you must come along a trail from above, which begins by climbing up through a break in the back wall just beyond the Dragon and Tristar Boulders in the Main Area. From here, follow the trail as it bends to the right. Most of the problems in this area are hidden on the undersides of boulders, and can be hard to find, and also photograph (sorry for the lack of photos). **They are described from the farthest right problem to the left.** Getting off of these problems is easy, just walk off.

☐ 62a **High Heel** V4
Start on flat edges in seam on the right side of the large roof. Climb straight up and out the short overhang above.

☐ 62b **Low Spark** V5 ⭐
"Sketchy." Start the same as for *High Heel* with hands on ledge at the right side of the roof, move left along good holds in crack to broad sloper and make a large move up and left to crimp edge and jugs. An uneven landing.

☐ 62c **Bones** V3 ⭐
This one starts way down at the lowest point of the pit, on the clean white wall on the right side if scrambling down. Stand start on crimper and climb the wall above, traversing right at finish along rail.

☐ 62d **V2**
The overhanging thin blade of rock down in the pit. Scramble down to reach it. Stand start with left on high sidepull and right on right arete of boulder. Move up to gain jugs and top out.

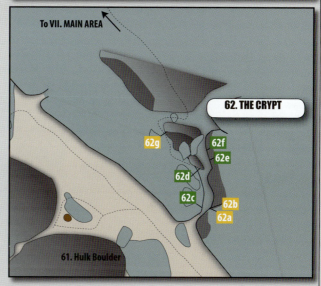

☐ 62e **Self Service** V3 ⭐
On the left side of the large open pit, directly behind 62d on the back wall, is a short hanging arete type block. Start here and climb directly out the tiered roof above, roughly following a thin crack weakness.

☐ 62f **Keystone Cops** V0
A few feet left of *Self Service*, at the left margin of the large roof. Start on jugs and climb upwards out the tiered roof on more big jugs.

☐ 62g **Six Feet Under** V6 ⭐⭐
In the cave completely underneath the ground. Wriggle down a hole to reach it, or climb around to the open side. Sit start in the very back of the cave on jugs. Work out the roof on flakes, climbing upwards, then back down, to top out on the open side of the cave. A fairly long problem.

X. THE DESTROYER BOULDERS

13 problems		
V0		
V1	🟩	2
V2	🟩	1
V3	🟩	4
V4	🟨	2
V5	🟨	2
V6		
V7		
V8	🟥	1
V9		
V10		
V11		
V12		
projects	⬛	1

The Destroyer Boulders are a group of large and densely packed boulders which reside right on the edge of the golf course. They are found next to Your Sister's Boulder, and downhill from the Super Crack Boulder and the Super Mario Area. For such a large group of boulders, you would expect that there would be more problems, but most of the accessible faces are low angle. Not to be missed is the arete problem called *the Destroyer*, although it is quite tall and you will need lots of pads and spotters. Be mindful in this area not to climb on the sides of the boulders which face the golf course, as these are closed by the golf course for climber safety.

This large group of boulders is easy to walk around, and you will find most of the problems along the outside of the group. To reach *the Destroyer* and the problems near it, walk downhill into the grass from below the Super Mario Area. Angle right into an open area with boulders on all sides.

NOT TO BE MISSED:

V3 Rely on Gimmics ⭐⭐ – This would be a perfect hand crack if it was about an inch deeper. Instead it is a shallow water runnel which presents a fun and interesting slabby problem.

V3 Destroyer ⭐⭐⭐ – One of the finest aretes around, but at the price of a sketchy landing. People have been injured here before, so bring many pads and spotters.

V5 Sunnie Rose ⭐⭐ – A rather obscure problem which never-the-less has some cool pockets and good movement on it.

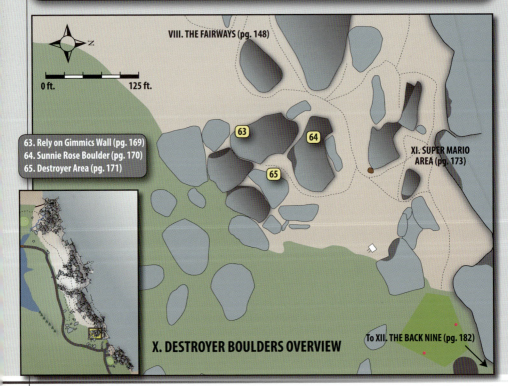

VIII. THE FAIRWAYS (pg. 148)

0 ft.   125 ft.

63. Rely on Gimmics Wall (pg. 169)
64. Sunnie Rose Boulder (pg. 170)
65. Destroyer Area (pg. 171)

63
64
65

XI. SUPER MARIO AREA (pg. 173)

To XII. THE BACK NINE (pg. 182)

X. DESTROYER BOULDERS OVERVIEW

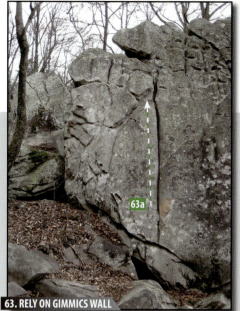

63. RELY ON GIMMICS WALL

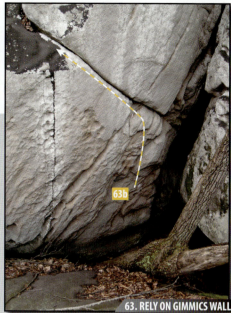

63. RELY ON GIMMICS WALL

63. RELY ON GIMMICS WALL

The Rely on Gimmics Wall is the large slabby wall which sits right next to Your Sister's Boulder. It includes the cool low-angle water runnel called *Rely on Gimmics*, and also describes the possibilities in a hole/cave that you can jump down into right of that. **The problems are described from left to right.** To get off this boulder, down climb one of its slabby faces.

☐ **63a** **Rely on Gimmics** V3 ⭐⭐
"Sketchy." The tall slabby water groove facing Your Sister's Boulder. Stand start at the bottom and climb your way up the cool feature. No gimmics needed, just balance.

☐ **63b** **Captain Cave Man** V5
Despite what looks to be some good potential in this hole/cave, there is nothing worth jumping down here for, except perhaps a stray golf ball. On the left wall is a problem. Start on the pinch and move up the dirty, granulated face above.

☐ **63c** **Project**
On the overhanging wall of the cave to the right of *Captain Cave Man* is a very hard project which climbs out the steep wall and then up the tall face above.

☐ **63d** **V3** ⭐
"Sketchy." Start down in the hole, on the opposite side from *Captain Cave Man*, on a good rail. Move straight up the slab on cool blobs, regaining ground level, and then up the face above, moving left to a good flake.

☐ **63e** **V1** ⭐
"Sketchy." On the slab about 10 ft. to the right of 63d, but starting at ground level. Stand start and climb awesome grips up the tall slab.

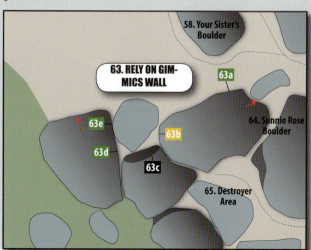

64. SUNNIE ROSE BOULDER

64. SUNNIE ROSE BOULDER

64. SUNNIE ROSE BOULDER

The Sunnie Rose Boulder is home to two problems on a short pocketed face which is just across the trail from the problem *Don't Tell My Daddy* on the Super Crack Boulder. Also described here are a couple of tall aretes in the corridor behind it. The problem *Sunnie Rose* is pretty fun and worth a go. **These problems are described from right to left.** To get off this boulder, you will have to down climb a slab perched next to it.

☐ 64a Sunnie Rose V5 ⭐⭐
The cool pocketed face right of the arete. Sit start low in pockets. Move up to flat jug, then up the bulging white face above on slopers and more pockets.

☐ 64b Peed on Me V1 ⭐
The overhanging arete to the left of *Sunnie Rose*. Sit start on the large obvious jug hole and climb up and left up the arete using pockets.

☐ 64c Pittman Arete V3 ⭐
"Sketchy." At the back of the corridor behind the Sunnie Rose Boulder, and past the *Pittman Arete 2*, is a tall right leaning arete. Stand start on a pinch block and ride it up and right with the slab rising beneath you.

☐ 64d Pittman Arete 2 V2 ⭐
"Scary." About 20 ft. to the left of the Sunnie Rose Boulder, and slightly around the corner, is a large overhanging arete which looms above a gap in the boulders. It is identified by its tiered shape, and has thin vertical cracks breaking off from it. Climb it to the top, but be very careful about your landing.

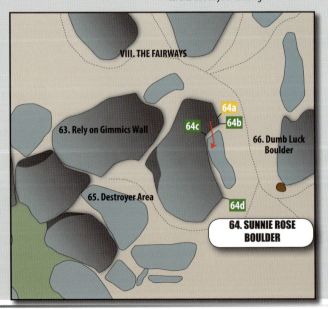

VIII. THE FAIRWAYS

63. Rely on Gimmics Wall

64a
64b
64c

66. Dumb Luck Boulder

65. Destroyer Area

64d

64. SUNNIE ROSE BOULDER

65. DESTROYER AREA

65. DESTROYER AREA

65. DESTROYER AREA

The Destroyer Area is the open area around the sweet arete problem called *Destroyer*. Be aware when you are hanging out around here that you are not far from the 18th hole tee box, and while you should be guarded by the boulders around you, it would not be a surprise for a golf ball to go whizzing by overhead. To access this area, walk down off the trail below the Super Mario Area into the grass. After about 30 feet, you will be able to head right into the middle of an open area amongst the boulders, this is the Destroyer Area. **The problems are described from right to left as you enter the area.** Getting off of these problems involves some slabby down climbing.

☐ 65a Drumm Problem V4 ⭐

The first problem encountered which climbs the short overhang and tall face on the right upon entering the area. Sit start on flakes and climb up and right to underclings in chossy rock, then over bulge to slab.

☐ 65b Johnson Problem V4

Stand start in the middle of the face to the right of the arete on left-facing flake. Move up to slab, then through rock scar to extremely dirty slab above.

☐ 65c Destroyer V3 ⭐⭐⭐

"Scary." Stand start at the base of the obvious 20 ft. tall arete. Long moves with good holds. Backbreaking slab behind, so spotters a must.

☐ 65d Pringle Problem V8 ⭐

"Sketchy." Climb most of the way up the *Destroyer* arete before moving out right across the face on sidepulls and pinches. Traverse these holds right before finishing up dirty top out.

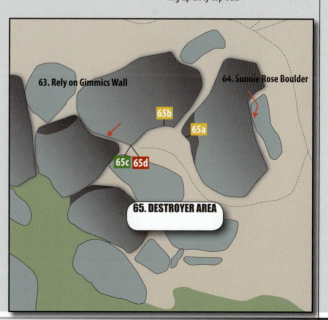

63. Rely on Gimmics Wall

64. Sunnie Rose Boulder

65b

65a

65c 65d

65. DESTROYER AREA

Jay Perry, Destroyer V3, Micah Gentry photo.

XI. SUPER MARIO AREA

The Super Mario Area is the last area before the 18th Tee Box on the golf course, and is home to the super classic Super Mario Boulder. One of the most popular boulders at the Stone Fort, it is rare that you walk up to this boulder and have it all to yourself. That said, there are a number of other worthy problems in this area, from the Dumb Luck Boulder, which is right below *Super Mario*, to the Boulder Problem From Hell Wall, which includes a number of quality high-balls and top-ropes.

To access this area, just walk along the main trail past the Super Crack Boulder in the Fairways Area. Follow the trail as it makes a left and heads up a short steep slope, depositing you beneath the Super Mario Boulder.

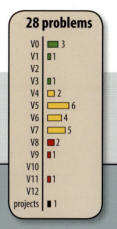

28 problems

V0	🟩	3
V1	▪	1
V2		
V3	▪	1
V4	🟨	2
V5	🟨	6
V6	🟨	4
V7	🟨	5
V8	🟥	2
V9	▪	1
V10		
V11	▪	1
V12		
projects	▪	1

NOT TO BE MISSED:

V4 **Super Mario** ★★★ – Like the original Nintendo game, for this problem you will start on the left side of the screen and make your way right. A cool long problem with interesting moves and varied grips, rightfully one of the most popular and memorable problems at the Stone Fort.

V7 **Red House** ★★★ – The straight up problem to the right of *Super Mario* is not quite as good, but is just as popular. It adds a burlier and lower percentage start to *Super Mario*.

V8 **House of Leaves** ★★★ – The serious, tall, and bad ass arete on the right side of the boulder. Be very careful up there, and make sure your pads and spotters are in place.

V11 **Jeremiah** ★★★ – Established by Jeremy Walton, this is one of the proudest and scariest hard lines here. It climbs the rippled orange rock up the middle of the tall rad face. Just watch your landing.

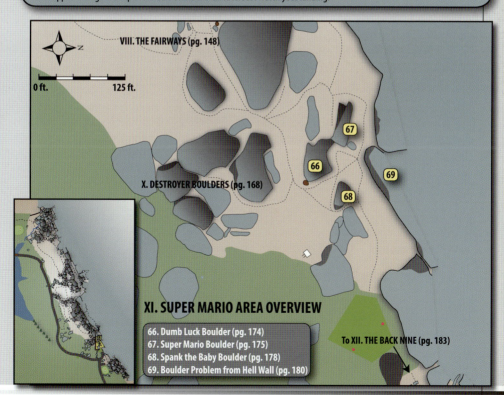

VIII. THE FAIRWAYS (pg. 148)

0 ft.   125 ft.

X. DESTROYER BOULDERS (pg. 168)

67

66

69

68

XI. SUPER MARIO AREA OVERVIEW

66. Dumb Luck Boulder (pg. 174)
67. Super Mario Boulder (pg. 175)
68. Spank the Baby Boulder (pg. 178)
69. Boulder Problem from Hell Wall (pg. 180)

To XII. THE BACK NINE (pg. 183)

66. DUMB LUCK BOULDER

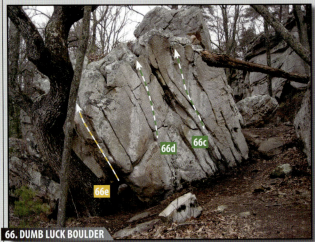

66. DUMB LUCK BOULDER

66. DUMB LUCK BOULDER

The Dumb Luck Boulder is the first boulder that you will come to in the Super Mario Area, and is the white face with cracks piercing it that is on your left as you ascend the short slope up to the Super Mario Boulder. These problems are fun and can serve as a good warm-up or diversion if you are in the area. **The problems are described from right to left, uphill to down.** To get off of this boulder, simply walk off the slab facing *Super Mario*.

☐ **66a** **Tennis Shoe Slab** V? ⭐
The blank slab across from *Super Mario*. Get a running start.

☐ **66b** **Plinko** V0 ⭐⭐
The low angle arete on the uphill side of the boulder. Stand start and climb slopers to the top.

☐ **66c** **V0** ⭐
Stand start to the left of *Plinko* on the face and climb up the face on good incuts to mantle.

☐ **66d** **Hand Me Down** V0 ⭐
The face to the right of *Dumb Luck*. Stand start on horn and climb up the face above using great incuts.

☐ **66e** **Dumb Luck** V5 ⭐
Sit start very low on flake underneath overhanging arete, awkwardly trying not to dab on tree. Climb the arete above.

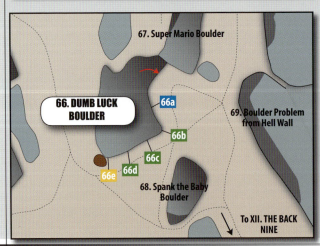

66. DUMB LUCK BOULDER

67. Super Mario Boulder

66a

69. Boulder Problem from Hell Wall

66b

66c

66e 66d

68. Spank the Baby Boulder

To XII. THE BACK NINE

67. SUPER MARIO BOULDER

The Super Mario Boulder is home to a number of classics from moderate to desperate, and is one of the most stacked boulders in the field. The most popular problems here are the classics *Super Mario* and *Red House*. To access this boulder, simply follow the trail towards the back of the field and keep an eye out on your left for the tall, pointy, orange face. **The problems are described starting in the back of the overhanging "cave" and heading to the right, all the way around the boulder.** There are many different ways off depending on the problem you climbed, so check the map for down climb arrows.

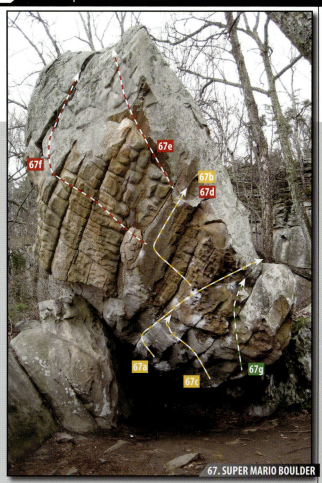

67. SUPER MARIO BOULDER

☐ **67a Super Mario** V4 ★★★
One of the most famous and classic problems at the Fort. Sit start low in the back of the cave on large holds. Move up to large sloper, then follow holds in seam straight right out the overhanging wall using incuts, underclings, a kneebar, and if you make it this far, don't forget to grab the 1UP found in the cool pockets. To finish, traverse off up and right.

☐ **67b Super Mario V6 ★★
Extension**
"Sketchy." The same as *Super Mario*, but when you get to the pockets at the end, move straight up on sidepulls to a long move out to shelf on the right margin of the boulder to top out.

☐ **67c Red House** V7 ★★★
Easiest V7 at the Fort? You decide. Sit start on underclings to the right of the *Super Mario* start. Move straight up into sloping rail pocket, then up and left via the vertical finger crack, gaining the incut holds on *Super Mario*. Finish up *Super Mario*.

☐ **67d Red House V8 ★★
Extension**
"Sketchy." The direct and extended finish to *Red House*. From the pocket holds, tack on two moves straight up on sidepulls and then make the lunge finish to the shelf out right. Mantle onto this and move off to the right.

☐ **67e House of Leaves** V8 ★★★
"Scary." The extension which tops out the arete and the boulder. Do the *Red House Extension*, but instead of mantling over to the right after the big throw, instead use a pinch and a sidepull to continue up the arete, eventually moving slightly left onto the face before reaching the top of the boulder. AKA *The Beautiful Struggle*.

☐ **67f Jeremiah** V11 ★★★
"Scary." The proudest line on the boulder! Sit start the same as for *Red House* and climb it into the extension. Before making the last throw out right, instead angle up and left across the orange bubble rock and top out the tall and proud face.

☐ **67g Underfling** V3 ★
The furthest right line on the face. Sit start on undercling flakes to the right of *Red House* and move straight up using footholds for the other problems to top out same as *Super Mario*.

Ronnie Jenkins on House of Leaves, V8. Andrew Kornylak photo.

68. SPANK THE BABY BOULDER

This small boulder is home to one problem, which gives it its name. It sits across the trail from the Dumb Luck Boulder and is recognizable by a short, steeply overhung orange face which faces downhill. Simply walk off to get off of this boulder.

☐ **68a** **Spank the Baby** V7 ★★

Climbs the short, steeply overhanging face on the boulder by the trail. Sit start low on pockets and underclings. Make your way up to slopey lip and mantle. The crux is avoiding the dab on the tree.

67. SUPER MARIO BOULDER

68. SPANK THE BABY BOULDER

☐ **67h** **Rage** V5 ★★
"Sketchy." The left line on the overhanging backside of the Super Mario Boulder. Start matched on pocket/pinch feature and climb straight out the overhanging prow, eventually finishing up and left to top out.

☐ **67i** **Fury** V6 ★
Start the same as for *Rage*, but move up and right onto the face into a pocket and undercling. Continue up and right to lip of the face, follow it left till you can top out.

☐ **67j** **Bent** V6 ★★
"Sketchy." Start low on the boulder with left in undercling and right in sidepull. Move up the right hand line of holds into the corner. Continue right along seam and finish at the apex of the boulder.

☐ **67k** **Slap** V5 ★
About four ft. right of *Bent*. Stand start left hand in undercling in seam/crack, right on crimp edge out right. Make a big move up the face to decent hold, then traverse rail left along good holds till you can rock over to top out.

☐ **67l** **Dribble** V7
On the right side of the face, where the lip of the boulder is lowest. Stand start on jugs at chest height and immediately move up the grey and licheny slab above.

Bethany Macke on Spank the Baby, V7. Corey Wentz photo.

69. BOULDER PROBLEM FROM HELL WALL

69. BOULDER PROBLEM FROM HELL WALL

The Boulder Problem From Hell Wall is the tall and sheer back wall along this section of the boulderfield, which also sits next to the Super Mario Boulder. It stretches from a clean white wall on the left, past some choss and a break, to a cool arete, then past a rather large roof, and further right to a massive dark cave where the trail meets the 18th Tee Box. These tall problems are commonly top-roped during the Triple Crown, so be smart about what you decide to do here. **The problems are described from left to right.** To get off of these problems walk backwards and to the right, towards the Back Nine until you can find a break to walk down through.

☐ **69a Bimbo Limbo** V9 ⭐⭐
"Scary." On the wall to the left of the chossy overhang is this tall problem. Stand start on undercling horn and climb the clean white bulge and face above using thin pockets, trending left. Eventually tops out the whole wall.

☐ **69b The Graduate** V5 ⭐⭐
"Sketchy." This problem climbs the arete on the back wall across from the Super Mario Boulder. The crux is high up, but with good spotters and pads, this makes for a feasible highball. Sit start on lowest holds left of the arete. Climb up into the scoop and grab holds around the arete, then proceed to the top on better holds.

☐ **69c Boulder Problem** V5 ⭐⭐
From Hell
"Sketchy." Sit start on the corner of the boulder underneath the arete on blocky holds just to the right of *the Graduate*. Move up and right on more blocky holds into corner underneath left margin of horizontal roof. Climb out the corner and make long move straight up into undercling and sidepull flake on face, finish straight up.

☐ **69d South Africa Arete** V7 ⭐⭐
"Sketchy." Start the same as for the *Boulder Problem from Hell* and move up into the corner at the lip of the roof. From here, move left along the lip of the overhang to decent edges and then continue left around the corner to gain scoop on *the Graduate* and finish up that problem.

☐ **69e Smell My Finger** V7 ⭐
"Sketchy." Start the same as the *Boulder Problem from Hell*, but at the lip of the roof, traverse slopers and thin crimps right along the lip till you gain a seam feature and move straight up to undercling flake. Follow pockets and sidepulls up the face above.

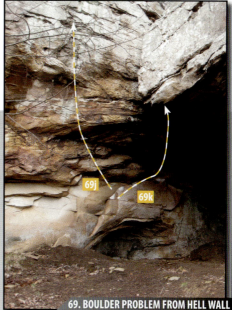

69. BOULDER PROBLEM FROM HELL WALL

☐ 69f **V1** ⭐
About six feet right of the *Boulder Problem from Hell* is a slabby orange face under the roof with some pockets on it. Stand start and climb this face to the roof, drop off.

☐ 69g **Project**
"Sketchy." The continuation of 69f through the roof. You must use small holds and have extreme body tension for this five foot roof.

☐ 69i **The Widowmaker** V6 ⭐
"Scary." About 30 ft. right of *Boulder Problem from Hell* is a chossy cave feature. Climb up into it and reach out it on its right hand side following a thin seam on decent holds up to cool incut holds on the face, then up the hard face above. Very tall, never been led, top-rope only.

☐ 69j **Baby Maker** V4 ⭐
"Scary." On the far right end of the wall is a large cave with a chalked flake on its left side. Follow holds out the steep wall to the left of the flake, eventually gaining an undercling pinch/pocket. Make long moves past this. Very tall.

☐ 69k **Tower Train** V5 ⭐
"Sketchy." Start on the left side of the chalked flake and follow it right, then bust straight up through the overhang to gain the offwidth crack above. Get your grovel on and top it out. Tall.

To XII. THE BACK NINE

XII. THE BACK NINE

The Back Nine is the final area in the back of the Stone Fort. It is made up of the largest blocks to be found here, all tightly packed one next to the other. The Back Nine is also home to some of the most classic rock formations to be found anywhere, in particular the crazy crack and seam laced grey walls of the Jigsaw Boulder and the Graham Cracker Boulder. Incidentally, it is also home to many of the Fort's hardest problems. A quick tour will inevitably be paused on the perfect viewing slab of the mind-blowing classic *the Shield*, easily one of the most beautiful problems you will ever see. The not-to-be-missed list for this area is long, as it is stacked with true classics. Be sure to bring your friends and their pads, as many of these problems involve some height.

To get to the Back Nine, follow the trail through the Super Mario Area. You will come to the 18th tee box. Continued access requires that climbers act respectfully here: wait until golfers have played and moved on until you walk through this area. Please be quiet out of respect, and if possible stay hidden until golfers have moved through. Walk across the tee box, over the cart path, and up a short stone staircase and trail which continues along the cliff line.

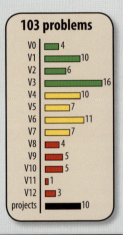

103 problems

V0	4
V1	10
V2	6
V3	16
V4	10
V5	7
V6	11
V7	7
V8	4
V9	5
V10	5
V11	1
V12	3
projects	10

NOT TO BE MISSED:

V1 **The Rib** ★★★ – A cool slab problem which climbs up a "rib" of iron bands. This is one of the best easy slabs at the Stone Fort, hands down.

V2 **Graham Crackers** ★★★ – A really cool tall arete, at a moderate grade! Similar in character to the *Incredarete*, this is just an awesome position.

V5 **The Mono Doigt** ★★★ – Very similar to *Shotgun*, and just as good, is this tricky pocket climb up a smooth face. Very much recommended.

V5 **White Trash** ★★★ – An incredibly varied problem, with some incredibly awesome grips. The rounded sloper groove that you lieback up is one of the cooler features at the Fort.

V6 **Cyclops** ★★★ – A classic Stone Fort patina crimper problem. The name refers to the "eye" hole which you climb past high up.

V7 **Deception** ★★★ – The striking line up the middle of the Jigsaw Boulder. This line is deceptively tricky and stunningly beautiful.

V7 **Junky** ★★★ – Locate the needle holes high on the face to identify this tall slabby classic. You'll use every slab trick you know to score yourself an ascent.

V7 **Heroin** ★★★ – A totally unique all points off lunge/glide move with enough air under your feet to really dilate your pupils.

V7 **Instinct** ★★★ – What's more instinctual – locking off or lunging? Either way, holding the swing is the real challenge to this perfect line of holds up an otherwise blank boulder.

V8 **The Brotherhood** ★★★ – The harder, and possibly even more deceptive start to the right of *Deception*. How can you resist not trying those moves?

V10 **Biggie Shorty** ★★★ – One of the most popular test pieces of the grade. Crimping is the ticket here.

V12 **The Shield** ★★★★ – Certainly one of the most beautiful boulder problems in the world. There are not enough stars for something this good. First climbed by visiting Frenchman Tony Lamiche.

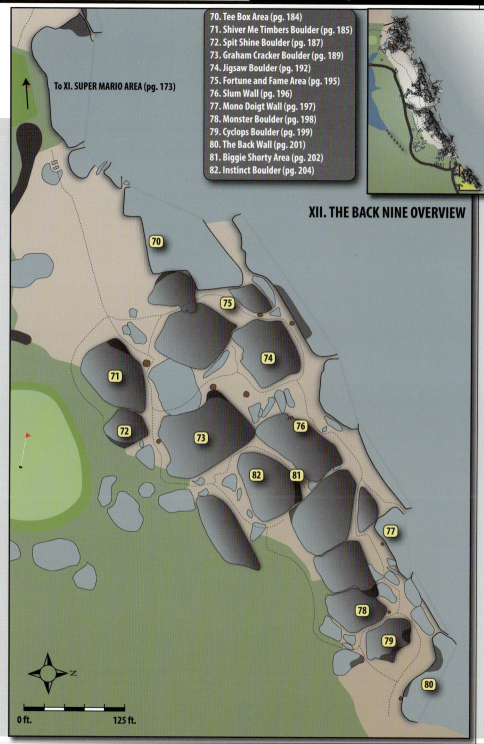

XII. THE BACK NINE OVERVIEW

To XI. SUPER MARIO AREA (pg. 173)

0 ft.   125 ft.

70. TEE BOX AREA

70. TEE BOX AREA

70. THE TEE BOX AREA

The Tee Box Area is used to loosely describe the problems and climbs along your left as you walk into the Back Nine. It includes problems on the back wall, as well as a few problems on the first two short boulders that you encounter on your left, across from the huge Shiver Me Timbers Boulder. **These problems are described from left to right as you encounter them.** To get off of the short boulders is an easy walk off or down climb. For getting off the back wall, the easiest way is to walk back and left and find an easy place to scramble back down through the cliff band.

☐ 70a V? ⭐
"Sketchy." The face and arete left of the crack in the corner has been climbed. Stand start at the base of the arete and climb up to break. Move up the slabby face above, aiming for shallow right-facing corner and climb it to the top. Unknown grade.

☐ 70b Chesnutt Crack V2
"Sketchy." Did you bring your rope and trad gear? Well, it could be bouldered. Stand start and climb the tall wide to fist to off finger crack in the corner. Traverse right to get off.

☐ 70c Water Groove V1 ⭐
"Sketchy." The obvious wide water groove feature on the face. Stand start at the bottom on good holds and follow the groove up more good holds. A bit of brush at the top, down climb to the left to get off.

☐ 70d Pittman Arete 3 V7 ⭐
"Scary." The tall arete which is to the left of the cave has some good holds on it but is a bit mossy. Quite tall, and with a precarious and off-balance crux very high up.

☐ 70e Segal Crack V5 ⭐
"Sketchy." The thin finger crack in the corner on the back wall. To access this, climb up onto the boulder left of *MC Hammer*. Climb the tall thin crack till you cannot get your fingers in anymore and trust that crimps will appear. Traverse right or left to get off.

☐ 70f V7 ⭐
The "beached whale" type lip traverse to the right of the cave. Start low on the right side of the block and traverse the very slopey and rounded over lip till you gain jugs in the crack and can mantle over.

☐ 70g Rodriguez Traverse V4
Start on slopers beneath water groove low on right side of the boulder and traverse the rail left across mossy and comglomerated rock till you gain the crack, finish up it.

☐ 70h Vulcans Do It With V2 ⭐ Straight Faces
On the boulder to the left as you are right next to the Shiver Me Timbers Boulder is a short pocketed bulge to slab. Start with left in bowling ball type grip and right on thin pockets. Move up to obvious jug pocket, then mantle out the slab above.

☐ 70i MC Hammer V6
About 10 ft. to the left of *Vulcans...* is a detached broken flake above ground level. Start above this on crimp pocket and move over the bulge and up the slab on pebbly rock.

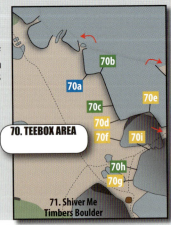

70. TEEBOX AREA

71. Shiver Me Timbers Boulder

71. SHIVER ME TIMBERS BOULDER

71. SHIVER ME TIMBERS BOULDER

The Shiver Me Timbers Boulder is a huge block which is the first one that you come to on your right as you enter the Back Nine. It is home to a handful of hard and classic problems, including it's namesake - *Shiver Me Timbers* – which involves long moves between small crimps. **The problems are described from left to right.** To get off of this boulder, head towards the Spit Shine Boulder and climb down onto it.

☐ **71a Kneed It** V9 ★★
Stand start and climb the blunt white prow using the left-facing corner. Carry on to the "worst top out in the world." You can probably guess which body part comes in handy.

☐ **71b Project**
Stand start with left hand on crimpers that form sort of an arete feature right of *Kneed It*. Attempt to move upwards to roundy ball type sloper up and right and use it to gain higher slopers and top out. Cool.

☐ **71c Devil's Cabana Boy** V7 ★
Sit start in the pod in the crack and climb the thin seam above to a high top out. Often wet.

☐ **71d Devil's Cabana Boy** V6 ★
Stand
Stand start on the horizontal rail above head height. Finish it up from here.

☐ **71e Shiver Me Timbers** V6 ★★
"Sketchy." This one will either make you shiver because of the high top out, or because of the size of the crimps! Stand start on incut crimps in hole on the face. Move up and right to sharp crimps in seam. Continue up and right around the corner on horizontal pocket edges to high top out.

☐ **71f Shiver Me Timbers** V8 ★★
Direct
"Sketchy." Start the same as for *Shiver Me Timbers*. Move up to sharp crimps in seam, then dyno up and left to decent edges at the lip of the boulder and top out straight up.

☐ **71g V3**
"Sketchy." Locate the overhanging orange and black scoop. On the face outside of the left side are two opposing sidepulls in a rock scar. Pull on using these and make moves up to crack break and finish it up along the crack.

☐ **71h The Ugly Roof** V8
"Sketchy." Start low in the back of the overhanging orange and black cave. Move up and right out the overhang using blocky holds for the left and black patina iron bands for the right and top out straight up. At the time of writing there was a bird's nest in this problem, please don't disturb wildlife for bouldering.

Caleb Boaz, Shiver Me Timbers Direct V8, pg. 177. Brion Voges photo.

72. SPIT SHINE BOULDER

The Spit Shine Boulder is a short boulder with some good problems on it which is just past the Shiver Me Timbers Boulder. The most popular line on the block is *Rail Rider*, a fun V4 which lacks the height of most Back Nine problems. **The problems are described from left to right.** To get off of this boulder, simply jump off where it is shortest next to *Kneed It*.

72. SPIT SHINE BOULDER

☐ 72a **Stupid Black** V4 ⭐⭐
"Scary." The tall angled finger crack on the left side of the face. Start on the right margin of the roof and climb the obvious crack. Watch out for the rocks beneath you in the landing zone.

☐ 72b **Paradox** V4 ⭐⭐
To the right of *Stupid Black* is a white and black rippled slabby face with a good landing. Climb holds up the left side of this face.

☐ 72c **Snap Decision** V3 ⭐⭐
The right side of the white and black rippled face, just to the left of the tree. Good thought provoking climbing.

☐ 72d **Spit Shine** V0 ⭐
Just to the left of *Tire Knockers* is a low angle scoop/corner with a thin seam in it. Stand start and climb it to the top.

☐ 72e **Tire Knockers** V3 ⭐
Sit start low on the sloping hold in rail the same as for *Rail Rider*. Climb straight up the arete above to a slopey top out.

☐ 72f **Rail Rider** V4 ⭐⭐
Sit start on a sloper at the corner of the arete. Move up and right along the ascending line of holds to a slopey top out.

☐ 72g **V3** ⭐
Sit start low on sidepull edges in the jagged crack. Make moves upwards to top out.

☐ 72h **V1** ⭐
Squat start on the far right side of the boulder and traverse the brushed good slopers and jugs left along the edge until you reach the crack to top out.

72. SPIT SHINE BOULDER

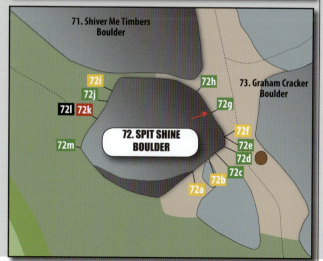

72. SPIT SHINE BOULDER

The following problems are on the Spit Shine Boulder, but around on the back side of it. To access them, walk around the Shiver Me Timbers Boulder and follow a faint path down towards the 17th green. The wall will be on your left. Although there is no danger of being hit by a golf ball here, you are quite close to the green and should be quiet and defer to golfers at all times.

❏ **72i** **Rodriguez Face** V5 ⭐
The short face to the left of the crack. Sit start with right in pocket sidepull and left in slopey pocket feature. Move up the face to left-facing sidepull and then left to crimpers to top out.

❏ **72j** **Crack** V2 ⭐
On the left side of this face is a crack which splits the boulder. Sit start and climb it to the top.

❏ **72k** **Bosley Traverse** V9 ⭐
On the left side of the overhanging wall, down low, where the line of cool pockets start. Begin here and traverse right using vertical pocket sidepulls, eventually making a large move to gain the arete and finish up it.

❏ **72l** **Project**
Start the same as the Bosley Traverse, move to the right along the low pockets, and eventually make a large move straight up to vertical pinch in seams, and straight up to top out. Really cool looking, will supposedly go at V12/13.

❏ **72m** **V3** ⭐
Sit start on red ledgey jugs on the right side of the boulder. Climb up and left along good holds on lip of the steep face till you can rock over to top out.

73. GRAHAM CRACKER BOULDER

73. GRAHAM CRACKER BOULDER

The wide grey concave face of the Graham Cracker Boulder which greets you as you walk into the Back Nine is surely one of the most impressive boulders at the Fort. Striped with jagged crack features, this boulder is home to many worthy problems, including the mega-classic *the Shield*. *Graham Crackers*, the tall arete on the downhill side is also a don't miss. **The problems are described from left to right around the boulder.** To get off of this boulder walk towards the back of the boulder and down climb a slab on its downhill side, towards the golf course.

☐ **73a** **The Shield** V12 ★★★
"Sketchy." Is this the most beautiful boulder you've ever seen? I think so! It's like a lightning bolt trapped in stone. Start on crimps down and right. Move up and left along the thin edges and seams, eventually topping out up and left around the corner.

☐ **73b** **The Shield 2.0** V12 ★★★
"Sketchy." The left hand start variation is a little harder. Start about six feet left of the original start on flakes and move right up thin seam to gain *the Shield* and finish on it.

☐ **73c** **Rodriguez Problem** V6 ★★
Start on the same holds as for *the Shield*, but move right fairly low across the face using seams and sidepulls to gain the bottom of *the Divide* and finish up that.

☐ **73d** **The Divide** V3 ★★
The furthest left continuous crack on the face, left of *the Shield*. Stand start on the vertical crack system and climb it to the top. Stick to holds only in the one crack for full value.

☐ **73e** **Twin Cracks** V1 ★★
"Sketchy." Climb the somewhat parallel cracks which start close to the top of the slab and just right of the last problem. Uneven landing.

73. GRAHAM CRACKER BOULDER

73. GRAHAM CRACKER BOULDER

☐ **73h** Star Child V6 ★★
"Sketchy." Start the same as for 73f, but about halfway up the right-angling crack follow it up and right to where it blanks out. Follow insipient seams further up and right to where they make a star-like pattern and top it out close to the arete.

☐ **73i** Graham Crackers V2 ★★★
"Sketchy." This tall arete is a classic for the grade. Stand start on the right arete of the face. Climb straight up the arete using sidepulls and crimps in the patina.

☐ **73j** Pleiades V4 ★
Around the corner from the other problems, on the left side of the flakey face and just left of a tree. Sit start low on flakes and crimp and make a couple burly moves up on slopey holds to fairly cruiser top out.

☐ **73f** V1 ★
Start on cracks down lower on the boulder right of *Twin Cracks*. Climb them up to a horizontal juggy feature in the middle of the face and head left into the *Twin Cracks* and finish up that.

☐ **73g** Scary Gary V5 ★
"Scary." A huge dyno. Climb up the same as 73f, till you gain the juggy horizontal crack, then do a huge dyno to cover the five foot span between you and the top of the boulder.

☐ **73k** Nick of Time V1 ★
"Sketchy." On the right side of the heavily flaked face. Stand start and climb flakes straight upwards along a vertical seam type feature at the top to a cool top out.

☐ **73l** Star Power V0 ★
"Sketchy." To the right of the last problem, in the scoop behind the tree. Climb the flakes up the tall wall.

Tony Lamiche

translated from French by Bonnie Sarkar.

What a surprise in this part of the US, overlooked and underestimated by American climbers, who think only the West has anything to offer and have no respect for the Southeast. But here's a bouldering spot with so many beautiful lines and rock worthy of South Africa! They should know about it! Well no...there are a bunch of projects in the area, like the famous "Sheild" which I think is one of the most beautiful bouldering lines there is. A rock like this presents the highest quality climbing a climber can experience, and this part of the climb remains one of my favorite memories of climbing. What can I say when so many enthusiasts were happy to take us to their secret spot. It's also next to a golf course, so it's even more necessary to respect nature, be aware that we're on private property, and to respect the people who live in this bouldering paradise. I've already taken two trips out here and something tells me I'm not finished with this area. The sandstone is big and the outcroppings numerous, earning it a place in two guidebooks that have come out recently. I hope that these aren't the last.

Good climbing everyone, Tony...

Tony Lamiche making the first ascent of The Shield, Stephen Denys photo

74. JIGSAW BOULDER

74. JIGSAW WALL

No need for superlatives here, just look at the picture. Or better yet, look at the boulder! The Jigsaw Wall is an impeccable piece of stone, obviously created specifically for bouldering. This one is home to a bunch of hard classics and undone projects. If you are climbing harder than V7, you will not want to miss it. **The problems are described from left to right.** To get off this boulder, make your way

to the top of the *Barndoor*, and then down climb off the corner of the boulder onto a slab beneath.

74a Barndoor 2000 V12 ★★★
This problem stood as one of the greatest undone lines in the field until recently falling to Jimmy Webb. Follow the shallow, arching flake to a long & awkward jump to slot above.

74b Project
The open stemming corner to the right of the *Barndoor Project*. It looks like it will go... for Tommy Caldwell maybe...

74c Project
Sort of an eliminate, but climb the right arete of the stemming corner as a squeeze problem. The wall to the right is off.

74d Open It Up V0 ★★
"Sketchy." The arete on the left side of the Jigsaw Wall. Stand start and climb pockets in ledges on the arete. A dirty top out awaits.

74e V3 ★
"Sketchy." Stand start the same as the arete, but after a move, traverse right along a ledge and then up. Often wet, the top out is a bit dirty.

74f Deception V7 ★★★
"Sketchy." The awesome line up the middle of the Jigsaw face. You'll probably understand the name very quickly, the first move is deceptively hard. Stand start in middle of face with left on black triangular corner crimp and right on sidepull crimp. Pull on and move into edge in crack, then continue straight up the edges and sidepulls above. Tall.

Barndoor 2000, V12. Spenser Tangsmith photo.

74. JIGSAW BOULDER

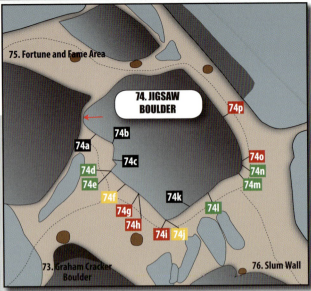

75. Fortune and Fame Area

74. JIGSAW BOULDER

74p

74b

74a

74c

74d
74e

74f

74g

74h

74i 74j

74k

74l

74o
74n
74m

73. Graham Cracker Boulder

76. Slum Wall

74. JIGSAW BOULDER

☐ **74g** **The Brotherhood** V8 ⭐⭐⭐
"Sketchy." Start in the holds in the vertical seam to the right of *Deception* with bad feet. Move up into the horizontal seam above, then move slightly left and top out on *Deception*.

☐ **74h** **Mind Freak** V8
⭐⭐⭐ "Sketchy." The direct finish to *the Brotherhood*. Stand start on the same seam as *the Brotherhood* and move up into the horizontal seam. Instead of moving left to gain *Deception*, continue straight up.

☐ **74i** **Dunky Doobie** V10 ⭐⭐
This one follows the horizontal seam that traverses across the entire face. Stand start on the arete same as for *Country Redneck Bitch*. Do a move or two, then head left across the face on the seam. Finishes past *Deception*, the same as for 74e.

☐ **74j** **Country Redneck V5** ⭐⭐
Bitch
"Sketchy." The arete on the right side of the Jigsaw Wall. Stand start and climb up a few crimps into a scoop, and then finish straight up the tall top out.

☐ **74k** **Project**
About four feet to the right of *CRB* is a brushed crimp about seven feet up the face. Pull up on this crimp and somehow use it to gain incuts about four feet above.

☐ **74l** **V1**
The short crack/seam in the middle of the face right of *Country Redneck Bitch*. Pretty pointless, since it doesn't take you anywhere. Pull onto the seam and do a move up to a ledge in the middle of the face. I wouldn't climb higher if I were you.

☐ **74m** **Rodriguez 2** V2
Stand start to the left of the arete on good holds and climb up and left following the angling seam/crack to eventually top out into the hole half way up the rock.

☐ **74n** **V3**
Climbs the detached pillar on the right arete of this face. The start is cool, but the ending not so much. Sit start with right on crimp and left on sloper sidepull near the crack. Climb upwards, eventually reaching into holds close to the crack. Drop off, top out not recommended.

☐ **74o** **Traylor Problem** V9 ⭐⭐
Just to the right of 74n. Sit start on small brushed crimps, move up on more crimps, then make big move up and right across the face a good distance to slopey pinch, and move straight up on more slopey divots to gain good holds.

☐ **74p** **Electric Boogaloo** V10 ⭐⭐
Stand start on the back wall of the boulder beneath a cool orange face with interesting shallow pocket/ripples. There are many different ways to start this problem, which depend on how high you stack your pads and which holds you choose to start on. For the V10 grade, start with opposing gastons as low as you can. Climb up and left across the face to the top out.

75. FORTUNE AND FAME AREA

75. FORTUNE AND FAME BOULDER

75. FORTUNE AND FAME AREA

The Fortune and Fame Area is a secluded little area tucked away behind the Jigsaw Boulder. You can get there by walking around the Jigsaw Boulder, or by scrambling through a gap in the rocks across from the Shiver Me Timbers Boulder. Here you will find some worthy hard slab and face problems. **The problems are described from left to right.** To get off of these boulders, head straight back, eventually encountering a gully which leads back down into the boulders.

☐ 75a Interplanetary V9 ⭐⭐ Escape

"Sketchy." This is one crazy problem. Stand start on the left side of the face with your right on a crimper and your left on either a really thin crimp sidepull, or a slopey sidepull right next to it. Jack your feet up and launch for the ear flake up and left. Finish up and right up the slab on holds which may be invisible from the ground but will hopefully appear when you get there. Has been done by traversing from the holds on the right side of the face, but that apparently doesn't add anything to the grade.

☐ 75b Project

Stand start on the right side of the face at the crimp in the middle of the wall. Climb directly up the glowing green face above.

☐ 75c Offwidth Crack 5.9

Have any plans to climb the *Steck-Salathe* in Yosemite Valley? If so, you may want to wriggle into this chimney and squirm your way to the top.

☐ 75d Fame V6 ⭐⭐

The slab to the right of the wide crack. Stand start on horizontal edges and figure your way past a long move in the middle. Unfortunately, way back in this corner, it probably won't make you famous.

☐ 75e V1 ⭐

The tall winding crack on the slab to the right of *Fame*. Stand start.

☐ 75f Fortune V6 ⭐⭐

Sit start in crack down low. Move up in decent holds to gain sidepull pocket and pocket on face, then rock over and stand up on the slab.

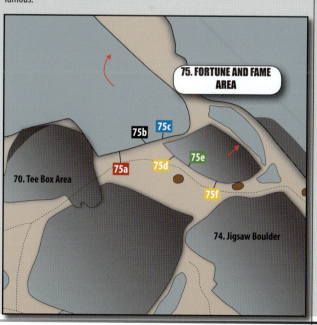

75. FORTUNE AND FAME AREA

70. Tee Box Area

74. Jigsaw Boulder

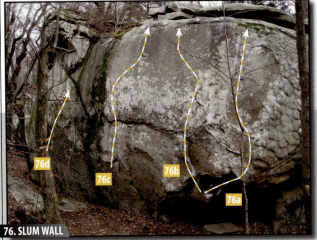

76. SLUM WALL

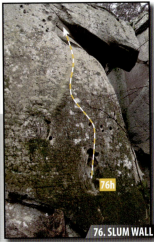

76. SLUM WALL

76. THE SLUM WALL

The Slum Wall is only host to a few problems, but they are some of the best and most unique tall problems at the Fort. Don't miss them. These climbs require a bunch of interesting techniques to overcome them, are exciting, and have incredibly cool grips. **The problems are described as you encounter them, from right to left.** To get off of this boulder, head to the right side of the wall past *White Trash* and down climb a groove using another boulder.

❏ **76a White Trash** V5 ⭐⭐⭐
"Sketchy." The right-hand line on this face is a super classic with lots of climbing. Sit start low on flat holds underneath overhang. Move right out the overhang on iron flakes to undercling, big move to flat edge on face, and up the water groove to the top.

❏ **76b Junky** V7 ⭐⭐⭐
"Sketchy." This one is recognizable by the "needle holes" high on the face. Sit start same as *White Trash* but move up a right-facing corner, then follow crimps up the slab to a long move to the holes, and on to the top.

❏ **76c Heroin** V7 ⭐⭐⭐
"Sketchy." One of the most unique problems around. About six ft. left of *Junky*, stand start on flakes and edges, move up to jugs, then left to good flake. I'll let you figure out how to get to the big slopey pocket in the middle of face. It ain't over till you're on top.

❏ **76d V6** ⭐
About 10 ft. left of *Heroin*, stand start in pods and move up pockets. Slap up and right on the slab above and top it out. Mossy and dirty.

❏ **76e Project**
Start the same as for 76d, but instead of moving up and right into pockets, go left to crimper flake, mantle onto it and finish up the slab above.

❏ **76f Project**
About 15 ft. left of 76d, stand start beneath twin undercling holes. Move up and stand as high as you can and reach for something in the blank water groove above.

❏ **76g Project?**
"Scary." The corner to the left of 76f has maybe been climbed? Start beneath the corner and make moves up the crack, eventually moving right around the arete onto the high face. Tall, inspect on a rope.

❏ **76h Ukrainian Gladiators** V6 ⭐
"Sketchy." This problem is on the slab on the next tall face, just past a short gap. Stand start with slab move into pockets on mossy and licheny face. More pockets lead to a right-trending sloper rail. Stand tall and reach for the top. Top it out, but don't expect the way off to be easy.

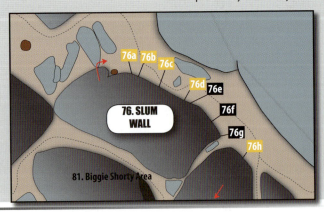

76. SLUM WALL

81. Biggie Shorty Area

77. THE MONO DOIGT WALL

The Mono Doigt Wall is a slabby face on your left as you head back towards the Cyclops Boulder. These are truly some of the best slabs of the grade at the Stone Fort. **The problems are described from left to right.** To get off of these problems, walk back off the top and then left down a trail back into the boulders.

☐ **77a** V1 ⭐
The rising lip traverse. Sit start low on the left side of the face and work up the slopey lip up and right to top out. A little sandy.

☐ **77b** The Rib V1 ⭐⭐⭐
"Sketchy." Probably the best slab climb of the grade at the Fort. The low angle slab on the left side of the face. It starts blank but little ribs appear as it gets steeper. It's all in the feet.

☐ **77c** V3 ⭐
"Sketchy." The tall black slab to the left of the tree. Stand start with hands on thin crimps. Stand up onto the starting holds and head up the blank slab above with very few handholds.

☐ **77d** The Mono Doigt V5 ⭐⭐⭐
The really cool face climb right of the tree looks like its littered with bullet holes. Stand start in obvious deep pocket and use the mono-divots above to gain the slab mantle.

77. MONO DOIGT WALL

☐ **77e** The Giving Tree V3 ⭐
"Scary." Across from 77a is a 25 ft. tall arete which has been climbed by Dan Rose. Was cleaned up at one time, probably needs a good top-down scrub before an ascent is tried.

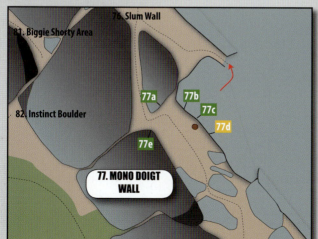

77. MONO DOIGT WALL

78. MONSTER BOULDER

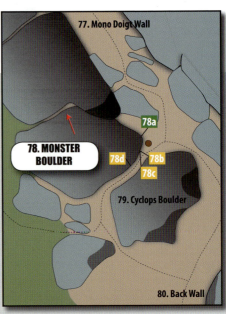

78. THE MONSTER BOULDER

The Monster Boulder is located right next to the Cyclops Boulder, but is easily overshadowed by its neighbor. The problems here are fun and revolve around incut patina holds. However, none of them garner classic status. **The descriptions run from right to left.** To get off of this boulder, simply down climb a slab on the opposite side of the boulder from the problems.

☐ 78a Sacrifice V2 ⭐

The stand start to the slabby prow which is the finish to *Monster*. Start by standing up on the shelf on the slab and climb the prow to the top.

☐ 78b One Eye V4 ⭐

Sit start matched on thin crimpy patina in the middle of the left face. Follow decent holds up and left to the inevitable mantle.

☐ 78c Monster V4 ⭐⭐

Sit start the same as for *One Eye* on the low patina crimps in the middle of the face. Use more patina holds to move right to gain the arete behind the tree, pull around the corner, and top out the slabby prow.

☐ 78d Monster Extension V5 ⭐

An extension to the previous problem. Sit start on the far left side of the face on a detached flake. Traverse crimps right to gain *Monster* and finish up it.

79. CYCLOPS BOULDER

79. THE CYCLOPS BOULDER

The Cyclops Boulder is an un-missable orange boulder which is at the end of the corridor and will be staring straight at you with its one eye as you walk up to it. It is home to a few worthy classics and generally the holds are sharp incut patina crimps. **The problems are described from left to right.** To get off of this boulder, walk to the right and down climb into the corridor right of the *Blacksmith*.

☐ **79a** **Cyclops** V6 ⭐⭐⭐
Climbs the obvious flat orange face at the end of the corridor. Sit start really low on flat flake and climb up the face out the left line of incut thin crimps, eventually gaining the break and the large Cyclops eye high on the face.

☐ **79b** **Cyclops Stand** V3 ⭐⭐
Stand start matched on the series of patina crimps at about face height and climb straight up as for *Cyclops*.

☐ **79c** **Cyclops Right** V6 ⭐⭐
Sit start on the low flakes the same as for *Cyclops*. Instead of moving up and left to the crimps, instead move up and right to thinner crimps and a shallow mono pocket, then make long move to the break before finishing as for *Cyclops*.

☐ **79d** **The Blacksmith** V9 ⭐⭐
An extension to *Cyclops*. Start about 10 ft. right of *Cyclops* on the left side of a large flat shelf. Follow blocks and edges left under the roof to gain the low crimps on *Cyclops*, and finish up it.

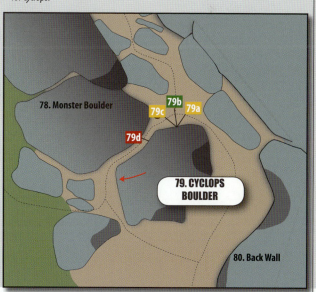

79. CYCLOPS BOULDER

Blacksmith V9. Micah Gentry photo.

80. THE BACK WALL

Past the Cyclops Boulder is one more wall with problems on it. These are the last problems in the field. Somewhat mossy, and not often climbed, these climbs are none-the-less better than they look and are worth the effort. I have not been able to uncover given names for these problems and it seems possible that they have never been named. **The descriptions go from left to right.** To get off of these problems, simply walk off straight back, and then head right and down climb the short wall past the last problem.

80. THE BACK WALL

☐ 80a V0 ⭐

Stand start in pockets under small roof at the far left side of the roof and climb straight up the face above on great incuts.

☐ 80b V1 ⭐

Stand start in crack underneath the roof and climb out the roof to large jug, then up the face above on good holds.

☐ 80c V4 ⭐

Stand start on jugs in crack underneath roof. Reach out to decent holds and surmount the shield above using thin edges and pockets.

☐ 80d V3 ⭐

"Sketchy." Starts just left of the tree on the right side of the roof. Sit start on big shelf. Climb up the white face and then out the roof above on jugs to sloper top out.

☐ 80e V3 ⭐

The furthest right side of the face and the last problem at the back of the Fort. Sit start on rail and move straight up the blocky face to slopers at the lip and a rockover top out.

80. THE BACK WALL

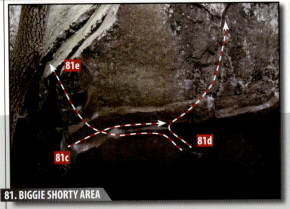

81. BIGGIE SHORTY AREA

81. BIGGIE SHORTY AR

81. THE BIGGIE SHORTY AREA

The Biggie Shorty Area is a narrow corridor stacked with hard problems and some cool tall slabs. To get there, head right at the Graham Cracker Boulder, past the Spit Shine Boulder, and then follow a trail up and left into the corridor. *Biggie Shorty* is easily one of the most popular hard problems at the Fort, probably cause it's good, and cause everyone loves to crimp! **The problems are described from the back of the corridor to the front, left to right.** There are many ways off this boulder, check the down climb arrows on the map.

☐ 81a 5.10 ⭐
"Scary." The tall fist and offwidth crack in the corner behind *Biggie Shorty*. Definitely worth roping up for.

☐ 81b 5.9 ⭐
"Scary." The tall offwidth/chimney crack on the right side of the pillar behind *Biggie Shorty*. Starts out as arm-bars and chicken wings and eventually you can get inside it. Or you could just lie-back up it...

☐ 81c Biggie Shorty V12 ⭐⭐ Extension
Start on jug flake on the far left side of the wall and traverse right along bad slopers to gain second hold of *Biggie Shorty* and finish up that.

☐ 81d Biggie Shorty V10 ⭐⭐⭐
This classic is all about the crimp. In the middle of the overhang, sit start low on two small crimps. Move up and left to edges, then up and right on thin crimps and finish the face above.

☐ 81e Bert V11 ⭐⭐
The *Biggie Shorty Extension* reversed. Sit start same as for *Biggie Shorty*, do the first move, then head left along the sloper rail, eventually heading up more slopers to mantle.

☐ 81f V4
Sit start about 10 ft. right of *Biggie Shorty* on flake crimps in the face. Move up the face on more flakes to reach large flat holds. Finish straight up onto the slab.

☐ 81g Crunk V3 ⭐
Start on wide sloping shelf at the right margin of the overhanging wall. Climb up and left along the lip of the overhang until you can rock over onto the slab.

☐ 81h WMD V4 ⭐⭐
"Scary." The tall slab which starts just to the right of the overhang. Not a bad idea to rope up for this one. Not a lot of holds, lots of footwork. You can climb the right corner of the boulder to reach the summit to set up a top-rope.

☐ 81i The Wax Museum V3 ⭐
"Sketchy." The slab about 10 ft. right of *WMD*. Starts by a hole in the rock at ground level. Climb up to blocky feature and continue on above.

☐ 81j The Mummy V3 ⭐
About 5 ft. right of the *Wax Museum*, climb the licheny slab using thin crimp edges on the face. Much shorter than the climbs to the left.

☐ 81k New Sensations V10 ⭐⭐
Across from the *Wax Museum* is this somewhat invisible problem. Start with your hands on a ledge in the middle of the face. Move a long ways to a thin pocket on a small block and go to the top up and left.

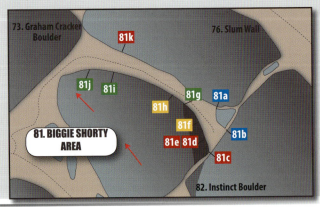

73. Graham Cracker Boulder

76. Slum Wall

81. BIGGIE SHORTY AREA

82. Instinct Boulder

The Rib V1, Micah Gentry Photo.

82. INSTINCT BOULDER

82. INSTINCT BOULDER

The Instinct Boulder is a large white boulder with a couple of classic problems on it. It is one of the last boulders in the field, and you can access it by following the trail right past the Graham Crackers Boulder and the Spit Shine Boulder. Look for the obvious rail coming out an overhang on your left, this is *Instinct*. The common way off this boulder is to step off onto the left wall and into a hanging corridor once you have established yourself on the upper face. Squeeze through this corridor and you will end up at *Biggie Shorty*, and can walk back around.

☐ 82a Instinct V7 ★★★

This awesome problem features holds which just look made for climbing on. Stand start on incut sidepull flake and follow the rail right till you can make a move to gain the hold at the lip. Hold the swing and follow holds upwards till you are standing above the roof. Step off left to get off. This has been topped out by Jeremy Walton, which would be very sketchy.

☐ 82b Instinct Low V10 ★★

Start matched on edge at the very left margin of the wall. Follow slopey edges right to encounter rail and the starting holds of *Instinct*. Often wet and a bit awkward, since the left wall is totally off.

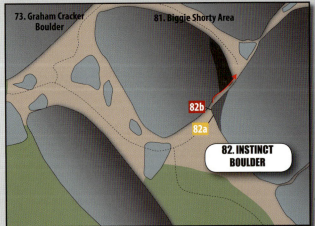

"MIRACULOUS SKIN HEALER"

-- Climbing magazine

ABOUT THE PHOTOGRAPHERS

Dan Brayack – Dan Brayack is a professional sports photographer and videographer out of West Virginia, though he travels throughout the country. Just a note for the record, Dan rarely if ever poses climbing photos. His action images are just that. Check him out at www. brayackmedia.com.

Andrew Kornylak – Andrew Kornylak has been climbing since '92, and has called Atlanta home for 10 years. A full-time photographer and video producer, he shoots for such diverse clients as Mercedes Benz, GEO Magazine, Outdoor Life, Discovery Channel, and Businessweek. Driven by his love of southern climbing, this year he has been working on a video series for Chattanooga's Rock/Creek Outfitters and the Triple Crown Bouldering Series.

Brion Voges – I've been living in Chattanooga my entire life and have spent countless days among the boulders at LRC climbing and taking photos. For the last few years I've been dividing my time between school at UTC and traveling to bouldering areas throughout the U.S. You can check out more photos plus words and video on my blog at brionvoges.blogspot.com.

Adam Johnson is a southern-born and raised climber and photographer from South Carolina. He has spent most of the last decade ticking away as many boulders as he could get his hands on throughout the southeast. Working full-time at a nuclear station as a licensed civil engineer has forced him to make the most of his weekend warrior status. Along with his wife Beth Anne, he continues to boulder in the southeast and all over the world, documenting as he goes.

Corey Wentz- www.coreywentz.com

Spencer Tangsmith : RVproj.com

V0-

	Route	Stars	Page
☐	Needless Things	★	42
☐	Costume Rings		42
☐	Left Blob Slab	★	55
☐	Right Blob Slab	★	55
☐	V0- (Fish Market)		112
☐	Downclimb Slab		123
☐	Slabatical		144
☐	V0- (Mystery Machine)	★	44
☐	V0- (Mystery Machine)	★	44
☐	Slab		42
☐	Easy Does It		45
☐	Arete		49
☐	Thin Flakes V0-	★	62
☐	Downclimb		67
☐	V0- (Mystery Groove)		68
☐	Downclimb Arete		87
☐	V0- (Blind Spot)		104
☐	V0- (Funhouse)		111

V0

	Route	Stars	Page
☐	Spare	★★★	60
☐	Five and Dime	★	67
☐	Dragon Traverse		145
☐	Plinko		174
☐	Open It Up		192
☐	V0 (Crack of Doom)	★	126
☐	V0 (Spyro Gyro)	★	62
☐	V0 (Crescent)	★	65
☐	V0 (Two Shoes Jack)	★	86
☐	V0 (Two Shoes Jack)	★	86
☐	V0 (Frumunda...)	★	107
☐	V0 (Sternum)	★	122
☐	V0 (Sternum)	★	122
☐	V0 (Dragon)	★	145
☐	V0 (Dumb Luck)	★	174
☐	Booger	★	45
☐	Farrah's Fawcett	★	48
☐	Chicken	★	54
☐	Magua's Revenge	★	57
☐	Editor's Choice	★	57
☐	Left Arete	★	61
☐	Low Constitution	★	66
☐	Murfreesboro Blues	★	67
☐	Tom Jones	★	87
☐	Kenny Loggins Road	★	95
☐	Red Tape	★	112
☐	Snipe Hunt		116
☐	Dihedral		124
☐	Old Maid	★	130
☐	Amen	★	142
☐	Cormany Wall 1	★	150
☐	Hand Me Down	★	174
☐	Spit Shine	★	187
☐	Star Power	★	190
☐	V0 (Back Wall)	★	201
☐	Keystone Cops		167
☐	Crack Traverse		49
☐	Mufassa		49
☐	The Lying King	★	49
☐	Right Arete	★	61
☐	Blithering Idiot	★	67
☐	Corner Crack		71
☐	Worm Drink	★	73
☐	Baby, One More Time		107
☐	V0 (Castaway)		110
☐	V0 (Funhouse)		111
☐	V0 (Funhouse)		111
☐	V0 (Crack of Doom)		126
☐	V0 (Tanqueray)		134
☐	Shits and Giggles		156

V1

	Route	Stars	Page
☐	Increderate	★	44
☐	The Crescent	★	65
☐	Storming the Castle		71
☐	Brian's Brian		144
☐	The Rib		197
☐	Black Label	★	46
☐	Split		60

	Route	Stars	Page
☐	High Times	★	65
☐	The Feature	★	66
☐	Slow Poke	★	86
☐	Dodge Swinger	★	90
☐	Mizzen Mast	★	110
☐	Moonminer	★	119
☐	High on Crack	★	138
☐	Jug Head	★	138
☐	Dragon Back	★	145
☐	Drag Me Down	★	156
☐	Uncle Punchy	★	156
☐	Twin Cracks	★	189
☐	Fire Crack Flake		42
☐	Shaggy	★	44
☐	Red Label	★	46
☐	Green Label	★	46
☐	The Puzzler		57
☐	Chachqua		57
☐	Cuervo	★	73
☐	Smoking Jacket		76
☐	Moss Man	★	94
☐	Vlad the Inhaler	★	107
☐	The Swollen Goat	★	111
☐	Warm-Up Traverse	★	113
☐	Blow by Blow		119
☐	Snoop	★	129
☐	Crackerjack	★	135
☐	Trailer Ball		136
☐	Boardwalk		131
☐	Stimey		139
☐	Butt's Up Stand Start		140
☐	Cormany Wall 2		150
☐	Cormany Wall 4		150
☐	The Horn		162
☐	Peed on Me		170
☐	Water Groove		184
☐	Nick of Time		190
☐	V1 (Slice and Dice)		48
☐	V1 (Wave)		52
☐	V1 (Bowling Ball)	★	60
☐	V1 (Spyro Gyro)	★	62
☐	V1 (Spyro Gyro)	★	62
☐	The Little German Girl		65
☐	V1 (Two Shoes Jack)		86
☐	V1 (Human Chew Toy)		101
☐	V1 (Blind Spot)		104
☐	V1 (Blind Spot)		104
☐	V1 (Frumunda...)		105
☐	Fish Tank		112
☐	V1 (Jerry's Kids)		113
☐	V1 (Jungle Gym)		117
☐	Tombstone Traverse		117
☐	V1 (Glamour)		119
☐	V1 (Crack of Doom)		126
☐	Jersey Turnpike		130
☐	V1 (Bonesaw)		130
☐	V1 (Rely on Gimmics)		169
☐	V1 (BPFH)		183
☐	V1 (Spit Shine)		187
☐	V1 (Graham Crackers)		190
☐	V1 (Fortune and Fame)		195
☐	V1 (Mono Doigt)		197
☐	V1 (Back Wall)	★	201
☐	Wide Wet Crack		44
☐	V1 (Mystery Machine)		44
☐	The Scalpel		49
☐	V1 (Art of Vogi)		56
☐	Middle		61
☐	Showtime		67
☐	Dos Cosanos		73
☐	V1 (Blind Spot)		104
☐	Full Moon		107
☐	V1 (Frumunda...)		102
☐	Oops, I Did It Again		107
☐	Funhouse		111
☐	V1 (Jigsaw)		192
☐	Between the Trees		130

V2

	Route	Stars	Page
☐	Moustrap	★★★	126
☐	The Pancake Mantle	★★	152

	Route	Stars	Page
☐	Graham Crackers	★	190
☐	Ruby Roo	★	44
☐	Odds My Bodkins		51
☐	Gutter Ball	★	60
☐	Tall Crack	★	67
☐	Dis	★	104
☐	Soapmakers	★	112
☐	Scully	★	123
☐	Traverse Start	★	126
☐	Block and Tackle		143
☐	Warm Up Arete		144
☐	Smog		145
☐	Dragon Traverse Loop		145
☐	V2 (Shotgun)		90
☐	Butt's Up	★	140
☐	The Shrine		44
☐	Mutiny		45
☐	Dice	★	48
☐	Roscoe		54
☐	Hauled Ass	★	65
☐	Mixer Elixir		66
☐	Runnel Funnel		67
☐	El Capitan		73
☐	Spacegrass		84
☐	Conway Twitty Twister	★	95
☐	Corn Grinder		100
☐	T-bone		100
☐	Farmer Slab		101
☐	The Shining		107
☐	Farmhand		111
☐	ABC's		119
☐	V2 (Bonesaw)		130
☐	By Jove		140
☐	Low Traverse		143
☐	Cormany Wall 3		150
☐	High Traverse	★	156
☐	Pittman Arete 2		170
☐	Vulcans Do It With Straight...	★	184
☐	Crack		188
☐	Sacrifice		198
☐	V2 (Mystery Machine)		44
☐	V2 (Slice and Dice)		48
☐	V2 (Turtle Tracks)		72
☐	V2 (Two Shoes Jack)	★	86
☐	V2 (Moss Man)		94
☐	V2 (Jerry's Kids)	★	113
☐	V2 (Chronic)		128
☐	V2 (Chronic)		128
☐	The Conformist		166
☐	Daddy Loves		54
☐	Milk Money		119
☐	V2 (Sternum)		120
☐	Paper Dragon		135
☐	V2 (Cell)		139
☐	V2 (Crypt)		167
☐	Chesnutt Crack		184
☐	Rodriguez 2	★	194
☐	The Undaclink		49
☐	Truth is Stranger		56

V3

	Route	Stars	Page
☐	Mystery Machine	★★	44
☐	Swingers	★	76
☐	The Ribcage	★	122
☐	Destroyer	★	171
☐	Increderate Sit		44
☐	Sister Sarah		44
☐	Pinch the Loaf		44
☐	The Boogie Man-tle		45
☐	Two Can Sam		48
☐	Strike		60
☐	Hairy Underclings		65
☐	Pit Fiend		79
☐	Clarence Bowater Survival		86
☐	Elephant Riders		90
☐	The Ghast		95
☐	Highway Jones		97
☐	Two Thumbs Up		116
☐	Glamour Boy		119
☐	A Face in ... Stand Start		125
☐	Phillip's Fury	★	136

Route	Stars	Page
These Feel Like Your Sister's	★★	156
Rely on Gimmicks	★	169
Snap Decision	★	187
The Divide	★	189
Cyclops Stand	★	199
Hot Java		46
Formula 1		46
Roscoe Extended		54
Maxine		54
TKO		55
Squatter's Rights		59
Jupiter		61
Puck Stick		66
Tight Like That		68
Turtle Tracks		72
Mescal Direct		73
V3 (Project Wall)		75
Pop Rocks		82
Holy Roller		95
Fish Lips		95
Diatribe		100
EFD Slab		101
Karmageddon		106
The Fish Market Traverse		112
Oracle Stand Start		114
Long Day Traverse		114
The Tombstone		117
The Cardinal Sin		118
South America		124
South Pacific		124
Jolly Roger		130
The Bronco Arete		131
Green Lantern		139
Jump		140
The Prison Planet		140
Keel Hauled		144
The Tempest		147
Burgos Problem		154
Boxing Your Shadow		162
Hocus Pocus		164
Pittman 1		164
Bones		167
Self Service		167
Pittman Arete		170
Underfling		175
Tire Knockers		187
The Giving Tree		197
Crunk		202
The Wax Museum		202
The Mummy		202
V3		64
Offwidth		56
Hog Jaw		61
Smear Campaign		84
V3 (Moss Man)		84
V3 (Human Chew Toy)		100
V3 (Jerry's Kids)		113
V3 (Jerry's Kids)		113
The High Traverse		117
V3 (Jungle Gym)		117
V3 (Tanqueray)		134
V3 (Barometer)		150
Swimming Pools, Movie Stars		166
V3 (Rely on Gimmicks)		169
V3 (Spit Shine)		187
V3 (Spit Shine)		187
V3 (Jigsaw)		192
V3 (Mono Doigt)		197
V3 (Back Wall)		201
V3 (Back Wall)		201
Seam Eliminate		42
V3 (Mystery Groove)		68
V3 (Turtle Tracks)		72
Where's the Downclimb?		85
Mistaken Identity		86
V3 (Funkadelic)		90
Toll Gate		96
V3 (Now and Zen)		97
Cling-On		100
Nutrageous		106
V3 (Fish Market)		112
V3 (Chronic)		128
Myrmidon		162
V3 (Tee Box)		184
V3 (Jigsaw)		192
Pittman Face		166

V4

Route	Stars	Page
Mystery Groove	★★★	68
Two Shoes Jack	★★	86
Tristar	★★	142
Dragon Lady	★★	145
Super Mario	★	175
Incredarete Left Sit		44
Boogie Mantle Sit Start		45
The Mane Event		48
Black Carpet		51
Green Machine		52
Art of the Vogi		56
Train Wreck		63
Mescal		73
Thundafrumunda		107
The Fish Market		112
The Big Much		113
Oracle		114
Cable Route		123
Pocket Pool		125
Short Long		134
Super Crack		157
Stupid Black		187
Paradox		187
Rail Rider		187
Monster		198
WMD		202
Slice		48
Humpty Dumpty		61
Body Glove		63
Fixer		66
Into the Owie		82
Lick the Stamp		94
Slow and Low		95
Black Hat		106
The Curse		106
Unusual Suspect		112
Clarice		113
Watermark		116
Boob Fight		116
The Crush of Love		118
Glamour Girl		119
Candy Corn		122
Thinner		124
Fight Club		128
Black Belt Jones		129
Geez-Us		130
Skeleton Crew		130
All In		134
The Relic		135
Sidewinder		138
Melon Theory		143
Crack of Pain		150
Mother Thrutch		150
Mother Trucker		150
Mosquito Deleto		162
Drumm Problem		171
Baby Maker		181
Pleiades		190
One Eye		198
V4 (Jerry's Kids)		113
V4 (Glamour)		119
Decidous Enima		144
V4 (Cleopatra)		154
V4 (Back Wall)		201
One Bad Hat		59
V4 (Crescent)		65
Injury Free Guarantee		97
Tanqueray		134
Rise to Rebellion		147
V4 (Backside)		147
High Heel		167
Johnson Problem		171
Rodriguez Traverse		184
V4 (Biggie Shorty)		202

V5

Route	Stars	Page
Genghis Khan	★★★	52
Galaxy 5000	★★	90
Diesel Power		105
The Sternum		122
Crack of Doom		126
White Trash		196
The Mono Doigt		197
First Knight		71
The Glove		79

Route	Stars	Page
Crystal Ball	★	86
Casper the Friendly Ghost	★	96
Drumm Arete		100
Bear Hug Arete		104
Fat Cat		107
Frumundathunda		107
Mayor for a Day		117
Finish Your Homework		118
Bonesaw		130
Clutch		138
Latin for Dagger		139
Slap Happy		142
Font Arete		147
Mother Thrutch Right Sit		150
Steamroller		152
Sunnie Rose		170
Rage		178
The Graduate		180
Boulder Problem from Hell		180
Country Redneck Bitch		194
Trailer Hitch		136
Bootleg		49
Are You Experienced?		51
IDYC Stand		51
High Gravity		61
Walk the Talk		84
Jungle Foot		96
Minerva		96
Thundatathunda		107
Big Wheel		112
Line of Scrimmage		119
Meeks Traverse		125
Chorizo		128
Blood Sausage		128
Short Long Traverse Start		134
Old Scratch		135
Superman		140
The Cutpurse		140
The High Arete		143
Font Right		147
Profits of Doom		151
Eiseman Corner		166
Pop Top		166
Low Spark		167
Dumb Luck		174
Slap		178
Tower Train		181
Segal Crack		186
Rodriguez Face		188
Scary Gary		190
Monster Extension		198
The Eyes Have It		96
V5 (Cell)		139
V5 (Tristar)		142
V5 (Barometer)		150
The Cheese Grater		72
Drumm Slab		79
Rodriguez Problem		164
Captain Cave Man		169
Tunnel Vision		79

V6

Route	Stars	Page
Manute Bol	★★	52
The Wave	★★	52
Kingpin		60
Shotgun		90
The Hulk		166
Cyclops		199
Aneardon		42
Heartbreaker		67
High Tide		94
Pure Rock Fury		95
Sink 'Em Low		113
Left Wing		129
Main Area Reverse Traverse		136
Main Area Traverse		136
Six Feet Under		167
Super Mario Extension		175
Bent		178
Shiver Me Timbers		185
Rodriguez Problem		189
Star Child		190
Fame		195
Fortune		195
Cyclops Right		199
Genghis Khan Right		52
The Fouling		59

Route	Page
Do Dat	75
High Slab Traverse	86
Slow-Fury Traverse	95
Pussy Patrol	97
Get Your Groove On	105
Olive's Oil	107
Stretch Armstrong	107
The Merovingian	113
The Ditto Traverse	118
The Bulge	119
One Man Stand	124
Undertow	126
Boro Traverse	138
Pockets of Resistence	140
Life is Goodlett	144
Dragon Ballz	145
Low Traverse	150
Fury	178
The Widowmaker	181
Two Up Two Down	82
V6 (Jerry's Kids)	113
V6 (Frontside)	144
V6 (Backside)	147
V6 (Slum)	196
Ukrainian Gladiators	196
Devil's Cabana Boy Stand	185
V6 (Art of Vogi)	56
Galapagos	84
Surfing the High Tide	94
MC Hammer	184

V7

Route	Page
Spyro Gyro	62
Kaya	63
Tennessee Thong	76
Now and Zen	97
Jerry's Kids	113
A Face in the Crowd	125
Celestial Mechanics	142
The Pinch	154
Cinderella	154
Red House	175
Deception	192
Junky	196
Heroin	196
Castaway	110
Instinct	204
Dirty Sanchez	45
The Mechanic	52
On the Fence	76
Pou	82
Watermelon Slab	85
Midway	87
Fire	94
Tooth Fairy	105
Blind Spot	105
Symmetry	125
The Chronic	129
Right Wing	129
Iron Man Traverse	140
Don't Tell My Daddy	157
Spank the Baby	178
South Africa Arete	180
The Eliminator	45
Crescent Slab	65
Special Agent	84
Iwo Jima	87
The Blast Tyrant	116
Pennzoil Arete	134
Drumm Problem	140
Webb Problem 2	140
Acid Drop	164
Smell My Finger	180
Pittman Arete 3	184
V7 (Tee Box)	184
Devil's Cabana Boy	185
The Barrier	95
Webb Problem	101
Dribble	178

V8

Route	Page
Space	84
Dr. Atkinson	97
Grimace	125
Spanky	139
Cleopatra	154
House of Leaves	175

Route	Page
The Brotherhood	194
Mind Freak	194
King of the Castle	71
Jut Strut	87
Simply Irresistable	101
Jerry Rigged	113
Fussili Jerry	114
Fatigue Syndrome	129
Red House Extension	175
Shiver Me Timbers Direct	185
Aneardon Low	42
V8 (Mystery Machine)	44
Dosey Twat	63
Jam Up	86
Headies	94
Man Hands	131
Gross Sit	150
Hoops	151
White Chili	152
Pringle Problem	171
Pocket Traverse	86
Riddim Warfare	164
The Ugly Roof	185

V9

Route	Page
Odyssey	85
Psychosomatic	136
Bedwetters	164
Tyrone Biggums	126
I Think I Can	45
IDYC	51
Robbing the Tooth Fairy	105
Blind Spot original	105
Ace of Spades	122
Dragon Man	145
Cleopatra – Cinderella Traverse	154
Bimbo Limbo	180
Kneed It	185
Bosley Traverse	188
Traylor Problem	194
Interplanetary Escape	195
The Blacksmith	199
Tommy Boy	45

V10

Route	Page
The Power of Amida	101
White Face	126
King James	143
Biggie Shorty	202
Dunky Doobie	194
Electric Boogaloo	194
New Sensations	202
Instinct Low	204
Reflections	45
AGR	87
Disparate Impact	106
Lurod/Gross Undercling	157

V11

Route	Page
Flying High	75
The Law	140
Jeremiah	175
Watch Your Back	75
Dragon Slayer	145
Clarien's Cherry	157
Bert	202
Made in France	142

V12

Route	Page
The Shield	189
The Shield 2.0	189
The Chattanoogan	87
Biggie Shorty Extension	202
Barndoor 2000	192

V13

Route	Page
Tall Tee	76

5.9

Route	Page
5.9 (Biggie Shorty)	202
Offwidth Crack	195

5.10

Route	Page
Neurotica	157
Exotica	157
5.10 (Biggie Shorty)	202

5.11

Route	Page
Human Chew Toy	101

5.12

Route	Page
Pittman Face	62
Baxter Traverse	166

V?

Route	Page
V? (Tee Box)	184
Gross Mantle	147
Big Fat Momma	139
Tennis Shoe Slab	174

Projects

Route	Page
Yin Yang Project	63
The Wedgie Project	76
Project?	98
Project?	98
Project?	105
High Five Project	110
Project (Jerry's Kids)	113
Project (Crack of Doom)	126
Project (Crack of Doom)	126
Project (Chronic)	129
Project (Tanqueray)	134
Project (Rely on Gimmics)	169
Project (BPFH)	183
Project (Shiver Me)	185
Project (Spit Shine)	187
Project (Jigsaw)	192
Project (Jigsaw)	192
Project (Jigsaw)	192
Project (Fortune and Fame)	195
Project (Slum)	196
Project (Slum)	196
Project? (Slum)	196

INDEX

About The Author & Publisher

Andy Wellman began climbing in 1997 and has been obsessed ever since. Over the years he has spent significant amounts of time focusing on all varieties of climbing. Recently he has devoted his climbing energy towards sport climbing and bouldering. After an incredible year spent living in the Southeast, he chose to settle back into his house in Rifle, Colorado.

Rockery Press is the realization of a local community effort that has been building for over half a decade.

It's generally well known that Chattanooga has had a reputation for being tight lipped with regards to publicizing our regional climbing resources. Whether this conservative stance results from our seemingly never-ending battle with area access, or from a tradition of 'do it yourself' guidance, or maybe simply from a trend of general guidebook skepticism – the Chattanooga climbing community has long been divided on what to do about the "guidebook question."

With this conflict as our backdrop, it's important as publishers and community members to see both sides of what a guidebook offers. Oftentimes, the immediate local response to publication is to focus on the impact that guidebooks bring. Studies show that guidebooks result in a 30% rise in user visitation. Outside of the disgruntled 'not what it used to be' local perspective, this increase in traffic, if not mitigated through appropriate planning, can result in forms of negative impact.

On the other hand, a community without a guidebook runs the risk of having its future gym and web reared generations loose, forget, or never learn the histories and tall tales that distinguish a community's legacy.

Rockery Press recognizes both sides of what a guidebook does. For this reason, it's our mission to produce the most unique, local-born content and multimedia designs that preserve the authentic Chattanooga rock climbing record for past, present, and future generations. And in addition, as proactive local publishers committed to area access and stewardship, we pledge a portion of profits to local grass roots organizations and efforts committed to developing, sustaining, and protecting our local climbing resources.

We hope that this balance between publication and protection will help carry Southeast rock climbing into a healthy and vibrant future as it continues to grow throughout the TAG region.